"In a moment when the public meaning of C
moral responsibility couldn't be more conte
text by Ellen Ott Marshall. *Introduction to Christian Ethics* bring-
on a journey of careful critical thinking rooted in clear methodology so we may engage the urgent collective question, 'How do we live a good life in the midst of ongoing conflict?' Marshall doesn't merely ensure that her readers take seriously tradition, reason, texts, and contexts; she also demonstrates that our engagement of such must include critique and reconstruction for the sake of justice and social transformation. She ably demonstrates how these are part of the social-ethical mission at the heart of the Christian tradition. I am eager to use this work with my own students and excited about what it will enable them to go forth and be and do in the world."

—Jennifer Harvey, Professor of Religion, Drake University

"Ellen Ott Marshall's new *Introduction to Christian Ethics* is grounded in the novel and timely claim that 'to study Christian ethics is to study conflict.' Deploying a methodology that is contextual, feminist, and Wesleyan, she masterfully explores major theological affirmations and methodological claims of Christian ethics through examples and case studies, all of which return again and again to conflict. This is an introductory text pitched as overview and demonstration, as illustrative, humble, and self-revealing rather than comprehensive, proud, and distant. Marshall claims that 'one cannot pursue the kingdom of God without entering into conflict.' She is absolutely right, and this introductory textbook helps us understand why. Highly recommended."

—David P. Gushee, Distinguished University Professor of Christian Ethics and Director, Center for Theology and Public Life, Mercer University; author of *Still Christian: Following Jesus out of American Evangelicalism*

"By acknowledging that conflict is at the heart of the human experience, Marshall offers a radically new and innovative approach to the task of Christian ethics, one that offers creative possibilities for deepening moral reflection. Imaginative, impassioned, practical, and eminently accessible, this book is an essential read."

—Rebecca Todd Peters, Professor of Religious Studies and Director, Poverty and Social Justice Program, Elon University

"If you have been looking for an innovative text to teach introductory Christian ethics, then Ellen Ott Marshall's new book is it. 'How do we live a good life in the midst of ongoing conflict?' Marshall uses conflict as an interpretive lens to explicate and rethink theological concepts, such as *imago Dei*, sin, and reconciliation and ethical theories, such as teleology, deontology, and responsibility. Her keen scholarly insights are also practical insights drawn from experiences of conflict in church and society. With this book, Professor Marshall provides a means to teach our students how to think ethically about and be moral agents who respond faithfully to the ongoing conflict of twenty-first-century life in church and society."

—Marcia Y. Riggs, J. Erskine Love Professor of Christian Ethics, Columbia Theological Seminary

Introduction to Christian Ethics

Introduction to Christian Ethics

Conflict, Faith, and Human Life

Ellen Ott Marshall

First edition
Published by Westminster John Knox Press
Louisville, Kentucky

18 19 20 21 22 23 24 25 26 27—10 9 8 7 6 5 4 3 2 1

Book design by Drew Stevens
Cover design by Eric Walljasper

Library of Congress Cataloging-in-Publication Data

Names: Marshall, Ellen Ott, 1970– author.
Title: Introduction to Christian ethics : conflict, faith, and human life / Ellen Ott Marshall.
Description: First edition. | Louisville, Kentucky : Westminster John Knox Press, 2018. | Includes bibliographical references and index. |
Identifiers: LCCN 2018025269 (print) | LCCN 2018033695 (ebook) | ISBN 9781611648904 | ISBN 9780664263447 (pbk.)
Subjects: LCSH: Christian ethics.
Classification: LCC BJ1251 (ebook) | LCC BJ1251 .M347 2018 (print) | DDC 241—dc23
LC record available at https://lccn.loc.gov/2018025269

Most Westminster John Knox Press books are available at special quantity discounts when purchased in bulk by corporations, organizations, and special-interest groups. For more information, please e-mail SpecialSales@wjkbooks.com.

For Katherine, Zoe, and Steve

Contents

Acknowledgments

I am fortunate to have wonderful students and colleagues who help me think carefully about the tasks and teaching of Christian ethics. I am grateful to all the students in my introduction to Christian ethics course over the years. My interactions with them in the classroom informed the writing of this book as much as my own notes and lectures did. I have also been lucky to have wonderful doctoral students as teaching assistants in this course. They help me to be a more creative and effective teacher, and their scholarship broadens and deepens my understanding of our field. I am also so grateful to my faculty colleagues in ethics and society at Candler and Emory: Liz Bounds, Robert Franklin, Pam Hall, Tim Jackson, Ted Smith, and Steve Tipton. This manuscript brings together material I have presented in different settings over several years, and I am aware of the many conversation partners who helped the drafts along. In its final stages, the manuscript received particular attention from Susan Hylen, Liz Bounds, Kyle Lambelet, and Ulrike Guthrie. I am incredibly grateful for their close reading and thoughtful suggestions.

I have worked in three educational institutions that perceive and value connections between peace and conflict studies and Christian theology and ethics: Elizabethtown College, Claremont School of Theology, and Candler School of Theology. Christina Bucher at Elizabethtown not only oriented me to my first academic job but also helped me to reunite master's-level work in peace and conflict studies with my doctoral focus in Christian ethics. Her invitation back to Elizabethtown as a Peace Fellow in 2014 also enabled me to think more fully about prominent theological themes running through the literature and practices of conflict transformation. In this world of conflict transformation and Christian ethics, Debbie Roberts has also been my teacher, good friend, and valued conversation partner. At Candler School of Theology, I am grateful for faculty colleagues involved in the Justice, Peacebuilding, and Conflict Transformation concentration: Liz Bounds, Luther Smith, David Jenkins, Beth Corrie, Jennifer Ayres, Greg Ellison, and Deanna Womack. With credit to Beth Corrie for our nickname, this "peace posse" provided me support when I first arrived at Candler, and a circle for guidance, friendship, and good humor ever since.

As always, I feel an overwhelming sense of gratitude for my family. My in-laws, Cynthia and Tom Marshall, offer unwavering support and encouragement. My husband, Tommy, and our terrific kids, Katherine, Zoe, and Steve, keep me connected to all kinds of things I would not follow on my own. Every day they bring me happiness, love, wonder—and they force me to think honestly about conflict! We also have a lovable, unruly dog, Cinder, who is my constant companion. When I am home, she is beside me, and I am always grateful for her company. My parents, Karen and Phil Ott, continue to care for all of us with a spirit of generosity that is astounding. They prepare meals, chauffeur kids, help with homework, and support me in this academic life that I learned from them. In writing this book, I became even more grateful for the ways that Mom and Dad taught me to see the moral life as shaped by grace and responsibility. I could not live so fully into this vocation I love if I did not have all of these amazing people in my life.

1
Christian Ethics in Conflict

This book takes conflict as the context for Christian reflection on the good life. Conflict cannot be an occasion about which Christians make decisions only periodically, for conflict is an ever-present reality that Christians cannot avoid. We live in conflict. The dynamics of conflict are the stuff of daily life, the movement of history, the making and remaking of community, and the vibrancy of faith. To be is to be in conflict. Thus, the central question of this book is this: How do we live a good life in the midst of conflict? The task of this introductory chapter is to explain why the question matters, and to suggest a path for pursuing it using the resources and methods of Christian ethics.

TO BE IS TO BE IN CONFLICT

"To be is to be in conflict" seems a rather pessimistic statement, especially if one has a negative understanding of conflict (and there are certainly legitimate reasons to have a negative understanding of conflict). Violent conflict destroys life and livelihood. Ongoing interpersonal conflicts rupture relationship, erode trust, and debilitate us emotionally and psychologically. Conflict costs time, sleep, health, and material resources. To assert that we exist in conflict seems to trap us in a fundamentally anxious situation. This makes the assertion uncomfortable, but not necessarily untrue.

At its root, *conflict* means "to strike together," the Latin *com* meaning "with" and *fligere* meaning "strike." The *Oxford English Dictionary* defines *conflict* in its noun form as "a state of opposition or hostilities," a "fight or struggle," "the clashing of opposed principles." To be in conflict means that elements are in opposition with one another; they strike together. We might think of this in contrast to confluence, where different elements flow together more smoothly. Conflicting elements are in tension, in opposition with one another. The power of this concept is that it describes a relationship between different elements. *Com-fligere* maintains the difference and the relationship. Because we exist as different elements (and of different elements) in relationship to others, our existence is one of conflict.

Conflict, in this way, is both natural and necessary. As parts of an ecosystem, we are organisms that are both different from and related to each other. Whether on the large scale of shifting tectonic plates or the small scale of worms and waste in compost, the world of which we are part is made and remade through conflict. We live as part of an ecosystem that undergoes constant change as elements strike together. To be is to be in conflict.

TO BE HUMAN IS TO BE IN CONFLICT

To this observation rooted in nature, we need to add a sociological description and a moral argument. Conflict plays a sociological function for human beings. More than a feature of our existence in the ecosystem, conflict plays an essential role in the formation and reformation of human communities. We may tend to fixate on the ways that violent conflict redraws national boundaries or changes the demographics of a society or fuels the emergence of social groups. However, as I will emphasize repeatedly in this book, not all forms of conflict are violent. Think of the way that, for good or ill, legislative jostling or conflict reshapes the policies that govern people's lives and prompts the formation of organizations for advocacy or resistance. Think of the way that nonviolent social movements and actions, such as the 2017 Women's March on Washington or civil rights sit-ins, protests, and marches past and present have used conflict to expose injustice, motivate negotiation, and force change. Every day, in small ways, conflict shapes human community. It affects the dynamics of friend groups, families, classrooms, work environments, and congregations. Conflict is a catalyst for change, and if approached constructively, it can be a catalyst for positive change. This view of conflict reflects the latest in a lineage of approaches: conflict prevention, management, resolution, and now transformation.[1] Rather than beginning with the assumption that conflict can be prevented, this approach understands conflict to be a normal and unavoidable part of life. Rather than perceiving conflict as something to be managed and contained, conflict transformation intends to work constructively with conflict as a "catalyst for change."[2] Rather than focusing only on a problem to be solved, this approach also tries to engage conflict in a way that begins something new and good.[3]

In everyday speech, we apply the term *conflict* to everything from interpersonal tension to international war. So it is crucial to understand that the literature and the practitioners of conflict transformation are not claiming that everything we associate with conflict is natural and necessary. Rather, they are calling for a more precise understanding of the term. They sharpen our focus to the place and moment in which perceptions, needs, desires, ideas, or convictions "strike together." Striking together is part of living in an ecosystem that is changing and interrelated. Conflict is natural and necessary. How we respond to these moments and circumstances of conflict warrants moral assessment and action. In other words, though we cannot choose whether to be in conflict, we can choose how to respond to it.

Violence is one response to conflict, but violence and conflict are not the same thing. To be accurate here, I need to distinguish firmly between the two, and then blur the distinction a bit. We experience violent conflict (a physical fight, for example) and nonviolent conflict (a verbal disagreement), and we respond to conflict with violence (a retaliatory strike) or nonviolence (a sit-in). When we conflate conflict and violence, we lose sight of a vast range of human interaction and the possibilities that reside in it. This distinction between violence and conflict is crucial, because one can also respond to conflict nonviolently and use conflict nonviolently for purposes of social change. If we lose the distinction between violence and conflict, we obscure the rich tradition and ongoing efforts of nonviolent resisters to engage conflict constructively for purposes of social change. Nonviolent resistance is also one response to conflict, one approach to or use of conflict. Moreover, nonviolence shares the umbrella of conflict transformation with practices of mediation, restorative justice, and circle facilitation, because all of these actions rest on the assertion that conflict can be a catalyst for constructive change in relationships and communities.

However, it is also important and honest to complicate these distinctions a bit. The lines between violent and nonviolent resistance are blurry because there are so many different kinds of violence. Violence is both overt and hidden; it is physical, structural, and psychological; it is already experienced and persistently threatened. Regimes and persons alike can behave violently in any number of ways without manifesting physical harm. Nonviolent resisters also blur the distinction between violence and nonviolence when they advocate sanctions that restrict access to basic goods or when they utilize resistance tactics that involve self-harm, for example. Similarly, it is exceedingly difficult to separate conflict from the forms of emotional, psychological, and spiritual violence that are inevitably part of striking together. So it is crucial to recognize conflict as a natural dimension of life in a related and changing system, and it is equally crucial to avoid romanticizing conflict or relaxing too much with this acceptance of necessity. Striking together, no matter how natural it is, is fraught with danger, and those dangers are compounded by issues of power and proximity. The costs of conflict land heaviest on those who are least powerful and closest to the dispute. When we reflect on contexts of conflict from a distance or from a position of comfort, we need to be particularly mindful of this. This is one reason why I privilege the perspective of victims of violence.

A second important distinction is between conflict and sin. One could read the preceding description of human life as situated in conflict and conclude that this is another way to talk about our fallen state, or our historical moment in the interim, the "not yet" in the Christian story. However, conflict as understood here is not a consequence of the fall, but a consequence of being interrelated and changing. Conflict is a dimension of createdness, not a result of sin. Our natural and social circumstance makes conflict a part of life. Moreover, unlike sin, conflict contains possibilities for good. Conflict can be a catalyst for constructive change. Thus, it is inaccurate to conflate conflict and sin, because possibilities for positive transformation reside in the dynamics of conflict. Through discussion with practitioners and trainers in conflict transformation, I have learned that they usually begin their work with Christians by helping them to disentangle conflict from sin. Such disentangling takes some doing because most of the Christians that these writers, practitioners, and trainers encounter still intuitively perceive conflict as being contradictory to Christian living, which they think should be marked by patience, forgiveness, kindness, and charity. To "strike together" seems to be unchristian or an indication of sin itself. Well-known peacebuilder John Paul Lederach writes, "During years of consulting, I have found this to be a common view of conflict in church circles. Conflict is sin. It shows that people are falling from the straight and narrow way. Working with and through conflict is essentially a matter of making sure people 'get right with God.'"[4] Lederach insists that being in conflict is not sinful. It is simply part of being created in relationship with the capacity for freedom and change.

Christian conflict transformation practitioners, like Lederach, regularly respond to this link between conflict and sin by providing a theological affirmation of conflict. In other words, conflict is not a consequence of fallenness, but of creation. As one practitioner-trainer told me, "For me, conflict is an ordinary and natural part of living. It's a part of life, it's a part of God's creation."[5] We see this in manuals as well: "Conflict is a natural part of a creation that is relational and diverse, a creation in which we are free to make choices. God declares it good. We will always have conflict."[6] Lederach articulates this theology of conflict as being a natural part of God's creation in a chapter aptly titled "In the Beginning . . . Was Conflict." There he identifies key theological convictions that affirm conflict as inherent in God's creation (that we are created in God's image and given freedom, that God is present within each person, and that God values diversity).[7] "By the very way we are created," he concludes, "conflict will be a part of our ongoing human experience."[8] Conflict is a given. It is a natural and necessary part of God's creation.

On this point, the practitioner-trainer explained that the task "is really about shaping an already existing, evolving process into something that might be life-giving and nourishing."[9] Conflict is happening. The moral dimension of conflict—that is, our assessment of it as good or bad—emerges in the active responses to it. Conflict *can be* incredibly destructive. It *can also be* a catalyst for constructive change in terms of interpersonal relationships or social justice movements. These destructive and constructive aspects of conflict arise as people act in response to the ontological realities of difference and friction. The things that we frequently attach to a conception of conflict—violence, separation, destruction, discomfort, or even constructive engagement and healthy change—are *activities*. They are not part of conflict essentially, which is simply what I defined earlier as a striking together; rather, they attach to conflict via our purposeful response to it. Sin enters as we fail to respond to conflict constructively. In chapter 4, I explore why conflict itself is not sinful, though we may respond to it in sinful ways.

We cannot choose whether to be in conflict, nor can we choose whether conflict affects the human communities in which we live; however, we can choose how to respond to conflict and what kind of change to bring about. How we respond to conflict is a moral matter. Conflict is a natural and necessary element of life. But our responses to conflict are weighted with moral considerations involving power, accountability, values, and beliefs. There is not one single response to conflict because conflict is highly contextual. There are myriad kinds of conflict, and people are positioned in conflict with various degrees of power and various kinds of responses. Conflicts range from interpersonal to international; they can be between couples or between countries. Conflicts may be violent, intense, and brief, or they may persist as a low-intensity "hum" that lasts for years. The nature of conflicts varies tremendously; so do our proximity to them and the extent of our power in the midst of them. One conflict may be a peripheral issue for someone who has the choice of whether or not to engage it, while that same conflict may be truly a matter of life or death for someone else. The same issue that one person opts to address with a postcard or phone call actually determines the future of an undocumented immigrant, a patient's access to affordable medicine, or the length of a soldier's deployment. Even within an interpersonal relationship, there can be a conflict that is perceived as a minor policy change for one person and causes deep personal harm to someone else. Consider, for example, the way that two colleagues might respond to their employer's family leave policy if it assumes a narrow definition of family. The worker who is a straight, married woman accessing maternity leave might well argue that the narrow definition fails to address the needs of nontraditional households. She sees it as unfortunate but does not feel its effects directly. For the gay man in a lifelong partnership contemplating adoption, a narrow policy is one more personal attack on the value of his family and his deep hopes for it. These contextual differences underscore the importance of conflict as a site for moral reflection. Because we are related to one another in a variety of ways, we are already in conflict, and we must respond. Disengagement is not an option. Moreover, given the differences in proximity to and impact of the conflict, our responses must be particularly accountable to those who will carry their weight.

The assertion that to be human is to be in conflict is thus also a moral argument. This is more than an ecological or sociological description;

it is also a normative claim. By normative claim, I mean that "To be human is to be in conflict" is an assertion about the way we *should* live, not only a description of the way we *do* live. As indicated above, the dynamic of conflict inherently reflects difference and relationship. To strike together, we must be different and somehow interacting. These claims relate to a view of human beings as autonomous *and* interrelated, different from one another *and* accountable to one another. In moral reflection, there are times when we emphasize autonomy over relationality, such as when we assert individual rights. At other times, we place greater weight on relationality—when, for instance, we speak of the common good. However, we are *both* autonomous *and* related.

Advancing the moral value of conflict is one way of affirming relationship *and* respecting autonomy. One of the pitfalls of relationality is that we obscure differences or downplay division in order to maintain the relationship. We say, "peace, peace when there is no peace" (Jer. 6:14). Autonomy can be a corrective to this effort at "peacekeeping" because it recognizes others rather than silencing them and because it respects the agency of others rather than denying their power. On the other hand, one of the pitfalls of autonomy is that we tolerate differences without seriously engaging them or feeling accountable to them. Under the guise of autonomy, we act independently (we do our own thing) despite its impact on others. Under the guise of autonomy, we live and let live. That separate living keeps us from being accountable to others, and it keeps us from challenging others. Conflict engagement is a practice of respect rooted in notions of relationship and accountability.

There are many reasons that people deny the presence of conflict, but one underlying reason is power. "There is no conflict here" is one way that those in power maintain the status quo and deny voice to others. When we acknowledge relatedness and take that seriously, we can no longer reframe a conflict as "her issue" or "their problem." When we respect the personhood and agency of others, we listen when they disrupt the peace, and we realize and acknowledge that peace never really existed. We also practice relatedness and respect when we challenge "the appalling silence,"[10] the counsel of "not yet," the feigned ignorance, or the outright denial from those who claim no connection to the issue that burdens, offends, and threatens us. These normative claims about conflict are not only attached to a view of human beings as independent and related, but also to values and beliefs rooted in the Christian tradition.

TO BE CHRISTIAN IS TO BE IN CONFLICT

Christ calls his followers into conflict with their most intimate relations, with cultural practices, with religious and political authorities, with their own inclinations, desires, and prejudices, and ultimately with the principalities and powers of life. Christians interpret and respond to these teachings differently, of course. Some focus on a calling to subordinate personal desires or partial allegiances in order to live according to the will of God. They often understand themselves to be in conflict with progressive forces in culture as they try to maintain faithfulness and obedience to God's law in a changing world. They may, therefore, choose to withdraw from the world in order to follow God's law and Christ's teachings in ways they deem to be more complete. Others emphasize Christ's solidarity with those on the margins and call Christians to resist the subjugation and exclusion of the vulnerable. For these folks, God's law and Christ's teachings call them into the midst of social struggle and political conflict as they work for social justice and liberation. Some Christians live in intentional communities where they practice a way of living in the world that bears witness to an alternative, kingdom vision. Whether they follow a personal piety at odds with contemporary culture, a political ideology that challenges systems of domination and power, or a way of living that offers an alternative to consumerism and materialism, there are Christians whose discipleship places them in conflict with other individuals and other social practices.

Christians also experience the dynamic of conflict as they live into the calling of Christ over a lifetime. The life of faith (or the process of sanctification in my Wesleyan tradition) is also an experience of conflict. We struggle to live faithfully in a changing world. Sometimes the conflicts are internal as we struggle through a discernment process or wrestle with a tension between competing commitments. Sometimes the conflicts are interpersonal as we interact with people whose perspectives differ or whose actions offend and/or threaten people we love and things we care about. And, to be fair, sometimes we are the ones who threaten and offend. Sometimes the conflicts are between groups of Christians who interpret the texts and teachings of their faith differently and reach different conclusions about contemporary issues.

Here again, I assert a normative claim. Clearly, Christian history and contemporary Christian churches are filled with conflict. "To be Christian is to be in conflict" is, in this sense, simply a description of the way things have been and continue to be. But I also suggest that this is the way things *should* be. Christians should be in conflict with one another because the Christian faith is a dynamic, historical development. Christians should be part of the contestations involved in shaping this living tradition. Ethicist Douglas Ottati writes that standing in a living tradition means "participat[ing] in a dynamic process of interpretation—one that moves between received heritage and the realities and challenges of the present world in order to express a continuing and vital orientation or identity."[11] To be a Christian is to locate oneself in a historical tradition that has developed and is developing through interactions of difference. To be a Christian is to be in conflict. While we tend to emphasize a Christian's conflict with "the world" in a sectarian sense, we must recognize that conflict is an integral part of the historical and ongoing development of the faith tradition itself.

Our ecosystem, our societies, and our faith traditions are intrinsically places of conflict, places where the elements or participants are related and different. Moreover, all of these places are under development, and conflict is a catalyst for change. How we respond and how we participate are moral matters. Thus, the central question of ethics as approached in this book is this: *How do we live a good life in the midst of conflict?* My response to the question—and the way that I approach it—reflects a certain understanding of Christian ethics. Not surprisingly, I understand Christian ethics to be a study of conflict.

TO STUDY CHRISTIAN ETHICS IS TO STUDY CONFLICT

Christian ethics is the study of morals and practices guided by the life, ministry, and teachings of Jesus. This object of study is dynamic, varied, and ongoing. Indeed, the object of study in this field is not so much a thing as a process. Christian ethics studies the ways in which people in particular places and historical moments understand their faith tradition to relate to the world unfolding around them, with its scientific discoveries, its cultural shifts, its political movements, and its ecological changes, not to mention its violence, beauty, pain, joy, sorrow, and resilience. This process is full of contingencies, moments in which the slightest variable makes a great difference.

Consider the tidy sentence above about being guided by the life, ministry, and teachings of Jesus. How do we understand those? How do I? How do you? How did our great-grandparents? How does someone in Bolivia? Or Baltimore? Or Berlin? We are immediately faced with different approaches to Scripture, for starters. One helpful resource for organizing different approaches to Scripture comes from an essay written by James M. Gustafson over thirty years ago.[12] Some believers, Gustafson explained, approach Hebrew and Christian Scriptures for instructions on behavior; they turn to Scripture to reveal morality to them. Yet they understand morality to be conveyed in different ways: as law, as ideal, as analogy, and as part of reflective discourse. Each of these four approaches also has variables within it. For example, in the Scripture-as-law approach, believers identify different content as the law. For some, it is the Decalogue (the Ten Commandments, Exod. 20:1–17); for others, it is the so-called hard sayings of Jesus (such as Mark 10:21: "Sell what you own, and give the money to the poor"); still others point to the dual love commandment as the law (to love God and to love your neighbor as yourself, Mark 12:30–31). Others point to the imperatives that Jesus communicates in the form of a story or blessing (such as "Blessed are the peacemakers," Matt. 5:9). Are those laws too?[13]

Another variable in Christian approaches to Scripture concerns matters of application. Consider, for example, those who understand biblical morality to be conveyed in the form of ideals for behavior.[14] Does Jesus' teaching to give up all and follow him apply to every Christian, in the same way, to the same degree? Did Jesus actually think we could achieve this? Or are we called to do our best and confess the rest? Is this an ideal that I should strive for so that my behavior is a little less awful than it might be otherwise?

The contingencies of approaching Scripture as analogy are particularly fascinating because of the power one wields in crafting the analogy.[15] Which biblical story does one choose to match with which historical circumstance? Which biblical characters does one choose to match up with whom in history? Clearly, this is a place where we can easily spot the instrumental use of Scripture, though of course this temptation accompanies every approach. At a panel discussion I attended after September 11, 2001, a person in the audience presented the panelists with an analogy. "It's like the terrorists are Goliath and we [meaning the United States] are David," he said. One of the panelists responded, "Well, what if we are Goliath and the terrorists are David? That is certainly the way they see it." Gustafson describes this as the problem of control: When we approach Scripture analogically, what controls the process? What determines our selection of a particular passage and our arrangement of the characters?

Gustafson refers to reflective discourse as the "loosest" of the four kinds of revealed morality, and indeed it is.[16] In this approach, Scripture is one source among many that the individual uses in a process of discernment. The content of Scripture continues to weigh heavily in one's moral reflection, but it does not necessarily outweigh insights from experience, teachings embedded in a living tradition, or arguments rooted in other sources of knowledge. Here again, the issue of control surfaces prominently: Which moral source (Scripture, tradition, experience, or reason, to use the Wesleyan quadrilateral as an example) holds the most weight?[17]

Gustafson's categories help us to make sense of some of the differences among Christians. One of the reasons why people sharing one faith tradition hold such disparate views on social issues, for example, is that they approach Scripture differently. When we consider that approaches to Scripture are just one variable in Christian ethics (though certainly a particularly weighty one), we become increasingly aware of the potential for multiplicity within Christian ethics. It is not just that Christians *do* think differently about any number of things; it is that Christians *can* think differently about any number of things—and still be Christians. I want to be very careful about this important point. I am not arguing that all Christian perspectives are equally valid. Rather, I am arguing that there is contingency in Christian ethics. The process of moral discernment for an individual Christian is filled with variables: one's focus on one Scripture passage and not another; one's appreciation for one interpretation of Scripture or theology and not another; one's formation in legalistic communities versus utopian communities; one's level of attachment to a particular tradition and that tradition's notions of authority; one's informal education about the relationship between Scripture and other sources of knowledge; one's social location; the influence of one Sunday school teacher, one religious studies professor, one really great sermon, one really horrible sermon; the impact of a current event and the way in which religious leaders do and do not respond to it. These variables—and many others—ensure a multiplicity of Christian views.

This variety alone is fascinating, but even more so is the process through which varieties emerge. It is a process of interaction. We see interaction between text and context, between interpretations and selections, between sources of authority and views of authority, between conceptions of an ideal and perceptions of historical necessity, between desire and obligation, between particular concerns and global commitments, between familiar ways and new ideas. And we see interactions between individual and community, between individuals, between communities, within individuals (navigating multiple allegiances or convictions in tension), and within communities (navigating differences differently). The dynamic and unfolding process of Christian ethics (and Christian faith more generally) naturally involves various kinds of interaction. And because each interacting element has its own boundaries and properties (whether it is a person, conviction, emotion, interpretation, or institution), there is a moment of striking together. The nature of this striking together varies, of course. But the fundamental nature of interaction—an ongoing, dynamic process of striking together—is constitutive of Christian ethics. Thus, to study Christian ethics is to study conflict.

Once again, this is more than a descriptive claim. To study Christian ethics should be the study of conflict. It should involve a full consideration of the differences and disagreements within this living tradition. This is one difference between Christian ethics and Christian morals. Though we tend to use these phrases interchangeably, Christian ethics is the study of Christian morality, the beliefs and values espoused and enacted by Christians. Christian morals is a more fixed category because it assumes that there is indeed a set of beliefs, values, and practices that reflect right belief (orthodoxy), while other assertions are heretical or at least questionable. Studying Christian morals, then, is studying orthodoxy, the right doctrine, the right view on moral issues. Studying Christian ethics involves studying the variety itself, analyzing it, and then engaging in careful discernment, debate, and argumentation. Christian ethics should involve more than assent to right doctrine; Christian ethics should involve contestation and conflict. More than the study of conflict, it involves *participation* in conflict as well.

TO DO CHRISTIAN ETHICS IS TO PARTICIPATE IN CONFLICT

My approach to this debate over orthodoxy and variety reflects the influence of a nineteenth-century German Protestant named Ernst Troeltsch. Troeltsch argued that Christianity is a historical development, one that reflects the dynamic interaction between faith and history. Troeltsch argued that Christians take up their core convictions—the kingdom of God, for example—differently in different sociohistorical contexts.

These convictions are not ahistorical kernels traveling untouched through space and time. Rather, they are interpreted and reinterpreted in light of changing historical circumstances by Christians in living communities over time. Troeltsch's colleague Adolf von Harnack shared Troeltsch's historical sensibility but argued that one ought to be able to sift through all of the accruals of meaning to identify the essence of the faith.[18] For Harnack, there has to be some red thread that captures the essence of the Christian faith, and one should be able to trace that red thread through history.[19] Yet Troeltsch raised concerns about such efforts to strip away everything that does not align with the essence of the faith. What happens to all of the developments in the faith declared inessential? What criteria does one use to distinguish between the essential and the nonessential elements of the faith?

In his own work, Troeltsch adopts another approach.[20] Rather than paring down to the essence, he offers a comprehensive view of Christianity that perceives variation as a quintessential part of the Christian faith and not as mere residue around its essence. His work examines the ways that Christians interpret faith claims anew in the midst of changing circumstances.[21] At the end of his two-volume work *The Social Teaching of the Christian Churches*, Troeltsch describes the interaction between the ideals of faith (primarily the kingdom of God) and the world in terms of *kompromiss* ("compromise" or "ongoing interaction"). He writes, "The history of the Christian Ethos becomes the story of a constantly renewed search for this compromise, and of fresh opposition to this spirit of compromise."[22] Troeltsch's approach helps us to see that the Christian faith is a dynamic and living tradition and that Christians remain active in their faith by working with the interaction between the core convictions and their changing historical circumstances. This work of interaction is not a heretical or prideful practice, but a faithful one. Indeed, this very interaction between faith and history keeps the tradition alive.

Troeltsch's description also makes it clear that we cannot describe, analyze, and critique Christian ethics without becoming a part of the dynamic interactions that continue to shape it. To study Christian ethics is also to do Christian ethics. To study the interactions, frame them, describe them, and analyze them is also to impact them by participating in their historical development. We cannot describe something without affecting it in some way, if only in the way it is received and perceived by those who hear our telling of it. This was actually one of Troeltsch's concerns about Harnack's "red thread"—namely, that directing people's attention to one place is an implicit criticism of everything else.

Contemporary scholars in the field of Christian ethics powerfully address the ethics of vantage point and of listening. Feminist ethicists, for example, share a fundamental commitment to resisting subjugation of persons. This commitment drives keen analysis of power dynamics and the development of forms of scholarship that listen to those who have been silenced or kept on the margins. Feminist ethicist Karen Lebacqz, for example, writes powerfully of the differences between the view from above and the view from below in the context of theories of justice:

> Because this logic comes from the birds, and the fish have not been heard, we are only now beginning to understand the limitations of what we have taken to be the inexorable laws of logic and the tools of traditional ethics. *What is logic to the birds is death to the fish.* To those swimming in oceans of sexism and usury or other injustices, the logic of the oppressor often seems like a "frozen" logic, a life-denying logic.[23]

The commitment to consider the view of the fish has been developed methodologically through the concept of epistemological privilege, meaning that one grants authority to those who have firsthand experience with the problems under discussion. Epistemological privilege means that we recognize the knowledge and wisdom of someone living on the streets when we are thinking about the issue of homelessness, for example. Rather than speaking and writing *about* the situation of others from a place of distant theory, we grant authority and privilege to their own voices and experience. Epistemological privilege also demands that scholars not only listen to these voices of experience, but that they remain accountable to them. For example, if I am developing an argument about how my church should respond to homelessness in the surrounding neighborhood, my proposal should be assessed by those who live on the streets, especially if I claim that my proposal would be somehow "good for them."

Kelly Brown Douglas is a womanist ethicist whose work reflects the commitment and the complexities of epistemological privilege. As a womanist, she attends to the tridimensional oppression of race, class, and gender and focuses her work on the experiences of black women. In her essay "Twenty Years a Womanist," Douglas affirms her methodological commitment to recognize the epistemological privilege of "everyday black women" and explains the ways in which that essential commitment complicates her work as a scholar. First, taking seriously the wisdom of black women challenges traditional, academic notions of knowledge and reveals the complicating dimensions of true "discursive power" (the power to speak and be heard). This methodological commitment also means that the scholar must "name [her] own relative points of privilege" and remain accountable to the women in the pews. Douglas writes, "It is not only from these women that we must learn, but it is also to these women that we are most accountable."[24]

Douglas makes explicit the scholar's interaction with her subject of study and works intentionally to interact with her subjects as subjects, recognizing their privilege and remaining accountable to them. Christian ethicists who adopt a more traditional mode may not listen to the "fish" in Lebacqz's analogy, but they still have a viewpoint and some sites of accountability that shape their approach and the work itself. Scholarship is never a neutral activity. If this is true for the descriptive dimensions of Christian ethics, it is even more true for the prescriptive dimensions. In the prescriptive or normative dimensions, Christian ethicists advance an argument, make a recommendation, or commend one thread of the tradition or one interpretation of Scripture or one application of a conviction or one way of being church over others. They are actively participating in the interaction, not only indirectly impacting it through description, framing, and retelling. Here we see most explicitly that Christian ethicists participate in conflict. This is true for Christian ethicists across the political and theological spectrum. All are involved in the interactions through description and prescription. We are all participating in conflict. Now, we certainly participate in different ways, with various levels of intensity, and with different levels of risk and cost, but the basic dynamics of our work are similar. With our descriptive and prescriptive work (scholarship, teaching, and actions), we participate in conflict.

Some Christian ethicists also participate in conflict beyond their scholarship through practices and actions related to the subjects they pursue academically. We might think of this in terms of a double-axis. The *x*-axis depicts the spectrum of moral reflection and debate on a topic; the *y*-axis depicts the range of activities related to it (from charitable work to advocacy, for example).[25] Christian ethicists participate in conflict through moral debate and argumentation and also through engagement in political acts and spiritual practices related to the subject of debate. The praxis—the ongoing interplay of action and reflection, of practice and theory, of activity and argumentation—is a praxis of conflict. To do Christian ethics is to participate in conflict.

The phrase "to do Christian ethics" is a relatively new development in the way Christian ethicists speak about our work. Those of us who use this phrase do so in order to draw attention to methodology, to describe and prompt critical reflection on approaches employed as Christians live out their faith through argument and action, as well as spiritual practices. This phrase is also used to emphasize that Christian ethics is more than a field of study and scholarship. Christian ethics must be enacted; it must be "done." For people who are frustrated with forms of Christian ethics that are somehow disconnected from practices and actions on the ground, this language of "doing Christian ethics" is powerful and important. For Christians who could not conceive of their faith as solely an academic enterprise in the first place, "doing Christian ethics" may seem an unnecessary restatement of "being a Christian."

Either way, it is important to underscore that Christian ethics is more than a field of study; it is also an arena of practice and a way of life. The central question of ethics—how to live a good life—is not just something to debate or reflect upon in the abstract. It involves embodied knowledge, conversation with others, serious engagement with multiple sources of knowledge, shared actions and mutual dialogue, participation in the life of a faith community, and involvement in the institutions of society. All of this takes place in contexts of conflict and involves conflict. Thus, the question again surfaces: How do we live a good life in the midst of conflict?

HOW DO WE LIVE A GOOD LIFE AMIDST CONFLICT?

The central question of this book is how to live a good life amidst conflict. As I hope the introduction has made plain, this is not an exercise in situational ethics. The question is not, If and when we experience conflict, how should we respond? The question emerges from an ontological reality—that is, one related to being—not an occasion: Given that we exist in ongoing conflict, how then are we to live well?

This introductory chapter has offered the first of several responses to this question and has identified others that are addressed in subsequent chapters. First, it is helpful to see conflict itself as part of the Christian story and the ongoing effort to live faithfully in a changing world. This response reflects a certain approach to Christian ethics, which I will explain in chapter 2. I understand the Christian faith to be a historical development, and I take active participation in this living tradition very seriously. As someone formed in the Wesleyan tradition, I draw on Scripture, tradition, reason, and experience in a process of moral discernment. All of these sources enter into each chapter, though I emphasize them differently. Chapters 3 and 5 work more fully with reason and tradition, while chapter 4 focuses on Scripture. Experience informs every chapter fully, because I cannot step out of my own social location and also because I intentionally attend to the experiences of others.

Chapter 2 orients the reader to the methodologies and contexts present in this text. One could approach the question of living a good life in conflict in a myriad of ways, so it is important to explain the approach this book takes and why. The first part of the chapter situates this book in the tradition of Christian social ethics and emphasizes its constructive approach. In other words, this is a book that takes the interaction between context and faith very seriously. It is important to me that faith informs our behavior in the world, but also that we think carefully and critically about faith in light of lived experiences in history. Chapter 2 also names the norms, approaches, and sources of authority (some of the building blocks in ethics) that inform the content of this book. All of these things occur above ground, as it were. The reader can see what norms and sources are utilized, and I will explain them as we go. But there are also convictions that inform this book and constitute methodological factors in play beneath the surface. Christian ethicists have different views about how transparent we should be about the convictions that inform the ethical positions we articulate. My view is that we cannot be self-critical of convictions that we do not bring into the light. Thus, the second part of chapter 2 describes the confessional context from which I write as someone formed in the Methodist tradition. The assertion that conflict can be a site of constructive change is, for me, also an expression of faith informed by grace and responsibility.

Chapter 3 begins with a description of the ways in which the *imago Dei* enters into contexts of conflict to affirm bodies under attack, to resist attack itself, and to guide the behavior of resisters. The resources informing this chapter include denominational and ecumenical statements responding to violence and injustice, as well as the teaching and behavior of individual Christian actors in some contemporary social movements. The statements and documents provide examples for studying the connection between the image of God, dignity, and human rights, and the Christian actors demonstrate the ways in which this theological conviction both inspires and sets parameters around resistance. By focusing on the ways that this theological doctrine informs principles for behavior, the chapter also offers a study of deontology. Rooting this study in contemporary struggles for human rights and social justice provides particularly fertile ground for considering the importance of universal principles for ethics and the challenges to universality posed by context and power. This chapter also explores the way that contexts of violence shed new light on the meaning of the *imago Dei*. As an example, I consider John Wesley's understanding of the *imago Dei* in light of recent literature on moral injury. By bringing these resources together, we can see that the *imago Dei* speaks not only about our created nature but also about the persons we become over time. In the end, we have an example of deontology that also teaches us about the interaction between principles and context and about the process of becoming as well as an affirmation of being. In contexts of ongoing conflict, we have the *imago Dei* to affirm us and to call us to remain accountable to the other. We live a good life by reflecting and responding to the image of God even in the midst of intense conflict.

Chapter 4 puts a central claim of this book to the test of Scripture. At the heart of conflict transformation is the assertion that conflict can be a site for constructive change. This assertion also distinguishes conflict from sin. However, this distinction is not too apparent in Scripture. Quite the contrary, in fact. There are many passages throughout Scripture that discourage participation in conflict as a threat to community and a sign of selfishness, foolhardiness, and intention to divide. The first part of this chapter examines some of those passages (in Galatians, James, 1 Timothy, 2 Timothy, and Titus) to argue that the criticism of conflict stems primarily from a concern about division. Thus, the goal of unity drives the identification of conflict as a vice. The second part of the chapter turns to a second set of texts, including two practical teachings from Matthew, two conflict stories recorded in Mark and Matthew, and one parable from Luke. In this collection of writings, we do not find a tidy answer to the question of conflict and sin, but we do find reason to challenge the assumptions that conflict always reflects disorder and breeds division. In addition to this example of the use of Scripture in ethical discernment related to conflict, chapter 4 also introduces virtue ethics through discussion of conflict behaviors, the purposes that orient them, and the processes they disrupt.

Chapter 5 turns to teleology through a study of reconciliation. It begins with discussion of the meaning of reconciliation in writings on violence and within the work of conflict transformation. It explores one dominant approach to reconciliation, which understands it through the narrative of atonement and then maps a process for human reconciliation that mirrors the self-giving act of God for humanity, which remains unworthy. This study helps us to see the connections between the conception of the telos and the ways we construe the relationship between here and there. Debates over the relationship between justice and reconciliation readily bring some concerns to the fore. The remainder of the chapter examines restorative conceptions of justice that provide an alternative purpose and path for reconciliation. The final move in the chapter is to consider the multiplicity of narratives that enter into the work of conflict transformation and to call for more open-ended conceptions of the process of moving from violent conflict to nonviolent conflict.

Chapter 6 turns to contexts of interpersonal conflict and to the "mundane" work of equipping people to engage those contexts constructively. This work entails self-assessment, conflict analysis, and mediation. I draw on feminist ethical methodology to argue that these low-profile and often private settings are also worthy of ethical reflection and, indeed, are sites of justice. This chapter also makes connections between self- and conflict-analysis, on the one hand, and H. Richard Niebuhr's approach to ethics as responsibility and discernment of the fitting response, on the other. Tools for analysis offer us a way to explore Niebuhr's fundamental question for ethics: What's going on? This chapter also brings in the feminist ethical methodology of care and explores mediation as a place where the ethics of care unfolds. The interaction between these ethical methods (responsibility and care) and the tools of interpersonal conflict work also provide space to think more critically about power and about fear. As recent work in unconscious bias teaches us, we are constantly being formed to fear. I suggest that we cannot think fully about responsibility and about care without attending to the misperceptions and misinterpretations that fear so regularly causes. The final part of this chapter is written to moral agents like me who occupy positions of relative privilege and are not under threat of direct attack because of identity. For us, living a good life in contexts of ongoing conflict requires that we respond to need rather than react to fear. I explore this point with a meditation on the garden of Gethsemane and the things we are tempted to do in our fear.

The seventh and final chapter responds to the question of how we live a good life in the midst of ongoing conflict with four assertions.

First, we live a good life in the midst of ongoing conflict by taking responsibility for the impact of our actions on others. Second, we live a good life in the midst of ongoing conflict by refusing to be afraid. Third, we live a good life in the midst of ongoing conflict by maintaining an awareness of relatedness. Fourth, we live a good life in the midst of ongoing conflict by discerning possibility. These proposals relate to the principles, virtues, and goals discussed in the rest of the book and place them into conversation with a variety of sources. The foundation for this proposal, and the framing mechanism for the final chapter, is a prayer that closes the baptism liturgy in the Episcopal Church. The prayer captures essential features of a good life in the midst of ongoing conflict: "an inquiring and discerning heart, the courage to will and to persevere, a spirit to know and to love you, and the gift of joy and wonder in all your works."[26]

2
Considering Method

CRAFTING QUESTIONS

When I teach Christian ethics, I require students to craft a moral question that they pursue through a series of steps in a semester-long writing project. With my guidance and in consultation with teaching assistants and with other students, they each spend several weeks crafting a good question. While the students' questions are particular to them, the work of crafting them becomes a shared activity of the class. We all work together to craft good, moral questions. Their initial questions tend to fall into one of three categories. The first (and most popular) category consists of "how to" questions. These exceedingly practical questions are important, of course. However, for a practical question to also be a rich, ethical question, we need to think about the moral foundation underlying the practical concern. This layer of consideration helps us to reflect in ways that are more than practical in nature. We consider not only what to do, but in what manner to do it, and we develop thoughtful rationales for choosing and acting one way and not another way. At this foundational level, we find the norms that guide us. Norms are one of the building blocks of ethics. They are the principles, goals, virtues, and values that give shape and texture to the moral life: Love God and neighbor. Be a good steward of creation. Do justice, love kindness, and walk humbly with your God. Care for the least of these. These examples of moral norms might enter into a process of moral discernment to guide (and often to complicate!) the practical questions we pose.

The second category of initial questions is descriptive. These questions primarily ask for information. When students begin with a descriptive question, my teaching assistants and I ask them what question might remain if they had all of the information. That is, if a student could locate all of the information necessary to address this initial question, what would the follow-up query be? What is the deeper question that still remains? Understanding the nature of a problem as fully as possible is essential to moral reflection. We need to know what is going on before we make any recommendations. This is the descriptive step in ethics, and it explains why ethics is an inherently interdisciplinary enterprise. We need to draw on multiple sources of information to understand the issues we address and the contexts in which they arise. Indeed, we need to know enough to ask good questions, questions that move us to a level of moral reflection on meaning, responsibilities, and implications related to the issue and context we have studied. These questions lead toward the prescriptive work of ethics.

The third category of initial moral questions is particularly tricky. In this category, we find words in the form of questions, but the words actually serve the purpose of teeing up an argument one wants to make rather than articulating a genuine inquiry. They are not truly open questions. They are posed with an agenda in mind rather than a spirit of curiosity. When students pose closed questions, my teaching assistants and I sometimes send them back to the drawing board. But most of the time, we invite them to be transparent about the area of certainty and then to locate an edge past which they feel unclear. The revised moral question arises out of that area of ambiguity, the gray area that persists on the edge of this circle of certainty. We push students to explore the gray space partly to resist the tendency to rush from description to prescription. We are trying to avoid snap judgments, the impulsive call to action, and the ready solution. I work closely with my teaching assistants to make sure that we, as a teaching team, are encouraging a moral pause. In the classroom context, we slow down the process of moving from *is* to *ought* by placing two writing steps between description and prescription (an analysis of moral sources and an explication of a point of view with which they disagree). I have implemented these writing steps in this book as well.

The question driving this text went through iterations that reflect these three categories of questions that need further work. An initial, practical version of the question was this: How do we respond constructively to conflict? I could answer this question with strategies and tools. And I do, regularly—that is, in workshops and in classes, I teach skills and share tools for understanding conflict and our responses to it, and for working more constructively with conflict in congregations, classrooms, and communities. This is valuable work, and the question that drives it is important. But it is not yet a deeply moral question. Underneath this practical question are deeper questions about human relationships, the shape of a "good life," the scope of responsibility and accountability, and the interaction between faith, hope, and lived experience. The moral question beneath the practical question concerns the nature of a life that makes constructive responses to conflict possible, desirable, and sustainable.

Informed by literature in religious peacebuilding, I have also pursued a more descriptive version of this question: What resources within the Christian tradition can help us deal more constructively with conflict? Clearly, Christianity has contributed and continues to contribute to various forms of violence. Can we also identify resources in our texts, traditions, and practices for reducing violence while still pursuing justice? In this search for resources, I have focused on the *imago Dei*, which sets parameters for our behavior and our treatment of others, and on reconciliation, which serves as the telos and ministry for many Christians in conflict. I also have explored passages of Scripture that discourage conflict and passages that offer examples of persons in conflict behaving faithfully. These resources—the information that "answered" my descriptive question—raise new questions, of course. How do we understand moments in history and lived experience that do not seem to follow the arc of reconciliation? How do we understand Scripture passages discouraging conflict in light of very real issues of dispute and injustice in church and society?

As these questions indicate, there are some things I am quite clear about. For example, conflict plays a crucial role in the work of justice, and Christians must neither avoid it nor respond to it violently. Like reconciliation, resistance is a ministry for Christians concerned with the least of these. I am also clear that we are called to behave a certain way in contexts of conflict. In a previous book, I argue that Christians who enter into contentious, pluralistic spaces must exhibit love toward those with whom they disagree, practice theological humility, and work honestly and constructively with moral ambiguity.[1] Around the edges of these positions, however, further questions arise. My clarity was mostly informed by study of nonviolent resistance movements and conflict resolution work, which places conflict within a defined space and time. That is, conflict is understood to be part of a circumstance in history, part of a social movement, or part of a dispute to be addressed. What happens, though, when we see conflict as a persistent feature of human life, not an episode or a circumstance to address periodically? Now, the question shifts from identifying the right resources for the right moment to thinking more fully about living a good life with conflict as a constant feature. The contextual features—the particulars—about conflict vary, of course, but the experience of striking together is a constant in our lives. How do we live a good life in the midst of ongoing conflict?

CONTEXT AND CONSTRUCTIVE PROPOSALS

Clearly, there are many different ways to answer that question. My proposal reflects not only personal convictions that I hold but also a particular approach to Christian ethics. In each of the following chapters, I will pause to explain elements of this approach, but I offer some overarching comments at this point. My approach is contextual and located in the tradition of Christian social ethics. It draws on material from four categories of moral source: Scripture, tradition, reason, and experience. It is constructive in nature, meaning that I critique and reconstruct elements of my tradition in light of conflict and violence. It reflects engagement with six methods of ethics (deontology, teleology, virtue, narrative, responsibility, and care) and the primary influence of responsibility and feminism.[2]

The first point to clarify is that the wording of the question itself reflects a contextual approach to ethics. In Western moral philosophy, we trace the question of "the good life" back to Aristotle's treatise *Nicomachean Ethics*, which begins with an assertion that all things "seem to aim at some good," and the good is "that at which all things aim."[3] What then is the good for human beings? Toward what do we aim? We aim toward excellent functioning as human beings, according to Aristotle: "The good of man is an activity of the soul in conformity with excellence or virtue."[4] Aristotle then describes this activity of the soul as *eudaimonia* ("happiness" or "well-being").[5] Near the end of these collected lectures, he pursues the subject of happiness in more detail, considering different forms of pleasure. He concludes that there is one form of happiness that most completely suits the nature of human beings, namely, contemplation. In contemplation, we function most excellently as human beings. Contemplation is the highest good for human life.[6]

I am certainly not the first person to notice that Aristotle's description of the highest good for human life is the life he was striving to live, the life of a philosopher. Is it possible that Aristotle's experiences in life and the philosophical school that trained him prompted him to pose and answer the question in this way? This brings us to the issue of context, a word that is as nebulous as it is important. Feminist philosopher Margaret Urban Walker notes that "context can be a loose and lazy word," and yet she insists that it is an essential "placeholder for information crucial to understanding what we and others are doing."[7] If we fail to attend to context in moral reasoning, we will reason poorly: "When context is ignored or effaced in theorizing, what we get is irrelevant or bad theory: theory that does not connect with life; theory that distorts, rather than reveals and clarifies."[8] Walker then describes two dimensions of context, both of which I alluded to in my observation about Aristotle. First, we have "the contexts that frame and guide ongoing moral thinking and action as we get on in our lives."[9] These are the circumstances of daily life, the places where we make choices, form perceptions, and enact judgments of various kinds. The second dimension of context points to the ways in which our academic, institutional, and professional places might "configure and constrain the *theories*" we craft. These contexts privilege some language over others, prioritize some values over others, and shape our questions as well as the answers.[10]

The question "How do we live a good life in the midst of ongoing conflict?" reflects both dimensions of context that Walker identifies. First, it takes seriously our varied experiences of conflict and an awareness that conflict in some way is ongoing. Daily life in the midst of ongoing conflict—from interpersonal conflict to social conflict to global violence—frames and guides my moral thinking about relationships, about scriptural teachings, about justice and reconciliation, and about notions of responsibility and care. An awareness of conflict serves as the locus for reflection on these things. However, attention to context does more than paint a landscape and assume all persons experience it the same way. I am situated differently in conflict than you are. Attention to context requires a recognition of variables and contingency. In this book, I use the first-person singular pronoun regularly as a reminder that one person's experience is not the experience of all.

Attention to context requires that we guard against assumptions about the experiences, perspectives, and agency of others.

However, in the framing of the question, I intentionally use the first-person plural pronoun. This reflects an awareness that I do not respond to conflict as an isolated individual or with a view from nowhere.[11] Here, "we" refers to fellow Christians and alludes to the tradition that forms and guides me. As a Christian, I carry with me into every experience of conflict and to every reflection on conflict a certain set of values and a frame for prioritizing them. I engage these contexts of conflict from the context of the Christian faith. My identity as a Christian—and a particular kind of Christian at that—configures and constrains my approach to this awareness of conflict, as well as the values and norms that guide my thinking in the midst of conflict.

I appreciate Walker's description of the two dimensions of context, because we often overlook the second one. That is, we tend to be more attentive to the places and circumstances we are engaging than we are to the frames of reference that we bring to them. Yet so much disagreement among Christians can be clarified (not necessarily resolved) by attending to the resources and approaches that we deploy in ethical discernment. These resources and approaches—or moral sources and methodologies—reflect our own contexts of formation and training. As such, they easily operate at the level of assumption, remaining invisible to ourselves and others. Yet careful ethical discernment requires that we render this ethical infrastructure visible and that we engage it critically. A contextual approach to ethical reflection, therefore, takes into account such particularities. It also prompts self-critical awareness on the part of the one reflecting, particularly on the influence of social location and formative experiences and traditions.

One effect of critical self-awareness is that we see more clearly the historical nature of our positions. We see ourselves standing in living traditions in which people of faith bring their convictions to bear on changing circumstances and also reconsider their convictions in light of changing circumstances. This book affirms and takes seriously the dynamic interaction between the contexts of daily experience and Christian contexts of formation and tradition. Tending to this interaction is not in itself a purpose, though. The reason why we pay attention to the interaction between faith and history, tradition and lived experience, conviction and circumstance, church and world is because "Christianity has a social-ethical mission to transform the structures of society in the direction of social justice."[12] This language from Gary

Dorrien captures the purpose of Christian social ethics, a tradition of scholarship and practice that informs this book.

In the introduction to their edited volume *To Do Justice*, Rebecca Todd Peters and Elizabeth Hinson-Hasty describe this tradition of Christian social ethics with a quick survey of church involvement in social movements such as abolition, worker justice, civil rights, nuclear disarmament, and sanctuary.[13] Their point with the historical survey is to demonstrate that "Christianity is not simply a personal and private matter between an individual and God; it is also about community responsibility and faithfulness in public life—social, political, and economic."[14] This is a key feature of Christian social ethics. In her discussion of methodology, Traci West expresses a similar conviction, but she clarifies that she is not aiming to Christianize the social order.[15] Christians bring their faith to social issues in part because it is impossible to shed it. But West cautions against projecting our beliefs onto others and assuming that Christianity can solve all of the problems of society. Rather, the work of Christian social ethics also requires critical reflection on our own faith tradition. West seeks a "kind of Christian ethics method that most constructively contributes to . . . shared communal responsibilities." Thus, her methodological proposal involves cross-boundary dialogue that "prepares us for the task of building shared ethics in a pluralistic world."[16]

In my book *Christians in the Public Square*, I argue for a similar approach using language of theological humility. By this, I mean three things: (1) admission of the limitations of knowledge and partiality of perspective, (2) explicit and deliberate hermeneutics, and (3) transparency about faith commitments and accountability to other sources of knowledge.[17] These three features of theological humility represent an attempt to make the internal contexts of our ethical reflection transparent. As in the tradition of Christian social ethics that Peters and Hinson-Hasty describe and carry forward, I believe that Christians should engage the work of social transformation for justice and peace. And like West, I think that social engagement should also prompt critical engagement with the resources, texts, and traditions of our faith. This willingness to critique and reconstruct our faith tradition is a mark of constructive Christian ethics. Reflecting such a constructive impulse, this book begins with a description of lived experience and reflects on elements of the Christian tradition in light of that experience. The starting point is the lived experience of conflict (interpersonal conflict, social conflict, and violent conflict), which raises questions about the care for bodies in conflict, our interpretation of Scriptures that speak of conflict, our hopes related to conflict, and our responsibilities to others in the midst of conflict. For example, chapter 3 focuses on experiences of social conflict and considers the *imago Dei* in light of those experiences. Specifically, I listen to the ways in which Christians reference the *imago Dei* in contexts of physical violence (such as police brutality) and of structural violence (such as unjust labor practices). In these contexts, I hear Christians making reference to the image of God as they condemn acts of violence and advocate for change. The first part of this chapter is primarily descriptive. Without weighing in myself, I describe the ways in which other Christians speak of the *imago Dei* as they respond to violence and participate in forms of nonviolent resistance.

The second part of the chapter becomes increasingly normative, meaning that I argue for particular interpretations of the image of God over others. For example, I argue that the image of God should ground responsibilities as well as rights, and I suggest that the image of God is dynamic not static. Although these points are normative (or prescriptive) more so than descriptive, they emerge from contexts of violent conflict (war) and of nonviolent conflict (nonviolent resistance). In keeping with traditions of social ethics, these contexts of conflict provide the starting place for ethical reflection and a site of accountability for the arguments I make. So I draw not only on the experiences of those in conflict but also on sources of knowledge that help us to understand the circumstances and dynamics of conflict. This is another feature of Christian social ethics, namely, that it draws on a range of disciplines to understand the contexts of reflection as fully as possible. These resources for understanding inform both description and prescription. In Christian social ethics, it is important that my assertions about the image of God have something more than biblically based revelation to commend them.

Constructive Christian social ethics, then, is marked by a heavy reliance on lived experience and disciplines of human knowledge that help us to understand the world. For readers familiar with the Wesleyan quadrilateral, we see here the importance of experience and reason as moral sources for ethical reflection. A contrasting point of view demonstrates the significance of this observation about methodology. In 2006, Mark Thiessen Nation (a theology professor at Eastern Mennonite University) published an essay titled "Toward a Theology for Conflict Transformation: Learnings from John Howard Yoder."[18] Nation begins by noting the growth in conflict transformation and the need to bring the resources of Mennonite theology more fully to bear upon it. Before proceeding to identify features of Yoder's thought relevant to conflict transformation, Nation clarifies his use of the preposition "for" and warns against the preposition "of." He references Yoder's criticism of "genitive theologies" in which the theological material is determined by whatever follows the preposition, and explains, "Yoder intentionally avoids this error. He does not begin with the 'givens' of some science called 'conflict transformation' that exist prior to his theological reflections. Rather, having read relevant literature in the field, Yoder offers 'a theological point of reference.'"[19] Nation, then, considers the ways in which several of Yoder's theological themes are helpful to the work of conflict transformation.

Nation's article constitutes a methodological foil to the approach in this book. I do not bring theological material into contexts of conflict unilaterally. Rather, what you will find here is a more dynamic interaction between contexts of conflict, sources of knowledge about conflict, and theological material from the Christian tradition. That dynamic interaction is intentional and reflects a historical approach and a constructive, social ethic. This approach to ethics insists that theological argument must also be accountable to what we know of the world through other sources of information. In more classical terms, we would say that faith must be accountable to reason.[20] In my view, this does not mean that we allow "some science of 'conflict transformation'" to determine our theology, although it does demonstrate that Christian ethics related to conflict emerges from the interaction of Scripture, theology, the sciences, and human experience. This multi-directional movement is much more dynamic than the prepositions "of" or "for" can capture. The theological assertions explored here (primarily *imago Dei* in chapter 3 and reconciliation in chapter 5) inform and are informed by the contexts of conflict.

This dynamic method of Christian social ethics is also shaped by an ethical commitment to form Christians to engage conflict more constructively. This is what the adjective "constructive" indicates. Projects like this one are not value neutral. We do not explore the relationship between ethics and conflict in a value-free space. Rather, I turn to these contexts of conflict with the desire for Christians to engage them more constructively. And as I have come to see conflict itself as a persistent feature of human life, I want to encourage Christians to live well in the midst of ongoing conflict, not only to behave better in a particularly overt moment of conflict. This requires that we understand the contexts of conflict and the way in which conflict is a regular feature of human life. But it also requires that Christians reflect critically on elements of our faith tradition that equip us to engage conflict constructively and elements that impede this goal. This dimension of constructive Christian social ethics explains the presence and approach of chapter 4, which turns to Scripture as a resource for Christian reflection on conflict.

I bring to Scripture a particular concern about passages that suggest conflict is a sin or at least a vice. Such a view stands in contradiction to the one that I assert and want to advance, namely, that conflict can be a site for positive change in human beings and human community. So I adopt toward Scripture a particular hermeneutic, modeled after liberationist hermeneutics. Hermeneutics refers to interpretation and draws our attention to the lenses that we bring to a text. Hermeneutics asks us to consider the ways that a lens or frame of interpretation affects what we see and what we value. A liberationist hermeneutic asserts that a central truth of Scripture is that God is a God of freedom. Through this lens, one casts a suspicious or critical look at passages that condone human slavery or the subjugation of persons. These passages are not as true or as binding as passages that affirm God's desire for freedom.[21] In an analogous way, I cast a critical look at passages that discourage conflict as divisive, heretical, foolish, and selfish. Rather than accepting these teachings as true because they are in the Bible, I ask what seems to motivate them. What is the concern behind the text? Why is conflict so strongly discouraged? These behaviors were construed as problematic in light of a goal for unity or cohesion, a goal that was clearly important to the newly formed community of Jesus followers. But if we bring different sensibilities to the text, we see this differently. Struggles for liberation and for justice have made it clear that tyrants and protectors of the status quo regularly appeal to unity as a mechanism for silencing dissent and resistance. Suspicion toward the goal of unity in Scripture also brings into light other biblical characters who risk resistance and model persistence. This conflict transformation hermeneutic, then, focuses on the Syrophoenician woman who resists Jesus' dismissal of her need and is then rewarded for her challenging and faithful word (Mark 7:28–29). It also pays special attention to the persistent widow who bothers the unrighteous judge until he vindicates her. Jesus tells her story in the context of a parable (Luke 18:1–5), through which he encourages his wearied disciples to remain faithful and to persist in hope.

Lifting up the Syrophoenician woman and the persistent widow also reflects feminist, liberative commitments to bring to the center those who have been marginalized. Feminist ethics resists forms of subjugation in both theory and practice. Christian feminist ethics requires that we interrogate our faith tradition for texts and practices that keep people on the margins, perpetuate physical and structural violence, and silence dissent. Informed by these feminist commitments, chapter 5 critically engages the telos (or goal) of reconciliation and a central text that calls Christians to ministries of reconciliation (2 Cor. 5:18–20). Like my interlocutors in that chapter, I feel bound to the goal of reconciliation and hear the calling in this text. Yet prioritizing the concerns of victims of violence makes me cautious about forms of reconciliation that might sacrifice justice for them, and interpretations of Scripture that commend the sacrifice of victims. Out of commitment to the needs of victims of violence, I resist an approach to Scripture that aligns their suffering with the voluntary suffering of Christ and then calls them to, like Christ, forgive the offenders. Attention to the needs of victims also prompts me to privilege descriptions of reconciliation that incorporate practices of restorative justice, and study of restorative justice approaches confirms the value of nonlinear descriptions of the journey toward reconciliation. In this chapter, then, is ongoing negotiation between moral sources of Scripture, tradition, reason, and experience. The reader will also sense the work required of Christian ethics to be faithful to traditions and texts as well as responsive to the changing needs of the world and the voices of those too often silenced there.

Chapter 6 turns from social and political contexts to interpersonal conflict. I continue the argument advanced by feminists who defend the private sphere of interpersonal relations as a worthy site for moral reflection and a place where justice is also at stake. This chapter places in conversation conflict analysis and H. Richard Niebuhr's responsibilist approach, as well as mediation and an ethics of care. The interaction between these conflict practices and the methods of ethics helps us to think more critically about issues of power and dynamics of fear. Out of this interaction comes a proposal to and for those in positions of power: that we live a good life in the midst of conflict by responding to need rather than reacting to fear.

The final chapter draws on liturgy, Scripture, experience, and literature to describe a good life in the midst of ongoing conflict. The liturgical frame for the chapter reminds us that these responses to conflict are not episodic, ad hoc, or occasional. Rather, they reflect—or should reflect—our identity as persons in the Christian tradition, formed in a way of life whether or not it is convenient, expedient, or practical. We are called and equipped to live a certain way in the world: with "an inquiring and discerning heart, the courage to will and to persevere, a spirit to know and to love [God], and the gift of joy and wonder in all [God's] works."[22] In contexts of conflict, this prayer takes on additional meaning because the behaviors named become increasingly hard to sustain. In contexts of conflict when we feel fearful or threatened, it is even harder to open ourselves to learn something new or to think differently about the things we think we know. When we feel daunted or exhausted by the need to fight the good fight yet again, it is even more difficult to remain courageous and to persevere. And when we feel anxious and preoccupied and harried, it is even more difficult to remain connected to God and to feel joy and wonder in the world around us. The liturgy does not define a good life; it captures a prayer for help in living well, especially when life does not feel good.

ETHICS, GRACE, AND RESPONSIBILITY

This chapter on methodology has thus far described the conceptual design for this book by explaining the motivating question and my general approach to it. I have also described the building materials (the moral sources and the norms derived from them) and led a tour through the rooms that represent different methodological approaches to this question of the good life. In other words, I have made plain the inner workings of this project, but only those that appear above ground. Underneath the question, the sources, the norms, and forms, and the structure of any project in ethics, there sit deeply embedded yet often unarticulated notions about human beings and the world we occupy. That is, beneath every project of Christian ethics, there is also a set of beliefs about the possibilities and limitations of human beings and history. When I assert, along with the conflict transformation school of thought, that conflict can be a site for constructive change, I am also communicating deeply held convictions about human beings and history. Christian ethicists have different views and practices about the confessional dimension of our work, how plainly or fully to communicate the convictions that undergird our interpretations and argument. I am of the mind that transparency increases our understanding of one another, our honesty about our engagement with subject matter, and the possibilities for critical exchange and learning.

Two of the most formative figures in contemporary Christian ethics debated one another in print only once, though they must have debated in private many times because they were brothers. In 1932, the *Christian Century* published an exchange between H. Richard Niebuhr and Reinhold Niebuhr about Japan's invasion of Manchuria and whether the United States should intervene. H. Richard begins his essay this way:

> It may be that the greatest moral problems of the individual or of a society arise when there is nothing to be done. When we have begun a certain line of action or engaged in a conflict we cannot pause too long to decide which of various possible courses we ought to choose for the sake of the worthier result. Time rushes on and we must choose as best we can, entrusting the issue to the future. It is when we stand aside from the conflict, before we know what our relations to it really are, when we seem to be condemned to doing nothing, that our moral problems become greatest. How shall we do nothing?[23]

H. Richard then describes three different kinds of inactivity: that of the pessimist who believes there is nothing to be done, that of the one who has renounced a possible action (violent intervention in this case) on moral grounds and stands by frustrated and morally indignant, and the inactivity of one who sees the current situation as a necessary prelude to something better. To these options, he adds the inactivity of the Christian who believes that "the fact that men can do nothing constructive is no indication of the fact that nothing constructive is being done."[24] The inactivity of the believer is rooted in an awareness of God's activity in history and human error in history. Driven by "rigid self-analysis," this believer knows that he cannot act in history as he needs to, in a disinterested (selfless) way.[25]

Reinhold Niebuhr absolutely agrees with H. Richard's assessment of human fault. We cannot act purely because we are too sinful, too selfish. But, Reinhold says, that does not mean we should not act. For Reinhold, the call to the necessary, imperfect historical action outweighs a "pure gospel ethic" that keeps the self-aware Christian inactive. He resists his brother's position that "it is better not to act at all than to act from motives which are less than pure."[26] Reinhold perceives in H. Richard's position something closer to a pure gospel ethic (which H. Richard himself never claims) that is ill-suited to history. Indeed, Reinhold understands history and our human experience within it as "perennial tragedy; for the highest ideals which the individual may project are ideals which he can never realize in social and collective terms."[27] Christians are called toward a behavior that is impossible to achieve in history. Thus, we must do what is necessary within the confines of history to approximate justice even by impure means.

In his response, H. Richard counters his brother's view of history as tragedy by describing it instead as "the prelude to fulfillment," because the "Kingdom of God comes inevitably." While Reinhold understood the kingdom of God as a transcendent ideal, one that obligates us but remains out of reach, H. Richard described the kingdom of God as an "'emergent,' a potentiality in our situation which remains unrealized so long as we try to impose our pattern, our wishes upon the divine creative process." He concludes by describing the human task as "eliminating weeds and tilling the soil so that the kingdom of God can grow" and "clearing the road by repentance and forgiveness."[28]

Reinhold and H. Richard Niebuhr shared a low view of human nature. They both believed that our human propensity to sin (primarily in the form of selfishness and pride) impedes our ability for Christ-like action in the world. For H. Richard, we respond to this reality with a posture of repentance and forgiveness of others (knowing our own faults) and a commitment to a form of inactivity that places trust in God's movement in history. The kingdom of God is emergent; it is a possibility if we can stay out of the way. Reinhold did not share the belief that the kingdom of God would emerge if we just got out of the way. Rather, he insisted that we must act even though we perpetually fall short of the ideals to which we are called. History is perennial tragedy. There is no emergent kingdom despite us. Our option is to do our best in history, to do what is necessary given the realities of our selfish nature and the moral obligations placed upon us.

This exchange clearly speaks to the question driving this book: How do we live a good life in the midst of ongoing conflict? While these two figures loom large in my field and over me personally, they do not offer satisfactory answers to this question. First of all, the persistence of conflict, as I understand it, is not a mark of tragic history. We might respond to conflict in sinful ways, but it is not the same thing as sin. The main difference here is that conflict contains within it a possibility for good that sin does not. In this sense, my concept of conflict persisting in history connects more closely with H. Richard than with Reinhold. In conflict, we also have an emergent, a possibility for constructive change, the possibility of transformation. To say that conflict continues is not to say that history is perennial tragedy; it *is* to say that history contains the possibilities for change because conflict is present. Our moral task is then to realize the possibilities for positive, constructive change. Unlike the Niebuhr brothers, I think that we imperfect human beings have the capacity to do this, to respond to conflict constructively for purposes of transformation. And to move fully into confessional mode: after twenty years of wrestling with the Niebuhr brothers, I am convinced that I do not share their view of human beings, primarily because I was formed in the Methodist tradition. My Methodist heritage continues to shape the possibilities I see for human behavior in history and the calling I feel to respond to the grace of God with every concerted effort to live a good life. These convictions run under every page of this book; they also shape its methodology and argument.

One intriguing time period for Methodists interested in questions of the good life is the 1740s, a time when the Methodist movement had grown enough to start getting into trouble. John Wesley was on the receiving end of theological criticism and in the midst of theological debates. He responded by insisting that Methodism is simply "genuine Christianity" living out the dual commandment to love God and neighbor.[29] He faced another kind of trouble in his visits to communities where the Methodist movement had been planted or had spread. He discovered people who had been captivated by the preaching of an itinerant or by Wesley himself but who had not really changed their ways of living. Faced with this backsliding, Wesley wondered how to support people in their journey toward perfection and how to hold them accountable.

So he clarified and codified the "United Societies." A society was "a company of [people] having the form and seeking the power of godliness, united in order to pray together, to receive the word of exhortation, and to watch over one another in love that they may help each other to work out their salvation."[30] In my view, there was a low bar for admission to the societies, but a high bar for continued membership in them. The one condition for admission was a desire for salvation. Does one say yes to God's extension of grace? Does one receive the offer of healing and redemption? An affirmative answer meant that the person could be admitted into a society. However, to remain in such societies, members had to show evidence that they were working on their own salvation, that they were responding to God's grace by living a holy life. Wesley wrote that all members of a society were expected to "evidence their desire of salvation."[31] They were expected to be *trying*. They needed to show evidence of effort.

My father's parents pursued their ministry in Methodist churches throughout southern Illinois. My grandfather was ordained in the Illinois Conference, and by the time I was old enough to pay attention, he was caring for a three-point charge of small, rural churches in his retirement. Clearly, one person could not meet the pastoral needs or even cover all of the worship services in three churches. So my grandmother, having received her "exhorter's license" in the early 1940s, continued with my grandfather in their joint ministry, preaching regularly on the circuit. In fact, we have a big folder full of her sermons, which were mostly written in the margins of the previous week's bulletins. Their context of ministry is the closest thing that I know to the early Methodist movement. Their flock was spread out; there were gatherings throughout the week led by other people in the congregation. They spent a lot of time traveling through the fields of southern Illinois and checking in on people. On the road as they often were, it was not unusual for my grandparents to pack a picnic lunch and stop along the side of the road to eat. They were not shy people, and they sat comfortably on the side of the road greeting people as they drove by. But this ease with being seen eating a picnic became more complicated when Coca-Cola started using cans instead of bottles. Although beer companies had started using cans as early as the 1930s, Coca-Cola did not use cans until the late 1950s. For a good twenty years, a passerby would see someone drinking from a can and *know* that the beverage could only be a beer. My grandparents, being good, old-fashioned, midwestern Methodists, definitely did not drink beer! So my grandmother would crouch down on the far side of the car to sip her Coke from a can, lest some passerby see her and think the worst.

This was not just a superficial concern about perception and reputation. Beatrice (Betty) Ott was living out the historical repercussions of membership in a Methodist society. When Wesley checked in on the society at Newcastle in 1743, he found that the members were so lax that he expelled sixty-four of them, seventeen of them for drunkenness. The other offenses included cursing and swearing; quarreling and brawling; habitual, willful lying; and habitual Sabbath-breaking. The number-one reason why members were expelled from this society, however, was "lightness and carelessness."[32] Two days after that visit to Newcastle, Wesley drafted "The Nature, Design, and General Rules of the United Societies" to clarify expectations.[33] These societies were intended to be a place where people could gather for fellowship and mutual accountability, to support one another in the journey toward perfection. Members were expected to show evidence of effort through holy living. But the rules reflect more than moralistic finger wagging. Viewed in the broader context of Wesleyan theology, the rules reflect an effort to craft a good life through grace and responsibility.[34]

According to Wesley, we are invited into relationship with a God who loves us and who continues to work with us to live well in the world and to channel God's grace into the world. We are called and accompanied by God on this journey toward perfection. Wesley took this invitation with utmost seriousness, and he demanded that those who claimed to be on the journey show evidence that they were actually doing their part. We cannot claim to be saved and then behave however we want. We cannot squander the gift. Wesleyan theologian Ted Runyon writes that Wesley understood grace to be "the transforming influence of God's love, present and active in human life."[35] If we claim to receive the grace of God, we should live that way. We must respond to the grace of God by working on ourselves, working in our communities, and working for the world.

This was the context in which Wesley codified the rules for the societies: do no harm, do good, and attend to the ordinances of God.[36] He explained that following these rules would show evidence of the members' desire for salvation. It is important to underscore that the rules themselves were not the motive for the behavior. We do not follow the rules because Wesley told us to. Rather, we strive to avoid harm, do good, and follow the ordinances of God because we are striving to live out our response to the grace of God and to channel that grace into the world. It is not enough for me to simply say that, yes, God is working in my heart. I need to also show evidence of my effort to respond to the way God is working in my heart. In language that is certainly not unique to Methodists, we need to do the right things in the right way for the right reason.

Wesley did not make up these rules himself. His moral source for them was Scripture, specifically Isaiah 1:1–17, in which the prophet scolds the people for focusing solely on ritual as evidence of faithfulness. Through the prophet, the Lord says, "I have had enough of your burnt offerings. . . . Bringing offerings is futile. . . . When you stretch out your hands, I will hide my eyes from you" (1:11–15). Rather than all of this, the Lord commands the people to "cease to do evil; learn to do good; seek justice, rescue the oppressed, defend the orphan, plead for the widow" (1:16–17). Wesley drew on this passage for the rules for the societies and, more broadly, when he preached about working out one's own salvation. The reference in that case is to Philippians: "Work out your own salvation with fear and trembling; for it is God who is at work in you, enabling you both to will and to work for God's good pleasure" (Phil. 2:12–13). In his sermon on this text,[37] Wesley insisted on a particular order and meaning for these points, the first being that God is at work in you. God's working in you makes it possible for you also to work. Prevenient grace makes it possible for all of us to begin the journey toward salvation, toward health and wholeness. But this is more than just a spark given to us once that we must then fan alone. Wesley insists that God "not only infuses every good desire, but that [God also] accompanies and follows it, else it vanishes away."[38] God is not only present with us; God is also at work in us, all the time, nurturing our best inclinations and encouraging our best thoughts.

Wesley's second point, intentionally ordered as such, is that because God is at work in us, we must also work, with fear and trembling. Wesley rejected the connotation of fear and trembling as a call to "stand trembling and quaking" before our master.[39] Rather, Wesley insisted, the apostle Paul used such strong expressions to compel us to work with "earnestness of spirit, and with all care and caution."[40] Because God is at work in us, we are able to work. And because God is at work in us, we must work. This raises the question, How must we work? What steps do we take "in the working out of our own salvation"? Wesley answered by pointing back to Isaiah. "The prophet Isaiah," Wesley preached, "gives us a general answer touching the first steps which we are to take: 'Cease to do evil; learn to do well.'"[41] When he then offered these rules to the Methodist societies, Wesley provided a long list of examples of behavior from which they should abstain. His list includes all of the behaviors that prompted him to expel those lax members in Newcastle. But it also includes various forms of mistreatment of others and various kinds of activities and preoccupations that distract us from God.

That is, of course, the point. The rules are not about the rules. The rules provide direction and give parameters as we journey toward perfection. If we focus on the rules, we lose the point of them. The point is salvation, the healing and redemption of the world. We participate in that work, we contribute to that process by doing all the good we can. But we also participate in the work of God by doing no harm, by avoiding evil, by saying no. The prophet Isaiah understood both avoiding evil and doing good to be required in order to seek justice, rescue the oppressed, defend the orphan, and plead for the widow. We seek justice not only by doing good, but also by saying no to policies that take advantage of vulnerable people. We rescue the oppressed not only by reaching out to those on the margins, but also by saying no to speech that disrespects them. We defend the orphan and plead for the widow not only through acts of compassion, but also by saying no to the violence that orphaned and widowed them. Sometimes we think of doing no harm as a minimalist posture, a commitment not to make things worse. But it is important to perceive the boldness and active engagement in acts of refusal and resistance. Saying no need not be a withdrawal from the world; it can be an active reorientation away from something harmful, an act of resistance to something hurtful. It is a refusal to participate in speech, actions, policies, and practices that thwart the renewing spirit of God at work in the world. Saying no is part of living a good life in the midst of conflict.

I have always loved that story of my grandmother hiding with her can of Coke. I love it because it captures a piece of my family history that is deeply important to me: I come from teetotaler Methodists who took seriously the call to live modestly in service to others, to live sober and serious lives of faith, to work hard, to refuse the temptations of materialism and vanity, and to celebrate every day the wondrous work of God. I approach the question of the good life not only from the context of constructive, Christian social ethics, but also from this context of embedded convictions, lived theology, and formation through faith and family. Before I actually read anything by Wesley or about the Methodist movement, I was formed in a tradition of grace and responsibility. I was taught that if we really do believe God's grace is at work in our lives, then there should be evidence of our effort to work with God in this ongoing process of salvation. We should be working on ourselves, in our communities, and for the world in courageous and loving ways. We should turn away from practices that do harm, then embrace ways of living that contribute to the health and well-being of all, especially the most vulnerable. I have not offered this discussion as formal instruction on Wesleyan theology and ethics, but rather as a description of the influence that my Methodist upbringing has on the way I frame and pursue this moral question about a good life in the midst of conflict.

My upbringing not only shapes my sense of human potential in history with the notions of grace and responsibility; it also shapes the way I think about conflict. My breed of midwestern Methodist does not complain or raise a ruckus. We simmer quietly and then scold ourselves and get back to work. In short, we avoid conflict. There are many reasons to avoid conflict, of course, and some of them are quite good. But one poor reason to avoid conflict is fear of the risk that it entails.[42] I see in conflict something that is disruptive and beyond my control; engaging conflict thus requires a willingness to risk. I have come to think that a hesitancy to risk is one of the downsides of my formation in responsible living. Or put more accurately, a fear of risk upsets the balance between responsibility and grace. When you are formed to do the right thing in the right way for the right reason, when you are taught to see action and character formation as entwined, when you have a deep sense of responsibility for the impact of your actions on others, and when you perceive a calling to channel God's grace into the world, it is very difficult to risk. This kind of formation prompts one to be deliberative and cautious so as to avoid errors in process and outcome. Engaging the literature of conflict transformation has helped me to put these things back in balance. Studying conflict, violence, nonviolent resistance, and peacebuilding underscores the importance of acting with care, of not assuming control; of deliberating fully while admitting partial perspective; of doing our very best while attending to ambiguity. In short, engaging conflict constructively requires an openness to risk that grace makes possible. From this particular (though in no way unique) context of formation, I am learning to respond to conflict with the conviction that God equips us to respond constructively, calls us to do our best, and welcomes us home when we come up short. I am also learning to engage conflict with a hope rooted in a gracious God who fills history with possibility.

CONCLUSION

The purpose of this chapter has been to explain the approach that this book takes to its driving question: How do we live a good life in the midst of ongoing conflict? I explained the journey toward the question itself and then named some of the norms and approaches I utilize to answer it. This chapter also emphasized the contexts in which I explore the question and from which I address it. Our response to this question is highly contextualized. We respond to conflict differently in different contexts, and the following chapter tries to reflect that. But I am also intentionally exploring ways to live a good life in a constant state of conflict, with the full recognition that we strike together simply because we are related and changing. Striking together is an unavoidable part of human life in relationship (and there is no other way to live). This is not a fallen or tragic reality, in my view. It is simply the way we live. And it presents us with the challenge to respond well, to approach conflict as an opportunity for constructive change. The views that I have shared from my Methodist heritage are not unique to me or to Wesleyans. But they are distinctive from other views of history as tragic, for example, and human beings as too sinful to respond constructively in history. I perceive in conflict possibilities for constructive change. And I practice a form of hope that requires searching out the transformative possibilities within history without downplaying the limits to realization and the losses we experience along the way.[43] These convictions will move back underground now, as I explore the views of others who seek a good life in the midst of conflict.

3

Affirmation and Accountability through the Imago Dei

Considering Deontology, Tradition, and Reason

This chapter begins to answer the question "How do we live a good life in the midst of ongoing conflict?" by pointing to the *imago Dei*, the theological assertion that we are created in the image of God. Of all the places to begin, why do I begin here? After all, the *imago Dei* has a very small scriptural basis, it has been deployed historically to exclude as much as it has to affirm, it continues to be interpreted in a variety of ways, it regularly draws fire when offered as a theological foundation for human rights, and it has been written about and extolled ad nauseum. And yet . . . when I first read that Boko Haram strapped explosives to the bodies of girls in Nigeria and sent them into crowded markets where the explosives detonated,[1] I found myself screaming about a desecration of the holy, because other language about violence against bodies was not strong enough to convey my fury. When violent religious rhetoric shoves young people struggling with gender and sexuality identity into closets and onto ledges, I do not want them simply to find vague comfort in the grace of God who loves them anyway. I want them to hear that *they are created in the image of God.* When yet another black body lies in the street or another brown body lies crumpled in a truck, I want to call on our strongest possible religious language to convey the depth of wrongdoing and exclaim, "This is sacrilege!" It is not just that I need the language of *imago Dei* to say how wrong these things are; the truth of *imago Dei* reminds us how wrong they are.

If only I could simply point to the *imago Dei* to condemn the actions of others and to defend people I care about and agree with! But that would constitute an instrumental use of this theological doctrine, which complicates my prophetic speech and politics considerably. *All* people are created in the image of God: the member of Boko Haram who strapped the explosives on the girl, the man on the corner holding a sign that says "God hates gays," the police officer who shot the black boy, and the trafficker who pocketed money from the now-dead migrant. This is also why I begin answering the question about living a good life in conflict by pointing to the *imago Dei*. We live a good life in the midst of ongoing conflict by remembering that all persons are created in the image of God—the victims and the perpetrators, the resisters and the bystanders, the advocates and the apathetic. This conviction places parameters around how we treat one another while we remain in conflict. I point to the *imago Dei* not only because we need parameters in conflict, but also because we simply must live as though one of the central tenets of the Christian faith actually matters. You are created in the image of God, and so is that person you despise.

In the midst of violent and nonviolent conflict, the *imago Dei* reminds us how *all* people should be treated. It functions as a principle that transcends our particular inclinations in the moment. It establishes rules for behavior to which we all must adhere. It provides a standard that policies and procedures should meet. Examining the *imago Dei* and contexts of conflict, therefore, gives us a lesson about deontology as well. The Greek root of deontology, *deon*, means "duty" or "that which is binding." Deontology is a branch of ethics that determines the right course of action by referring to rules and principles. It also assesses moral action and actors according to their adherence to rules, principles, or laws.[2] In *The Responsible Self*, H. Richard Niebuhr assigns the metaphor of "citizen" to the moral agent in a deontological system. This metaphor captures the point that those operating with a deontological approach see themselves as governed by a rule or principle to which they must adhere. The primary question for the deontologist is: What should I do?[3] Deontology emphasizes what we should and should not do more than who we should and should not be or become. A concern with being indicates that character or virtue ethics predominates, as we will see in chapter 4. Deontology focuses more on intention than outcome, which distinguishes it from teleological ethics, which we will examine in chapter 5.

In deontology, our capacity to adhere to a principle rather than give in to personal biases is perceived as a mark of moral maturity. And to hold people in different situations accountable to the same principle is an issue of fairness. In other words, deontologists perceive my tendency to yield to my own partial concerns and interests as a threat to fairness and to ethical consistency. Correspondingly, deontologists understand rules and principles to safeguard against self-interested bias and partial concerns. Psychologist Carol Gilligan refers to this ethical stance as a justice orientation or justice perspective: "From a justice perspective, the self as moral agent stands as the figure against a ground of social relationships, judging the conflicting claims of self and others against a standard of equality or equal respect (the Categorical Imperative, the Golden Rule)."[4] Deontologists assert that we need criteria external to ourselves in order to make ethical judgments. Without these external or transcending principles, I would continue to make judgments that serve primarily my interests and to advance goals that are best for my relations. Ethical behavior requires adherence to rules that transcend my particular context and concerns.

These features of deontology present us with a picture of transcendent, universal principles that we pull into our historical location as needed. Deontology, as presented so far, does not seem to allow for the fact that the principle must also reflect some historical influence. Yet that is exactly what we see with the *imago Dei*, a rich theological-ethical doctrine that accrues meaning over time and remains binding across time. This chapter begins with an honest account of the small scriptural basis on which this massive Christian doctrine rests. It then explores a variety of conflicts and the way that the *imago Dei* functions in them. This journey helps us to see something important about Christian ethics. Living a good life means more than applying the tenets of faith to history; it demands that we also reflect on our faith in light of history. We learn about the beauty and power of the *imago Dei* by attending to bodies in their destruction, brokenness, healing, restoration, and transformation.

IMAGO DEI IN THE TEXT

Given the frequent and weighty presence of *imago Dei* in Christian ethics, one might expect an expansive scriptural basis for this stance and a consistent and clear meaning. However, what we find is a mere handful of scriptural references and a variety of interpretations. The primary reference for *imago Dei* comes from Genesis 1:26–27:

> Then God said, "Let us make humankind in our image, according to our likeness; and let them have dominion over the fish of the sea, and over the birds of the air, and over the cattle, and over all the wild animals of the earth, and over every creeping thing that creeps upon the earth." So God created humankind in his image, in the image of God he created them, male and female he created them.

Beyond this key text we find a few more references. The genealogy offered in Genesis 5 opens with this reminder: "When God created humankind, he made them in the likeness of God" (5:1). In Genesis 9, we find God's covenant with Noah, which includes this mandate: "Whoever sheds the blood of a human, by a human shall that person's blood be shed; for in his own image God made humankind" (9:6). We find two more references in the New Testament. In Paul's first letter to the Corinthians, he mentions the image of God but adds a distinction based on gender to explain why women should cover their heads: "For a man ought not to have his head veiled, since he is the image and reflection of God; but woman is the reflection of man" (1 Cor. 11:7). James also references the image of God in the course of his appeal to tame the tongue, which utters both blessings and curses: "With [the tongue] we bless the Lord and Father, and with it we curse those who are made in the likeness of God" (Jas. 3:9). Noting these few references, theologian Ian McFarland comments, "Though the phrase is certainly evocative, such a sporadic pattern of use would seem to suggest caution in according it excessive anthropological weight."[5] Yet since the time of Irenaeus, McFarland continues, theologians have viewed the *imago Dei* "as the key to formulating the Christian doctrine of human being."[6]

In the field of Christian ethics, *imago Dei* features prominently in moral discernment and ethical argumentation over social, political, economic, and biomedical questions. Sometimes, like Paul, Christian ethicists refer to the *imago Dei* to make distinctions among persons or to set persons apart from the rest of creation. In other places, one finds argumentation akin to that of James: concern about the way we treat others in light of the fact that all are made in the image of God. The introduction to this chapter demonstrated how readily Christians turn to the *imago Dei* to convey outrage at violence and to call for more caring and just treatment. It also noted the way that the image of God connects with the notion of human dignity and functions as a theological foundation for human rights. These connections are both plentiful and fraught with complications.[7] So what are we to make of this cartoonish discrepancy between the massive history of engagement with a theological concept and the small scriptural basis on which it rests?

This book takes a historical approach to Christian ethics, meaning that it observes and appreciates the interaction between faith and history as a resource for new insight as well as grounding for ethical positions. A historical approach to religion perceives and values its development over time through a dynamic process that involves the interaction of texts, communities, and lived experience. Applying the historical sensibility to the image of God, we can see how this central doctrine has accrued meaning over time. The historical approach considers the massiveness of the concept currently as a reflection of its development as Christians have interacted with it across time and space rather than encapsulating it from historical developments in a dogmatic fashion. Considering the dynamic interaction between the theological concept and changing sociohistorical contexts gives us new understanding and demonstrates the power of principles that are both universal and lived out in the particular contexts of faith.

THE *IMAGO DEI* IN CONTEXT

In her book *Ferguson and Faith*, Leah Gunning Francis shares the experiences and convictions of Christian ministers who participated in social activism in Ferguson, Missouri, after the shooting of Michael Brown on August 9, 2014. Francis writes:

> For the clergy, standing up for justice on behalf of Michael Brown was about joining the work of God in the world. This was a tipping point in the fight against black lives being deemed as disposable. The people I interviewed, and many more, heeded the call of God to call for justice on behalf of Michael Brown and all black bodies that are deemed less than human. This movement has beckoned all of us to see black people as human beings created in the *imago Dei*—the image of God.[8]

One of Francis's interviewees explains this underlying conviction in his own words: "And so, yes, black lives do matter, and yes, they matter because there's a God who believes that all life is sacred. . . . There's a God who cares and there's a sacredness of person because we're all created in the image of God."[9] There are many reasons why Christian ministers near Ferguson joined this movement. But one fundamental reason was the conviction that Michael Brown was created in the image of God. The killing of Michael Brown was not only criminal; it was sacrilegious. And because this killing was (and is) part of a pattern of treatment of black and brown bodies deemed "less than," the killing of Michael Brown was something not only to mourn but also to protest. Michael Brown's body lying in the street demonstrates not only an unlawful use of force, but also an act of dehumanization and a violation of the holy.[10]

In her book *Stand Your Ground: Black Bodies and the Justice of God*, Kelly Brown Douglas places this experience of dehumanization in historical context, tracing the persistent framing of the black body as a guilty body. Douglas provides this historical framing as a way to understand how Trayvon Martin, a fourteen-year-old boy in a Florida subdivision, could be construed as dangerous enough to warrant being shot dead by George Zimmerman, who enacted the violence rendered legally justifiable by Florida's Stand Your Ground law. Stand Your Ground laws justify force against someone perceived to be a threat. But how could a grown man with a gun perceive a fourteen-year-old boy with a pack of Skittles to be a threat? Zimmerman's perception of Trayvon as threatening only makes sense when Trayvon's fourteen-year-old black body is perceived through the lens of historical patterns of seeing black bodies as dangerous and guilty. These historical patterns are certainly not accidental. As Douglas demonstrates, they reflect social conditioning to whiteness and blackness. Douglas traces the "sociocultural conceptions that coalesce to deem the black body—especially the black male body—as not just inferior to the white body but as a threat to it."[11] Stand Your Ground is not just a social policy justifying violence when one is under threat. Stand Your Ground reflects a racialized sociocultural conception in which white spaces and naturally free white bodies are constantly under threat by black bodies that therefore must be constrained. Stand Your Ground enacts a form of white supremacy that assumes white bodies are free to occupy any spaces they choose and black bodies are a constant threat to white bodies and white space. The black body must justify its presence because it is always presumed guilty.

Douglas's analysis illumines the chasm between the conception of the black body as dangerous and guilty and the conception of the black body as created in the image of God. Douglas explores the power of this theological assertion as well:

> To be created in the image of a God that is free means that the human person is meant to be free. That is, like God, free from all human constraints and constructs that prevent one from being fully who one is and that threaten one's very life. Because humans are created in the image of God, and not the other way around, black life has meaning beyond the images constructed by narratives of a stand-your-ground culture.[12]

Douglas emphasizes the absurd truth of this faith in a world that denies it. This is a hard-won faith, one that has been tested over generations and refuses to shatter. Despite all historical evidence to the contrary, this faith insists that black bodies are created for freedom.

Violence against black bodies tests Christians' commitment to the *imago Dei*. In the words of Brian Batnum, "Churches must ask themselves if they reflect an unqualified commitment to the full humanity of one another that is exhibited in Christ's life and work."[13] Do we just *say* that all persons are created in the image of God, or do we actually try to live that way and to build societies that treat every person that way? As the movement for black lives continues in a variety of forms, we do see Christian participation rooted in this fundamental claim of theological anthropology. When Christians provide religious reasons for participation in or affirmation of the movement, they reference the image of God as a theological conviction that is both deeply meaningful and applicable. All persons are created in the image of God. But when some bodies are treated as less than, it is crucial to affirm their sacredness explicitly: black lives matter.

With these convictions and the actions they engender, Christian participants in contemporary movements such as Black Lives Matter continue a tradition of Christian advocacy for personhood rooted in the theological doctrine of *imago Dei*. As one formed in the brutality of and resistance to apartheid, Archbishop Desmond Tutu gives this point powerful expression. After asserting that human beings are endowed with dignity and worth, he continues:

> To treat such persons as if they were less than this, to oppress them, to trample their dignity underfoot, is not just evil as it surely must be; it is not just painful as it frequently must be for the victims of

> injustice and oppression. It is positively blasphemous, for it is tantamount to spitting in the face of God.[14]

Consider the power of this language, particularly in contexts of systematic oppression and violence, contexts where persons are attacked, marginalized, and silenced because of an attribute that renders them "less than." In these places, which of course are all around us, this universal theological affirmation of personhood is, in Tutu's words, both "marvelously exhilarating" and "staggering."[15]

The theological assertion that "we are all, each one of us, created in the image of God"[16] functions prophetically to denounce perpetrators and systems of dehumanization, to inspire resistance, and to implicate bystanders near and far. In discourse and action, this assertion has played a crucial role in resistance movements around the globe. In each movement, the universal assertion is applied to particular bodies that are devalued, neglected, or violated. The application of the conviction to particular, concrete bodies is absolutely crucial if it is to avoid becoming an empty platitude. And Christians apply the conviction by participating in actions of witness, resistance, and affirmation. This belief is enacted by bearing witness to bodies that are violated, resisting policies and practices of violation, and affirming the dignity and sacredness of every human life. For example, Christians stand outside of a private (meaning for-profit) detention center in South Georgia to insist that the people who have no papers and no "status" are in fact bearers of the divine image. Similarly, a Christian enacts this theological conviction by standing with a woman whose body bears the scars of violence and insisting that the violence she has experienced is a desecration of the holy. Christians embody this commitment by joining in a movement that declares that the black body lying in the middle of the street is sacred and the destruction of that body is blasphemy.

Christians have also enacted or practiced the *imago Dei* through denominational statements that convey resistance to violence or affirmation of persons. Sometimes this kind of work is aimed at forms of structural violence as well as overt, physical violence. Consider, for example, language used by the National Council of Churches in its "Social Creed for the 21st Century." This document was issued in 2008 to continue the 1908 social witness of the Federal Council of Churches, which called on Christians to stand "for equal rights and complete justice for all men in all stations of life," for safe working conditions and a living wage, for the abolition of child labor, and the abatement of poverty.[17]

The 2008 statement, by necessity, continued to appeal for safe working conditions, a living wage, and an end to child labor, poverty, and hunger. Unlike its predecessor, though, this document made explicit the theological affirmations that undergird the language of rights: "the full humanity of each woman, man, and child, all created in the divine image as individuals of infinite worth."[18] Rather than acquiesce to the forces of industrialization and capitalism, the writers of these statements illuminate the gross inconsistency between human beings as created in the image of God and human beings as exploited in the economic machinery of society. In the rich tradition of Catholic social thought, the dignity of the human person grounds economic, social, and political rights *and also* constitutes the criterion by which one judges policies and practices. The National Conference of Catholic Bishops articulated this criterion in 1986: "Every economic decision and institution must be judged in light of whether it protects or undermines the dignity of the human person."[19] Policies and practices that undermine the dignity of the human person are unjust and must be resisted and dismantled.

We see a similar argument in some denominational statements related to human sexuality and gender identity. The United Church of Christ, for example, has a history of issuing statements regarding the civil and human rights of same-gender-loving people; more recently, it has issued similar statements about transgendered persons. In 1975, the Tenth General Synod of the United Church of Christ issued a pronouncement that articulated a foundational commitment often referred to in more recent statements: "In faithfulness to the biblical and historical mandate, we hold that, as a child of God, every person is endowed with worth and dignity that human judgment cannot set aside."[20] It is significant that this statement takes a stand on discrimination and civil rights but not on the morality of same-gender-loving relations: "Therefore, without considering in this document the rightness or wrongness of same-gender relationships, but recognizing that a person's affectional or sexual preference is not legitimate grounds on which to deny her or his civil liberties, the Tenth General Synod of the United Church of Christ proclaims the Christian conviction that all persons are entitled to full civil liberties and equal protection under the law." The statement focuses on the incompatibility between discrimination and Christian concern for the oppressed and commandments to love God and neighbor. And the statement insists on the inherent worth and dignity of persons as children of God. However, it stops short of offering theological affirmation for same-gender-loving relationships.

Thirty years later, the Twenty-Fifth General Synod continued this resistance to discrimination by adopting a statement on marriage equality.[21] This document reiterates the commitment to inherent worth and dignity and the resistance to discrimination based on sexual orientation and preference. It also opens with an affirmation of love and partnership and reference to the *imago Dei*: "The Bible affirms and celebrates human expressions of love and partnership, calling us to live out fully that gift of God in responsible, faithful, committed relationships that recognize and respect the image of God in all people." This suggests movement in the denomination to affirm the goodness of same-gender relationships, and the closing section of the statement indicates persistent disagreement about this: "In recognition that these resolutions may not reflect the views or current understanding of all bodies," the document encourages continued prayer, study, and dialogue.

These statements, thirty years apart, help us to see two things about the *imago Dei*. Sometimes the image of God provides a basis for resisting discrimination; as one created in the image of God, every person should be treated with dignity and inherent worth—that is, not discriminated against. We make this move theologically by either digging beneath or looking beyond particular differences to assert that all are created in the image of God, no matter what. This aspect of the theological assertion places all persons in one generalized category: created in the image of God. This constitutes a *universal* dimension of the *imago Dei*. There is also a *particular* dimension to the *imago Dei*: not "no matter what, you are created in the image of God" but "in every bit of matter, you are created in the image of God." The second point directs attention not to a general, universal assertion about all people, but to their createdness in the image of God in bodies that are very different from one another. This dimension of the *imago Dei* affirms you in your unique embodiedness as also created in the image of God. This assertion, with its particular attention to difference, becomes prophetic when different bodies come under attack, be they differently abled, ethnic minority, or gender nonconforming. That all persons are created in the image of God is not only a universal statement of inherent value no matter what our bodies look like; it is also an affirmation of the different ways our bodies look: we are created in the image of God not only as a *category* of creature but in our embodied *particularity*. It may be more diplomatic to affirm the image of God in all bodies no matter what, but it is radically prophetic to affirm the image of God in the actual flesh-and-blood bodies with all of their differences.

This is the kind of particular, embodied affirmation (body-love) that the preacher Baby Suggs conveys to those gathered in the clearing in Toni Morrison's novel *Beloved*:

> "Here," she said, "in this here place, we flesh; flesh that weeps, laughs; flesh that dances on bare feet in grass. Love it. Love it hard. Yonder they do not love your flesh. They despise it. They don't love your eyes; they'd just as soon pick em out. No more do they love the skin on your back. Yonder they flay it. And O my people they do not love your hands. Those they only use, tie, bind, chop off and leave empty. Love your hands! Love them. Raise them up and kiss them."[22]

I cite this powerful and well-known passage here because it so beautifully conveys the double move of affirming the body in its intricate particularity and calling out those who threaten and destroy it. This is the dual impact of affirmation of bodies through the image of God: we affirm the body and resist its denigration.

Because of its universal affirmation, the *imago Dei* often functions as a principle in contexts of social conflict. As we have seen in this chapter, Christians whose bodies are under attack assert themselves and condemn their mistreatment by referencing the *imago Dei*. We have also observed denominational statements that reference the *imago Dei* to denounce mistreatment, affirm persons under attack, and call for more just policies and practices toward them. We see the *imago Dei* connected to claims about inviolability of persons, about inherent worth, and about dignity. Tracking the *imago Dei* through these contexts of conflict, we can see how it functions to place parameters about human behavior, to buttress efforts to resist mistreatment, to hold the powerful accountable. The second part of this chapter invites you to reposition yourself from observing Christian usage of the *imago Dei* in contexts of conflict to thinking about how these contexts help you to see the *imago Dei* differently. Such repositioning makes deontologists nervous because it detaches the principle from its more transcendent location and brings it into dynamic interaction with context, where it might be subject to influence! In my view, however, the insight that occurs in the interaction between faith and history enriches our understanding of the belief and enlarges our ability to enact it in the real contexts of our lives. It is important to see ongoing interaction between theological convictions and lived experience, noting that changes in our interpretations of theological doctrine do not weaken their authority in our lives. Christian ethics does not depend on a set of unchanging rules that transcend the particular circumstances of history. Christian ethics exists insofar as Christians labor to understand the deep truths of our faith in a world that challenges them. Rules and principles are certainly important, but it is a degree of elasticity that makes them endure. Christian ethics is so fascinating and demanding because it requires so much more than the application of an objective standard; it requires that we enter into a dynamic, living tradition of responding faithfully to the image of God *within* the world.

FROM AFFIRMATION TO ACCOUNTABILITY

As noted earlier, Archbishop Tutu describes the universal affirmation of personhood as marvelously exhilarating and also staggering. Surely we must stumble a bit when we recall that *all* persons are created in God's image: not only the oppressed but also the oppressor, not only the victim but also the perpetrator, not only the advocate for justice but also the guardian and beneficiary of the status quo. The officer who shoots the unarmed man, the anti-immigrant protestor who blocks the bus of unaccompanied minors and screams at them, the mother who planned the death of her husband and lied about it, the abuser, the terrorist—each and every one of them is also created in the image of God.

In contexts of violence, therefore, this principle inspires resistance *and* places parameters around it. Religious peacebuilders empowered by a universal affirmation of personhood cannot then violate the dignity of their opponent in the context of conflict. John Paul Lederach captures this paradox perfectly in his discussion of "the dilemma of dignity": "How do I protect my/our dignity and yet recognize and acknowledge the dignity of the other?"[23] In this essay, Lederach examines the interplay between the "lived internal world [of the religious peacebuilder] that seeks meaning and purpose and the *external life* that seeks safety, understanding and respect." He wonders at the religious peacebuilders' capacity to perceive the sacredness within the enemy-other, precisely in a space that defines their relationships in terms of threat. Lederach asks, "How is it that humanity was noticed and recovered in spite of imminent threat and fear?"[24]

We see this awareness in the writings and work of Jean Zaru, a Palestinian Quaker, who writes, "My enemy, too, is a child of God."[25] In the context of Israeli occupation of the Palestinian territories, Zaru resists nonviolently because she perceives the presence of God in the persons who are suffering and perpetuating multiple forms of violence. She argues that "a real revolution must concern itself with the triumph of human value and human rights," and she finds "Christian teaching relevant to such a revolution."[26] (She demonstrates the interplay between the internal world and external life that Lederach describes above.) Zaru continues: "Although these teachings are essentially nonviolent, they can never be characterized as encouraging passivity or disengagement in the face of injustice. Rather, Christ's teachings are activist, highly political, and often controversial. They sometimes involve dangerous forms of engagement in social and political conflict."[27] The affirmation of human dignity inspires resistance, but it also shapes it. The form of resistance must continue to recognize the presence of God in the enemy-other. Indeed, for Zaru, that recognition of God's image in the enemy-other makes resistance possible. "It is really only in the light of love that I am liberated to work for peace and freedom," she writes.[28]

"That of God" or "the presence of God" becomes a criterion for the means of resistance. It shapes standards for behavior and informs the principles of nonviolence. Respecting the humanity of the other—or continuing to love the enemy—is a core commitment that shapes the actions of nonviolent resisters. We see this concretely in historical documents from the civil rights movement, which include commitment cards and codes of conduct calling on participants to "walk and talk in the manner of love" and "to refrain from the violence of fist, tongue, or heart."[29] Here again, we see deontology enacted as adherence to principles in contexts of conflict.

Zaru articulates a commitment that is core to nonviolent resistance, namely, "that means and ends should be consistent."[30] The way in which one engages conflict must be consistent with the goals for social change. Particularly with relationship to human dignity, one cannot create socially just institutions that safeguard and respect human dignity through efforts that violate the image of God. Zaru expresses this in practical terms as a matter of consistency: "I cannot endorse acts of violence in my day-to-day confrontations and, at the same time, be taken seriously when I speak of an ideal for the future that exalts wisdom, sensitivity, fairness, and compassion as basic requirements for running the world."[31] In an observation parallel to those of Lederach, she conveys the paradoxical power of nonviolent methods of social change: "the offering of respect and concern on the one hand while meeting injustice with non-cooperation and defiance on the other."[32] It is important to note that living according to the image of God in contexts of conflict sustains both elements of this paradox: it calls one into conflict with societal forces that violate the person, and it calls one to treat as fully human the violator as well. When taken seriously, the image of God muddies our lives, our politics, and our speech. It does not allow us to divide the world neatly between good guys and bad guys. It binds us to people from whom we might prefer to get away. If one takes the *imago Dei* seriously, one cannot dismiss anyone as unworthy of care or beyond redemption. In this sense, the *imago Dei* is a Christian's greatest affirmation and most challenging truth.

FROM RIGHTS TO RELATIONSHIP

We have seen how *imago Dei* functions as a principle to govern treatment of others, whether they are under assault or on the attack. We must treat all persons as created in the image of God. This sentiment connects clearly with the language of rights, and we have also seen rights language surface in most of the contexts considered thus far. The framework of human rights is another excellent example of deontology, a set of principles that transcend context and provide standards for behavior to which one should adhere. Yet as the previous paragraph suggests, the *imago Dei* calls us to do more than respect the rights of another person; it actually calls us into relationship with the other person. In fact, rights are inherently relational. One cannot talk meaningfully about rights without also talking about obligations. Rights concern what one is owed as an individual, and this concept has no real content unless the individual is among other individuals.[33] Yet we do tend to think of rights as belonging to individuals rather than informing the relationship between them. And deontology as a method does nothing to discourage that.

One of the downsides of deontology is that it privileges one's adherence to a principle over one's relationship to a person. Recall that deontology values one's ability to rise above particular attachments and partial concerns and act according to an objective standard. Thus, we heard Carol Gilligan's description of the justice orientation as a "figure against a ground of social relationships, judging the conflicting claims of self and others against a standard of equality." In the justice orientation, of which deontology is an example, the moral agent stands apart from relationships in order to make judgments according to a standard of fairness. In her research, Gilligan uncovered another moral perspective, however, which she refers to as a care orientation. In this approach, "the relationship becomes the figure, defining self and others. Within the context of relationship, the self as a moral agent perceives and responds to the perception of need."[34] Rather than responding to a situation by adhering to a principle that transcends it, those with a care orientation respond to the concrete need of the person in front of them. In care ethics, one's relationships are not a hindrance to clear and careful moral reflection, but the stuff of it. The body in front of me is not only a category of person with particular rights; it is a human being to whom I am related. My moral task is to discern that person's needs and respond appropriately.

Care ethics also has its share of critics. Responding to needs can also engender paternalism if one practices this ethic without appropriate collaboration, conversation, and accountability. Care ethics also raises questions about fairness when I respond differently to the needs around me. And the emphasis on unidirectional care can be a prescription for sacrifice and exhaustion especially for those prone to doing for others. However, I bring care ethics into the conversation at this point because it is a crucial counterpoint to the nonrelational dimension of deontology. In contexts of conflict, we need both perspectives. We need to respond in concrete and specific ways to the needs in front of us, and we need to zoom out to consider broader issues of justice across other contexts. As I hope the examples have demonstrated, the *imago Dei* functions in both of these ways. Affirming the image of God draws me close to other bodies and holds me accountable to the bodies I do not know and am not inclined to care for. I must acknowledge that other persons are not only created in the image of God like I am, but are created in the image of God with me. Because God is related to all of creation, we cannot be in the image of God as isolated beings. Rather, we are connected to one another through the image of God as well.

As someone formed in the Wesleyan tradition, I was happy to find some consonance between the relational view of the *imago Dei* and a trusted, contemporary view of John Wesley's image of God. In *The New Creation* (1998), Wesleyan theologian Ted Runyon describes the theology beneath Methodist social witness in the areas of human rights, the environment, and poverty. He highlights a soteriology that "sees the 'great salvation' . . . as nothing less than *a new creation* transforming all dimensions of human existence, both personal and social."[35] Central to this is an understanding of the image of God that reinforces relationality. Runyon explains that Wesley understood "the image more relationally, not so much as something humans possess as the way they relate to God and live out that relation in the world."[36] Wesley described three ways that human beings bear the image of God. First, the "natural image" refers to the endowments that make us "capable of God," or able to enter into relationship with God. These include understanding, will, and freedom. Recognizing that the natural image echoes the more traditional views on capacities, Runyon argues that even here we see that the qualities of the natural image are in the service of relationship. Second, Wesley referred to the political image in order to capture the place of human beings in governing the earth. He argued that human beings are assigned a place of privilege and responsibility but that this place is nested in a context of relationship to the creator of all things and requires certain behavior toward others. Runyon explains: "Humanity is the image of God *insofar* as the benevolence of God is reflected in human action toward the rest of creation."[37] Third, in the moral image of God, the human being receives continually from the Creator and mediates to the world that which is received. This is the context of Wesley's proposal for "spiritual respiration"—the ongoing breathing in of the spirit of God and the channeling of that spirit out into the world. This "unceasing presence of God" underscores our relationship with the Creator, a relationship that we maintain through "a life of service to God, our fellow human beings, and all creation."[38] There is much more to explore here historically, theologically, and ethically. But for the purpose of this chapter, it is helpful to take note of this resource from tradition. It reminds us that relationality is not only a hard-won lesson and enduring commitment in the contexts of transitional justice and nonviolent resistance; it is also already embedded theologically in an understanding of the *imago Dei*. To be human is to be in relationship with God and the rest of creation. In contexts of social conflict, one of the most important and challenging dimensions of the *imago Dei* is that it affirms the inherent dignity *and* interrelatedness of *all* people. Perpetrators of violence are not only made in the image of God like I am; they are made in the image of God *with* me. Our relationship to the Creator locks us into relationship with one another. The *imago Dei* is not only a declaration of personhood; it is a declaration of relationship.

FROM HAVING TO BECOMING

The first part of this chapter focused more on the victims of violence; the second emphasized the interrelatedness of victims and offenders. The third part turns our attention more fully to those who perpetrate violence. Thinking about the image of God within perpetrators of violence not only affirms their humanity in spite of their worst acts, but it also draws our attention to the ways in which the image of God is built up and diminished (and then, hopefully, built up again) over time. One of many things I have learned through studying violence is that an act of violence is never an isolated and encapsulated event; it is always part of a larger story. Indeed, I find it much more accurate to think about narratives of violence rather than acts of violence. Similarly, the violation or denial of the image of God is not an isolated and encapsulated event; rather, violation and denial are always part of a larger story. The image of God may be violated in a moment, but it is diminished over time through repetition of abuse, systematic discrimination, or a never-ending barrage of humiliation and ridicule. Attending to experiences in specific ways, we see the formation and transformation of personhood over time. We see the ways in which the *imago Dei* gets buried beneath acts of abuse, patterns of neglect, and speech that belittles and betrays. Moreover, we see that this burial occurs in the life of those inflicting violence as well as those receiving it.

The growing literature on moral injury helps us to understand the impact of participation in violence over time. Psychologists and veterans use the term *moral injury* to capture a certain kind of wound experienced by soldiers who act in ways contrary to conscience. Jonathan Shay, a psychologist with the U.S. Department of Veterans' Affairs who worked with Vietnam veterans, identifies three elements of moral injury: betrayal, legitimate authority, and a situation of great weight. According to Shay, "Moral injury is a betrayal of what's right by someone who holds legitimate authority (e.g., in the military—a leader) in a high stakes situation."[39] Soldiers and veterans experience this kind of wound when they perform a duty that is contrary to conscience. They experience a sense of guilt or shame because of the action and also a sense of betrayal at having been asked to do it by an authority they trusted. It is a complex dynamic involving personal wrongdoing and also a sense of duty, a lack of autonomy, and a feeling of betrayal. In a particularly helpful account, Iraq veteran Tyler Boudreau makes it clear that the depth of moral injury does not necessarily correspond with the intensity of violence in which one participated. In his experience, moral injury occurs through ongoing participation in the low-level violence of occupation, during which soldiers repeatedly perform actions that transgress morality. He writes, "What I've found most difficult for people to grasp (and for a while this was hard for me, too) is the full range of 'moral injuries' sustained in Iraq; because it's not always about the killing."[40] Boudreau tells of being with veterans of Iraq and Afghanistan as they "described the daily grind of driving in and out of towns, patrolling through streets, searching houses, detaining suspected insurgents, questioning locals, and all the while trying to stay alive."[41] Boudreau very carefully uses the word *occupation* to describe the form of violence that these veterans exacted. He does not deny their role in the atrocities of war, but he focuses on the way occupying a land is also morally injurious even though the stories and events seem more mundane.

Boudreau's point is powerfully illustrated in a narrative by Michael Yandell, another Iraq war veteran.[42] Yandell tells the story of offering a bottle of water to a young Iraqi boy who had asked for candy. When the boy refuses the water, Yandell becomes angry. He writes:

> I rip the cap off the liter bottle in my hand, dump some of it out on the ground, and throw it at him. An old man, most likely his grandfather, rushes up, grabs the boy, and pulls him away. The old man looks at me, not with anger, hate, or even sadness. His eyes are full of fear. He's afraid of *me*. In that moment, I don't recognize that look, because I don't recognize myself. How can he be afraid of me? I'm one of the good guys, after all.[43]

Yandell will never forget the way that the Iraqi man looked at him, nor will he ever forget that feeling of losing himself, not recognizing the person he had become. Like Boudreau, Yandell felt that his moral center had eroded over time through participation in a system that demanded his transgression of moral boundaries—momentous and minor—every day.

Thinking of veterans like Yandell, Boudreau writes, "Through these ostensibly mundane stories, we cried out to the world, 'Our moral fibers have been torn by what we were asked to do and by what we agreed to do.'"[44] After returning home, Boudreau searched for some explanation of why he was hurting in a way that neither the PTSD diagnosis nor a monolithic label of guilt could capture. Moral injury gave language for this experience: "Moral injury is about the damage done to our moral fiber when transgressions occur by our hands, through our orders, or with our connivance. When we accept these transgressions, however pragmatically (for survival, for instance), we sacrifice a piece of our moral integrity. That's what moral injury is all about."[45]

One of the first books to gather stories of veterans experiencing moral injury was published in 2013 by Rita Nakashima Brock and

Gabriella Lettini of the Soul Repair Center at Brite Divinity School. The descriptions, narratives, and poems collected in this volume provide rich resources for thinking about human dignity and transformation of persons. Brock and Lettini summarize the experience of moral injury this way: "Moral injury results when soldiers violate their core moral beliefs, and in evaluating their behavior negatively, they feel they no longer live in a reliable, meaningful world and can no longer be regarded as decent human beings."[46] They continue, "Moral injury can lead veterans to feelings of worthlessness, remorse, and despair; they may feel as if they lost their souls in combat and are no longer who they were."[47] Brock and Lettini include the story and poetry of Camilo "Mac" Bica, a Marine veteran of the Vietnam War, who insists, "No one truly 'recovers' from war. No one is ever made whole again." So he strives every day "to forgive and absolve [him]self of guilt and to live with the wounds of war that will never heal."[48]

As this chapter has underscored, those who participate in violence, whether it is morally justified or not, are also created in the image of God. They do not forfeit the *imago Dei* when they participate in violence. Yet the experiences of veterans suffering moral injury illustrate the ways in which a perpetrator of violence or a participant in an ongoing system of structural violence loses his or her moral center, comes to feel transformed into someone else, and perhaps feels unworthy of love and care. Much as years of abuse and neglect diminish the sense of self, participation in actions contrary to one's sense of morality diminish a person's identity as one created in God's image. Connecting these descriptions with Wesley's threefold understanding of the image of God is illuminating not only for veterans' experiences but also for our understanding of the *imago Dei* and the relationship between human dignity and transformation. When one violates one's conscience, whether in the performance of duty or in the madness of war, the natural image of God is diminished. Violation of conscience constitutes an attack on understanding, freedom, and will—the very qualities that give us the capacity to connect with God, according to Wesley. In the description from Brock and Lettini, we can hear the diminishment of the political image by which we represent a benevolent God in the world and the diminishment of the moral image by which we receive and channel the grace of God in the world. One of the most powerful features of the narratives of moral injury that veterans are now courageous enough to share is that moral injury accrues gradually. It is not so much the result of one dramatic event, but the erosion of one's moral fiber over time as one participates in a system that is both demanding and totalizing.

If violation of the image of God is not an act but a process, the same things must be said of restoration or recovery of the image of God. This too is a process, a journey of healing or restoration. It is a process of becoming that which we were created to be. This process is a social process; it involves an interactional dynamic. Another veteran profiled in Brock and Lettini's work gives expression to this. Camilo Ernesto Mejia is a veteran of the Iraq War who describes his preenlistment life as "self-absorbed." He did not see the connections between his problems and the problems of others. But his experience in the war changed his perspective:

> Moral injury is painful, yet it has also returned a sense of humanity that had been missing from my life for longer than I can remember. I have come to believe that the transformative power of moral injury cannot be found in the pursuit of our own moral balance as an end goal, but in the journey of repairing the damage we have done unto others.[49]

Repairing the damage we have done to others, in a Wesleyan sense, recovers the moral image of God. As Runyon envisions it, contemporary Wesleyan theology involves a call to reflect God's image in the world. One is not only created in God's image; one is also called to recognize the image of God in others and to reflect God's image in the world.

CONCLUSION

This context of conflict helps us to think differently about the image of God as part of a process of becoming rather than something we have. This difference turns us toward virtue or character ethics, which is the subject of chapter 4. The discussion of moral injury also highlights an important, critical concern about deontology. With its attention to adherence to duty or principles, deontology emphasizes intention more so than outcome. In the context of military combat, then, one judges the behavior of a soldier according to intention. Did the soldier adhere to duty? One of the lessons in moral injury is that this focus produces an incomplete moral picture. In order to reflect fully on these experiences of conflict, we must also pay attention to outcome, to relationship, and to formation of persons. Only with this expanded view can we consider all of the complicated features of the moral life of soldiers. Adhering to principles is one dimension of the moral life. But as we have seen here—and as we all know from our own experiences—principles and the intention to follow them constitute but one piece of the story. The moral life requires more than adherence to principles. And in contexts of ongoing conflict, the moral life requires accountability for the outcomes of our actions on others and attention to the shape of our own character in formation.

As we have seen, the relationship between this theological doctrine and conflict is complicated. The conviction that all persons are created in the image of God sets the parameters for treatment of others and also for personal behavior. I should treat others as bearers of the divine image, and I must also reflect the divine image in all I say and do. Treating others as bearers of the divine image requires more than being kind and respectful. It requires acts of resistance as well. The image of God not only inspires resistance in this way; it also sets parameters for the behavior of the resister. As a Christian activist, I cannot dehumanize my opponent any more than I can allow the dehumanization of someone on the margins. Or, put another way, I cannot claim the *imago Dei* as a reason for resistance without also reflecting it in the form of my resistance. This is why the *imago Dei* is both inspiring and challenging, and why its relationship to conflict is particularly complicated.

What do these reflections on the image of God in contexts of violence help us to see about deontology? In the first part of this chapter, we saw that the *imago Dei* functions as a rule for behavior. Mistreating human beings is wrong because (among other things) it violates the image of God. In Christian ethics, this theological concept, *imago Dei*, sets parameters for human behavior. We must treat others as beings who are created in the image of God. Correspondingly, I have a right to certain kinds of treatment because I, too, am created in the image of God. The image of God is reified into a principle most concretely when it is taken to be the foundation for human dignity and when human dignity functions as the foundation for human rights. As Christians speak about human rights and human dignity, they also use language that reflects another feature of deontological ethics, namely, that the rules and principles transcend particular contexts. "No matter what, all persons are created in the image of God." "Created in the image of God, all persons have inherent dignity and value." These sentences point beyond contextual particularities to a rule or principle that is universal in nature.

However, we have also seen that rules grounded in theological assertions can be historically dynamic. If one is relying on a fixed foundation for a rule that transcends context and history and functions as an impermeable objective standard, lived theology is problematic. However, when we understand Christian ethics as more than an application of reified rules to changing circumstances, then lived theology is not the problem but the practice. When we participate in a die-in, stand vigil at a detention center, counsel young people in crisis, sit at someone's bedside, or begin a conversation with someone whose views offend and threaten us, we are not only adhering to a principle, but living out the theology of *imago Dei*. When we reflect on the *imago Dei* in light of conflict and violence, we also move beyond the method of deontology to affirm the relational dimension of ethics and to consider the formation of moral agents over time.

We are experiencing one of the ways in which Christian ethics betrays the categories and branches we assign to it. Deontology is a discrete method of ethics, and we can define its features and see it functioning through insistence on principles, appeals to fairness, and adherence to duty. These are all crucial dimensions of the moral life, but they do not constitute its entirety. Christian ethics also involves the interplay between principles governing behavior and acts of care for the bodies being governed. It includes a declaration of rights and responsibilities, but it also includes a process of reflection on our interaction with the people whose rights we affirm and responsibilities we extol. It includes proclamation and declaration in the face of wrongdoing, and penance when the wrongdoing is ours. In these descriptions, we see attention to the living out of principles within context, and the work that this requires of us. We also see the interplay between doing and being. We reflect the image of God in the world not only by our actions but through ways of being and processes of becoming. This moves us toward the next chapter, which turns to the branch of ethics most focused on character formation, namely, virtue ethics.

4

The Vices and Virtues of Conflict

Considering Virtue Ethics and Scripture

In chapter 1, I introduced an argument about conflict that is central to this book, namely, that conflict is a natural and necessary element of human life and can be a catalyst for positive change. In order to advance this argument among Christians, most mediators, circle facilitators, and trainers regularly spend time detangling conflict from sin. We may respond to the realities of conflict—the inevitable striking together—in ways that are sinful, meaning ways that further rupture relationship or deny the image of God in the other. However, conflict itself is not the same thing as sin, nor does the inevitable situation of conflict reflect our fallen nature. Quite the contrary—we are created as interrelated and changing beings. We are, in this sense, created in conflict.

Yet one who insists that conflict is sinful has plenty of Scripture passages to cite for support. If we are to pursue a Christian ethic that calls and equips us to live well in the midst of ongoing conflict, we need to spend some time with the texts that describe conflictual behavior as foolish, divisive, selfish, immature, twisted, and unholy. Therefore, this chapter considers passages from Galatians, James, 1 and 2 Timothy, and Titus that teach that conflict is a mark of unholy living and is destructive to community. But these are not the only New Testament teachings on conflict. This chapter also considers passages, from the Synoptic Gospels, that treat conflict as something to be expected in the community and something to be addressed through habits of forgiveness, rebuke, dialogue, and persistence.

For purposes of initial introduction, I describe these as two rather cohesive and clear clusters of teaching. However, the turn to Scripture in ethics is never straightforward, and the results of engagement are rarely tidy. This reality invites us to think carefully once again about method. This chapter employs an approach to Scripture called revealed morality. James M. Gustafson uses the term *revealed morality* to describe a way of using Scripture in ethics to provide moral guidance.[1] In this approach, one turns to Scripture for moral instruction on how to behave and what to do. Gustafson notes that we might find answers to our moral questions in the form of law (one should and should not do X), or ideal (one should strive toward X), or by way of analogy (in a situation such as this, we should do X).[2] In this chapter, I turn to New Testament writings to see whether we understand conflict properly as sinful and, more broadly, to see how we are to behave in moments of conflict. As in Gustafson's framework, I identify some insights that function as laws or rules, some that offer ideals for us, and other passages that provide analogies to interpersonal conflicts today.

Gustafson also identifies several questions about this revealed morality approach.[3] How does one go about identifying certain teachings as revealed morality? And how does one apply these teachings to contexts so drastically different? As Christians draw on Scripture for moral guidance, we are inevitably selective and unavoidably subjective. Turning to Scripture does not mean running away from other sources of knowledge and authority. We cannot step out of our bodies, forget tradition, and ignore everything we have learned when we turn to Scripture. All that we are and all that we know come right along with us. They shape the questions we pose to Scripture, they affect our decisions to focus one place and not another, and they inform our interpretation and application of the text. Again, we find contingency in ethics: many variables shape what comes next. This is true for everyone whether we admit it or not. Such an admission may lead us to relativism, but it should lead us instead to a greater sense of responsibility. Noting the variables in a process of moral discernment does not render all positions equally true; rather, it demands transparency and accountability along the way. The onus is on us to explain the conclusions we reach by being transparent about process and accountable to those who see things differently. Transparency and accountability are not only important scholarly habits; they are also crucial practices for living a good life amidst conflict.

This reference to *practices* of transparency and accountability raises a second methodological consideration to address. The previous chapter discussed deontology, choosing to act according to principles. This chapter explores a second form of ethics in which one focuses on questions of character, on being a certain sort of person in accordance with a suitable end. The question is not so much what one *does* in the midst of conflict, but how one *is* in the midst of conflict. In a very helpful way, given the complications of responding well to conflict, character ethics encourages us to think about how to *be* even when we do not know exactly what to *do*. Even more than that, making a decision or choosing an action are no longer the crux of the moral moment; rather, they follow from being the sort of person one is called to be.

Traditionally, we speak of three categories of virtue: intellectual virtues are learned through study, moral virtues are developed through practice, and theological virtues are infused in us by God and orient us toward God. For the most part, contemporary virtue ethics does not focus on the lists and categories of virtue, but it does take seriously the connection between character formation and action. In the 1985 film *Witness*, in which a Philadelphia police detective lives among an Amish community to protect a boy who witnessed a murder, the boy eventually discovers the detective's handgun. His grandfather sits down with him to explain why he must not touch the unclean thing: "What you take into your hand, you take into your heart." This statement captures a core feature of virtue ethics. The actions we take reflect the person we are, and they shape the person we are becoming.

Contemporary virtue ethics may not focus on debating lists of virtues per se, but such lists nonetheless spark important debate in the field of Christian ethics. What counts as a virtue and why? This is not a neutral question. Rather, it reflects skepticism about the motivations, for example, behind extolling the virtue of meekness or humility or patience. In contexts of oppression, who benefits from practicing these virtues? In contexts of conflict, it is important to ask who commends which virtues to whom and why. We might point in an innocent way to Scripture or tradition to justify our mention of a particular virtue. But equally present in the calculation is our sense of purpose. Remember that a virtue is a disposition that orients us toward a suitable end. In this chapter, we will examine why conflict is named as a vice while obedience is recognized as a virtue. Understanding the goal of cohesion and unity helps us to see why conflict was perceived as vicious. It also opens up a space for critical engagement with these texts. Is conflict always a vice? Is unity always a suitable end?

Obedience was a profoundly important virtue in the ancient world, and cohesion in the community of Jesus' followers was profoundly important in the years after Jesus' death. However, as Christians today take up these admonitions against conflict, I think we feel or should feel at odds with the call to obedience as a mark of faithfulness. Challenging this thread of tradition and the virtues attached to it is one reason why I lift up the Syrophoenician woman and the persistent widow in this chapter. In these Gospel stories, we locate another formative tradition, in which practices of resistance and persistence become marks of faithfulness orienting one toward the kingdom of God more than to unity of the community.

Wrestling with some texts and affirming others reflects a particular hermeneutic in play here. Hermeneutics is the study of interpretation, and it draws our attention to the lens we bring to a text. I bring particular values and commitments to this work of turning to Scripture. I want to understand those texts that identify conflict as a vice, and I want to lift up other texts that present conflict behaviors that reflect faithfulness of the individual and contribute to the well-being of the community. In other words, this chapter demonstrates a hermeneutic of conflict transformation. In the New Testament, we find the assertion that conflict stems from disobedience, pride, jealousy, greed, and ambition. These things are contrary to Christian living, which should be marked by gentleness, mercy, humility, and patience. Christians should be known by the way they live, and there should be harmony within the community. In these first generations after Christ, it was necessary to mark a new identity and to function cohesively as a community. Conflict was not only a mark of individual vice but was also disruptive to the community. Thus, the New Testament letters admonish followers of Christ to avoid conflict and those foolish people who stir it up. The traits of this new community are in keeping with Jesus' teachings as recorded in the Gospels. Jesus did indeed commend humility, a forgiving spirit, meekness, gentleness, and patience. But we do not find Jesus explicitly admonishing his followers against conflict per se. Indeed, conflict marked Jesus' presence in the world, and he interacted in welcoming ways with people who were at odds with the community.

Although we find consistent discouragement of conflict in other New Testament writings, the Gospels depict various types of conflict and a corresponding variety of responses from Jesus to it. As we will see, this makes it difficult to respond with a simple answer to the question "How did Jesus respond to conflict?" Of course, this is not bad or unusual. Although Christians find timeless truths and core commitments rooted in Scripture, we recognize that Scripture was compiled over a long period of time and with multiple motivations. Without blurring these important differences to reach for something tidier than what is really there, I do identify a few consistent themes in Jesus' speech and behavior related to conflict.

First, Jesus expects conflict, and he prepares his disciples to expect it as well. There never seems to be a question of whether one will encounter conflict, but rather how one should respond to it. Jesus commends behaviors that help us to live well with one another in conflict. This suggests that conflict itself is not sinful, but that there are sinful ways of responding to it. Second, Jesus' speech about conflict behaviors and his actions in response to behavior are contextual. What he says and how he behaves depend on the context of the conflict and, particularly, the intentions and position of the person he is facing. Third, Jesus' engagements with conflict and teachings related to conflict consistently point toward the kingdom of God. One of the core arguments in this chapter builds on these three observations: Jesus teaches and models behaviors in conflict that respond to the particular circumstances of the conflict and keep us oriented toward the kingdom of God. However, conflict itself did not make the list of behaviors befitting Jesus' followers. To understand why, we need to examine the texts more closely.

CONFLICT VERSUS COHESION

A quick check of a concordance reveals that the English word *conflict* appears regularly in lists of behavior that is unwise, problematic, and discouraged. The Common English Bible (CEB) uses the word *conflict* forty-one times. (By contrast, the New Revised Standard Version uses it only seven times.) One-quarter of these citations are found in Proverbs, which includes lessons such as these:

> The empty-headed cause conflict out of pride; those who take advice are wise. (Prov. 13:10)
>
> Hotheads stir up conflict, but patient people calm down strife. (Prov. 15:18)

> Destructive people produce conflict; gossips alienate close friends. (Prov. 16:28)

> Remove the mocker and conflict disappears; judgment and shame also stop. (Prov. 22:10)

> Greedy people stir up conflict, but those who trust in the Lord become prosperous. (Prov. 28:25)

If we were to read forty-one similar condemnations of conflict, it would be difficult not to conclude that conflict is a vice or a reflection of ungodly behavior. However, many different Hebrew and Greek words are translated as "conflict." This leaves the reader with a strong negative association with one term rather than clarity about different kinds of behaviors and the distinct ways in which they are problematic. Using conflict as the catch-all term also, unfortunately, obscures from view the ways in which conflict might be appropriate to a situation or helpful to a community. In these five passages from Proverbs, for example, the English word "conflict" is used as a translation of the Hebrew word *madown. Madown* is more precisely translated as "strife" or "contention."[4] The CEB also translates *massah, medanim,* and *hamas* as "conflict," although these words are more precisely translated "contention," "dispute," and "violence," respectively.

The CEB continues to use "conflict" as an umbrella term in the New Testament, where we find another twenty references. In the New Testament letters, conflict is regularly listed as a feature of communities that are in trouble, an action that individuals should avoid, and even a behavior that keeps one from entering the kingdom of God. In 2 Corinthians 7:5, we read that Macedonia was beset by "external conflict" and "internal fears" such that Paul had his work cut out for him and could not rest. In other places, conflict is not only a characteristic of the setting for the writing but also a behavior that is explicitly discouraged. I will focus on this in five passages: Galatians 5:19–21; James 4:13; 1 Timothy 6:3–5; 2 Timothy 2:22–25; and Titus 3:9–11. Here, conflictual behaviors reflect ungodly living and threaten the community.

Again, the CEB translates several different words into the English word "conflict." In 2 Timothy 2:23, the Greek word is *machai*, which can also be translated as "quarrels and fights." Titus 3:10 and Galatians 5:20 use the word *hairetikos*, which refers to factions or one who is disposed to form sects. This is the Greek word from which we derive "heresy." In Galatians 5:20 and also 1 Timothy 6:4, we find the word *eris*, which means "strife." In these texts, we find a theme of caution against discord, strife, contention, and quarreling. This behavior reflects an unsettled character, a foolish mind, a disobedient heart, and a person bent on division. It is clearly and strongly discouraged. But why?

Let's look at these passages in more detail. In his letter to the Galatians, Paul includes conflict in the list of "actions produced by selfish motives," actions that keep one from inheriting the kingdom of God:

> The actions that are produced by selfish motives are obvious, since they include sexual immorality, moral corruption, doing whatever feels good, idolatry, drug use and casting spells, hate, fighting, obsession, losing your temper, competitive opposition, conflict, selfishness, group rivalry, jealousy, drunkenness, partying, and other things like that. I warn you as I have already warned you, that those who do these kinds of things won't inherit God's kingdom. (Gal. 5:19–21 CEB)

Similarly, James attributes conflict to internal cravings, jealousy, evil intentions, and a lack of faith:

> What is the source of conflict among you? What is the source of your disputes? Don't they come from your cravings that are at war in your own lives? You long for something you don't have, so you commit murder. You are jealous for something you can't get, so you struggle and fight. You don't have because you don't ask. You ask and don't have because you ask with evil intentions, to waste it on your own cravings. (Jas. 4:1–3 CEB)

In Galatians and in James, the primary concern about conflict seems to be that it represents an untamed spirit or a lack of discipline. Paul's letter to the Galatians lists strife among the works of the flesh that are contrasted to the fruits of the Spirit, which include "love, peace, patience, kindness, goodness, faithfulness, gentleness, self-control" (Gal. 5:20–23). As Philip Esler argues, this is much more than a moralistic list of norms for behavior. Paul is trying to articulate a new identity for Jesus' followers, to set them apart, to distinguish them from others.[5] In his letter, James makes the connection between internal character and external conflict. In the passage immediately preceding the one quoted above, James draws a sharp distinction between one who is "wise and understanding" and those who have "bitter jealousy and selfish ambition in [their] hearts" (Jas. 3:13–14 RSV). The wisdom of the latter group comes not from above, "but is earthly, unspiritual, devilish." And, more precisely to our point, jealousy and ambition lead to "disorder and every vile practice" (3:16 RSV). It is also worthwhile to recall James's admonition about the power of the tongue, which seems related to a concern about forms of conflict. He writes that "the tongue is a fire" that cannot be tamed. It is "a restless evil, full of deadly poison" (3:6, 8 RSV).

In 1 and 2 Timothy, conflict is associated with false teaching and with thoughtless disagreements and foolishness. The letters contrast these behaviors with acceptance of true teachings and being patient and kind to people who are wrong:

> If anyone teaches anything different and doesn't agree with sound teaching about our Lord Jesus Christ and teaching that is consistent with godliness, that person is conceited. They don't understand anything but have a sick obsession with debates and arguments. This creates jealousy, conflict, verbal abuse, and evil suspicions. There is constant bickering between people whose minds are ruined and who have been robbed of the truth. (1 Tim. 6:3–5 CEB)

People who know the truth do not argue; they do not stir up conflict. This point continues in 2 Timothy as well:

> Run away from adolescent cravings. Instead, pursue righteousness, faith, love, and peace together with those who confess the Lord with a clean heart. Avoid foolish and thoughtless discussions, since you know that they produce conflicts. God's slave shouldn't be argumentative but should be kind toward all people, able to teach, patient, and should correct opponents with gentleness. Perhaps God will change their mind and give them a knowledge of the truth. They may come to their senses and escape from the devil's trap that holds them captive to do his will. (2 Tim. 2:22–25 CEB)

We also find direct teaching about how to avoid conflict. For example, in Titus we read this:

> Avoid stupid controversies, genealogies, and fights about the Law, because they are useless and worthless. After a first and second warning, have nothing more to do with a person who causes conflict, because you know that someone like this is twisted and sinful—so they condemn themselves. (Titus 3:9–11 CEB)

The Revised Standard Version begins verse 10 this way: "As for a man who is factious . . . ," which more precisely captures the author's concern. Although earlier scholars attributed 1 and 2 Timothy and Titus to Paul, current scholarship suggests that these letters were written by followers of Paul after his death.[6] It is likely that the writers used unpublished excerpts of Paul's writing and then expanded on them to address issues facing the early community. Dominant concerns of Jesus' followers at this time were unity and the corresponding threat of other teachings.[7] Thus, 1 Timothy begins with an admonition to "charge certain persons not to teach any different doctrine nor to occupy themselves with myths and endless genealogies which promote speculations rather than the divine training that is in faith" (1 Tim. 1:3–4 RSV). This overarching concern about division provides the context for the admonition in 2 Timothy: "Have nothing to do with stupid, senseless controversies; you know that they breed quarrels" (2 Tim. 2:23). The concern about false teachings persists in the letter to Titus and constitutes one of its main themes.[8]

These letters weave together a concern about false teaching with broader appeals for obedience and submission, all under the theme of faithfulness and for the purpose of cohesion: "Remind them to be submissive to rulers and authorities, to be obedient, to be ready for any honest work, to speak evil of no one, to avoid quarreling, to be gentle, and to show perfect courtesy toward all men" (Titus 3:1–2 RSV). Continuing the theme from Galatians and James named above, the letter to Titus insists that Jesus inaugurated a new way of living: "For we ourselves were once foolish, disobedient, led astray, slaves to various passions and pleasures, passing our days in malice and envy, hated by men and hating one another" (Titus 3:3 RSV).

We see in these passages that conflict is associated with disobedience, lack of control, and divisions. For James and in Paul's letter to the Galatians, conflict is described as an external expression of internal disorder. In the Pastorals (Timothy and Titus), the overarching concern is with division and fraction in the fledgling community. Why? In the ancient world, hierarchy and social order were central values, and obedience was a corresponding virtue.[9] It is not surprising, then, that obedience and submission are named as virtues for Jesus' followers, reflecting not only the values of the larger sociocultural context but also the goal of cohesion in this fledgling community. Conflict is a problem insofar as it is framed as contrary to obedience and submission and a threat to cohesion. Conflictual behaviors were associated with disobedience, lack of control, and the unruly passions. These forms of conflict—strife, factiousness, quarrels, contention—are indeed discouraged as sinful behavior, a mark of internal turmoil in an individual and a sign that the community is in trouble. Being quarrelsome and contentious is out of keeping with the new identity of Jesus' followers. Strife is associated with works of the flesh, with jealousy, with greed, with anger. Contention is a mark of disobedience.

Drawing from these Scripture passages, then, in what sense is conflict (as strife, contention, factiousness) sinful? I see two clear answers to this question. From Paul and James, we learn that quarrels, divisiveness, and strife reflect the works of the flesh. These things stem from jealousy, greed, ambition, and foolishness. Such conflictual behaviors, then, are sinful in an individualistic, moralist sense. They do not reflect godly living. Specifically, for James, jealousy, greed, and ambition reflect a turning to the world rather than placing faith in God (Jas. 4:4). The presence of Christ in the world and in our lives should enable us to live differently. The marks of a Christian are not jealousy, ambition, and greed (which lead to strife, quarrels, contention, divisiveness), but gentleness, patience, kindness, and meekness (which lead to peace; Jas. 3:17–18).

The Pastorals (1 and 2 Timothy and Titus) raise the stakes a bit. Here we find an awareness that jealousy or greed that lingers in an individual is also a problem for the community. There is an emphasis on contrary teachings in these letters, a concern that there are individuals in the community who are breeding division, creating factions through false teachings. The concern about godly living certainly persists here, but the overarching frame for these letters is obedience. Strife, quarreling, and divisiveness, then, reflect disobedience to God. People who breed division are not only foolish because they turn from God to false teachings; they are also disobedient, sowing disorder in the community.

We undoubtedly receive strong messages from these texts against conflictual behaviors. However, Christian ethics entails wrestling with sources of authority, not just accepting them uncritically. So let's pause a minute to think about these passages. We cannot accept the Timothy and Titus passages without question. The Pastorals contain some of the more disturbing teachings on submission—of women to men, of slaves to slave owners—and these teachings come under the umbrella of maintaining order in the community and perceiving order and submission as marks of faithfulness to God. Of course, these sentiments are not only present in Scripture; they have been used throughout Christian history. Christians have employed these texts to suppress difference, to subjugate persons, and to deny theological authority to women. So what do twenty-first-century readers of Scripture do with texts that not only offend us but that also have been used to subjugate and oppress others?[10]

My approach in this chapter is twofold. First, I keep the focus on the reasons why conflict is a problem and then consider whether or to what extent those reasons apply today. Second, I look to the recorded teachings and ministry of Jesus to see whether the admonitions and rationale appear there as well. As we have seen, a concern about social cohesion and a new identity drives these admonitions against conflict and conflictual behaviors in Paul, James, and the Pastoral Letters. The Gospel writers certainly convey similar teachings for a new way of living in the world. But time and again, these new dispositions point beyond the community itself to the kingdom of God. In other words, the Gospel writings related to conflictual behaviors connect these teachings and stories to a telos that is greater than the cohesion of the community. When cohesion is the goal, one puts away conflict as an act of obedience and faithful submission. When the kingdom of God is the goal, one enters into the inevitable forms of social and spiritual conflict in a way that opens space for the kingdom to emerge. Turning to the Gospels, I find evidence that recognizes conflict as unavoidable and suggests that our responses should reflect the particular conditions of conflict. But I also find what to me is a much stronger argument: that one cannot pursue the kingdom of God without entering into conflict.

It is difficult to recognize this argument if we allow conflict to function as an umbrella term for a variety of contexts and behaviors. Contention, quarreling, strife, and divisiveness are certainly related to conflict. They can be contributing causes to conflict, elements of ongoing conflict, or consequences of conflict. However, when we use "conflict" as the English translation for all of these different words, we conflate a variety of intentions, behaviors, and consequences, and (by the negative implication that has accrued to the term *conflict*) we denounce them all. Moreover, we leave unchallenged two faulty assumptions: first, that conflictual behavior is unloving and disordered (i.e., always negative); second, that conflict is always bad for the community. In other words, conflict is assumed to be a vice. Turning to the Gospels, however, we find additional forms of conflict, reasons to question these two assumptions, and some space to consider the virtues of conflict.

CONFLICT IN COMMUNITY

The admonitions against conflict/strife/contention are both ironic and perfectly understandable for followers of one who came to bring division (Luke 12:51). They have seen how powerful and effective quarreling can be! But let's look now at the one they followed. The Synoptic Gospels are so full of conflict that it is difficult to know where to begin. Moreover, as they do with so many topics, the different Gospel accounts thwart our efforts to identify a uniform response and extract a clear and transferable lesson. We find a variety of teachings and actions attributed to Jesus. Jesus is involved in and responds to many different kinds of conflict, and his behavior varies accordingly. We do not find admonitions against *machai* (quarreling, fighting, contention), *hairetikos* or *hairesis* (heresy), or *eris* (strife) as in the other New Testament writings. But we do find teachings regarding behavior in conflictual situations and teachings regarding behaviors that are somehow related to conflict. We also find Jesus in many different kinds of (often overlapping) conflict: rhetorical, interpersonal, cosmic, religious, social, economic, and political.[11] This chapter does not attempt to provide a comprehensive survey of such variety, but it does analyze a few representative passages in order to challenge the assumptions named earlier: that conflict is always attached to negative behaviors and that conflict is always destructive to community.

Conflict is one of the defining characteristics of Jesus' life and ministry. We see this most explicitly in the pronouncement recorded by Luke:

> Do you think that I have come to give peace on earth? No, I tell you, but rather division; for henceforth in one house there will be five divided, three against two and two against three; they will be divided, father against son and son against father, mother against daughter and daughter against her mother, mother-in-law against her daughter-in-law and daughter-in-law against her mother-in-law. (Luke 12:51–53 RSV)

The Greek word used here is *diamerismos*, meaning "breaking up," "discord," or "hostility." Its verb form, *diamerizo*, means "divided up" or "divided against itself." (This is the same word that Jesus uses in Luke as he divides up the bread during the Passover meal with his disciples.) The author of Luke-Acts uses this word eight times (whereas it appears in Mark only once and in Matthew twice) and reflects the prominence of the theme of division or separation (of righteous from unrighteous) in Luke's Gospel. A similar verse to Luke 12:51 is Matthew 10:34: "Do not think I have come to bring peace on earth; I have not come to bring peace, but a sword." Matthew uses the word "sword" (*macharain*), rather than "division" to connect Jesus to the prophet Ezekiel: "I will summon every kind of terror against Gog, says the Lord God; every man's sword will be against his brother" (Ezek. 38:21). Matthew's Jesus does not suddenly embrace violent weaponry; rather, he uses sword imagery as a powerful metaphor for severing ties.[12]

Indeed, from the very beginning of his teaching, Jesus promised division and disruption, with his choice of the Isaiah scroll:

> The Spirit of the Lord is upon me, because he has appointed me to preach good news to the poor. He has sent me to proclaim release to the captives and recovering of sight to the blind, to set at liberty those who are oppressed, to proclaim the acceptable year of the Lord. (Luke 4:18–19)

He might as well have said, "The Spirit of the Lord is upon me to do disruptive, contentious, and quarrelsome things"! The theme of conflict runs right through the Gospels, from the temptations in the wilderness to the crucifixion. Sprinkled throughout are teachings on conflictual behaviors and a variety of conflictual moments. There are also passages that provide concrete instructions on responding to conflict. Yet the words *machai, hairetikos* or *hairesis,* and *eris*—translated as "conflict" in the Common English Bible—do not appear in the Gospels at all, let alone in the context of admonition.

The following pages focus on two practical teachings (Matt. 5:23–24 and 18:15–17), two conflict stories (both recorded in Mark 7:1–30 and in Matt. 15:1–28), and one parable (Luke 18:1–8). In this collection of writings, we do not find a tidy answer to the question of conflict and sin, but we do find reason to challenge the assumption that conflict always reflects disorder and breeds division. These readings suggest that conflict is part of community life, part of the social fabric, and thus they stand in contrast to the first collection of texts that present conflict as a threat to community (Galatians, James, 1 and 2 Timothy, and Titus). Matthew 5:23–24 and 18:15–17 provide practical instruction in a moment of conflict. Mark 7:1–30 and Matthew 15:1–28 first place Jesus in a rhetorical debate with a conflict pronouncement and then place him in an interpersonal version of a social conflict. Luke 18:1–8 tells the story of the persistent widow, one commended for her faithfulness, which she exhibits through her "continual coming." There is nothing remarkable in these passages: no miracles, no dramatic conversion, no extraordinary revelation. Rather, there are mundane, familiar, painful, awkward, and tiring interactions. There is a wedgelike offense and attempts to address it, there is a disagreement among teachers and religious authorities, there is a racial slur and a cunning retort, and there is an advocate who refuses to give up.

In these texts, I see recognition that conflict is part of social life and a call to cultivate habits for living well together amidst conflict. I do not claim to draw these insights from Scripture alone, nor do I claim to have stumbled across these passages by happenstance (or providence!). I am very aware that I bring certain commitments to the Gospels: a conviction that conflict is a natural element of social life and potential catalyst for positive change, and a commitment to equipping Christians to deal with conflict more constructively. This set of commitments, and the experiences and information that inform them, constitute a hermeneutic of conflict and, more specifically, a hermeneutic of conflict transformation. I look through Scripture for passages that depict conflict or teach about conflict, and I am particularly attentive to those that suggest actions and behaviors to engage conflict constructively for purposes of positive change. In the first part of this chapter, I considered passages that seem to admonish persons for participating in conflict, and I cast a suspicious eye over the motivations driving those admonitions. In this part of the chapter, I consider passages that help us to see conflict as an integral part of community rather than as a threat to it, and I lift up passages that indicate the positive potential of conflict.

Matthew 5:23–24 and 18:15–17 are often cited as Jesus' instructions for dealing with conflict in the church:

> "So when you are offering your gift at the altar, if you remember that your brother or sister has something against you, leave your gift there before the altar and go; first be reconciled to your brother or sister, and then come and offer your gift." (Matt. 5:23–24)

> "If another member of the church sins against you, go and point out the fault when the two of you are alone. If the member listens to you, you have regained that one. But if you are not listened to, take one or two others along with you, so that every word may be confirmed by the evidence of two or three witnesses. If the member refuses to listen to them, tell it to the church; and if the offender refuses to listen even to the church, let such a one be to you as a Gentile and a tax collector." (Matt. 18:15–17)

If we take these passages side by side, we find two sets of instructions for addressing conflict with a fellow disciple. In the first passage, Jesus casts the listener as the one who has done wrong—that is, the one who is angry without cause, the one who speaks slanderously or offers insults to another (5:22). The onus is on the offender to make amends even before proceeding with a religious observance. In the second passage, the advice is for the victim of wrongdoing and urges confrontation with the offender. Taking these two lessons together, we hear that the disciples must not allow hurts or trespasses between them to go unaddressed. Rather, they must prioritize and pursue addressing the violation until the two parties reach either reconciliation or separation.

In Matthew 18:15–17, Jesus speaks to the one who has been wronged. The victim should confront the offender (18:15). If the offender does not admit wrongdoing, the victim should bring in some others to witness the rebuke. If the offender still refuses to admit wrongdoing, then the others may treat him as a Gentile or tax collector. Because of its concrete and practical nature, this pericope regularly appears in manuals, texts, and workshops on conflict in churches. For example, in *Reconcile: Conflict Transformation for Ordinary Christians*, John Paul Lederach turns to these verses to identify a four-step approach to conflict: (1) "go directly," (2) "take along one or two witnesses," (3) "tell it to the church," and (4) "relate as with a tax collector."[13] By no means does Lederach suggest that these steps are easy. His approach is therefore not a simplistic one. But it does provide an example of the way this pericope is used to articulate a Scripture-based procedure for addressing interpersonal conflict in the church. He writes, "These interesting verses give direct and practical teaching from Jesus. They provide specific guidelines for how we are to proceed when we feel we have been wronged or when we feel that a sister or brother has erred."[14] Lederach goes on to argue that this text not only offers instruction for Christian behavior in conflict but that it also affirms the presence of God within communities in conflict. ("For where two or three are gathered in my name, I am there among them"; Matt. 15:20). Even when the two or three are in conflict, God is present. This affirmation then grounds Lederach's call for Christians to move "toward conflict and toward the other," knowing that God is there to meet them.[15]

This theme of moving toward conflict and toward one another also informs the way that Lederach interprets the fourth step, that of treating an unrepentant offender as a Gentile or tax collector. Citing an Anabaptist theological method of discipleship, Lederach observes how

Jesus treated Gentiles and tax collectors: "What stands out is this simple answer: Jesus ate with them."[16] Lederach's interpretation of the fourth step is that one must "maintain relational and emotional contact" with the offender on a journey toward reconciliation.[17]

Bridget Illian argues differently. She places the fourth step in the context of other Jewish teachings and cultural practices known to Matthew and also in the context of Matthew's other references to Gentiles. She connects the private rebuke with Leviticus 19:17–18 and Ben Sirach 19:13–17, which commend rebuke and reproval as part of care for the neighbor.[18] She explores debates among communities over whether a semipublic reproof is helpful and when a public rebuke is warranted.[19] And she makes the case that the fourth step in Matthew's account of Jesus' teaching reflects an escalation of consequences for one whose refusal to repent continues to threaten the community. Illian insists that the fourth step means expulsion from the community, while noting that the purpose of expulsion was repentance and reintegration (the purpose of all four steps of this process).[20] After reviewing some of Matthew's other references to tax collectors and Gentiles, Illian concludes, "'Tax collectors and Gentiles' are outsiders in Matthew's Gospel and to treat someone as such is to regard them as outsiders too."[21]

The larger point of Illian's article is an assertion that Matthew's Jesus demonstrates the importance of rebuke and of discipline in the maintenance of healthy communities.[22] Understanding the practices of and teachings on rebuke and even expulsion as formative influences on this text provides a counterbalance to calls for patience and forgiveness. When members of a community wrong each other, they must prioritize confession and rebuke because the offense will continue to damage the relationships and the community until it is properly addressed. Moreover, the unrepentant offender constitutes a particular threat to the most vulnerable members of the community. Thus, confrontation and expulsion (if necessary) are not only essential to the health of the community; they are also necessary for caring for the community's most vulnerable members.

Jeffrey A. Gibbs and Jeffrey J. Kloha expand this point about community care even further, arguing that Matthew 18:15–17 "is not about 'conflict resolution' per se. It is about deep concern for a brother who has been overtaken in a trespass."[23] Gibbs and Kloha assert that this pericope must be kept in thematic coherence with Matthew 18:1–20, where they find displayed a "crescendo of care." Jesus instructs the disciples to care first for children (who have the most needs) and then the lost sheep, and then to extend that same care to a disciple/brother who has sinned against them.[24] The rebuke and discipline (the focus in verses 15–17) is undertaken as part of caring for the community, not out of anger or vengeance or self-righteousness. In other words, Jesus commends a process of engaging in conflict that is motivated by care and that is helpful to the community. Keeping verses 15–17 connected to the surrounding material reveals more than a set of step-by-step instructions. In this broader frame of reference, we see attention to being as well as doing, to relationship as well as procedure. We also see clearly that engaging conflict well—even rebuking a brother or sister—is good for community.

However, the form and intention of the rebuke matters. Indeed, an angry outburst that belittles and insults a brother or sister renders one "liable to the hell of fire" (Matt. 5:22). Lederach's call to follow Jesus' practice and eat with offenders may seem at odds with Illian's support for expulsion, and Illian's focus on care of the victim may seem in tension with Gibbs and Kloha's argument for caring for the offender, but they all share two important commonalities. In each of these interpretations, the goal is reintegration into the community, or reconciliation. And throughout each process, the emphasis is on practices that are grounded in care for the community and its members. In other words, neither practice commends treatment that insults, belittles, or dehumanizes the offender. Given this commonality and given the presence of Leviticus 19:17–18 in the background here, it seems fruitful to move from Matthew 18:15–17 to Matthew 5:22: "If you are angry with a brother or sister, you will be liable to judgment; and if you insult a brother or sister, you will be liable to the council; and if you say, 'You fool,' you will be liable to the hell of fire." Moving from the procedures for rebuke to this condemnation of anger reminds us how fluid the identities of victim and offender really are. There are many ways that we can be wrong when we are doing right.

Victim and offender identities are not static, and moments of conflict do not have tidy demarcations around them. In the flux of history and human relationship, we often occupy victim and offender positions simultaneously. This does not mean that we occupy them to the same extent in every moment. But it does mean that over the course of our lives in community, we have moments for apology as well as rebuke and many moments that require both at the same time.

"So when you are offering your gift at the altar, if you remember that your brother or sister has something against you, leave your gift before the altar and go; first be reconciled to your brother or sister and then come and offer your gift" (Matt. 5:23). James Bailey suggests that the reference to the offense in this verse "seems intentionally vague."[25] This vagueness persists in verse 25: "Come to terms quickly with your accuser." We do not know the nature of these offenses. In verse 23, "you" remember that a brother or sister has something against you; in verse 25, "you" are in the company of your accuser. Bailey writes, "What hearers do know is this: there is rupture in the relationship between the one offering the gift at the altar and someone else in the community."[26] In Bailey's interpretation, the rupture is more than a "one-time angry outburst that arises spontaneously in reaction to a situation but rather a long-term holding of hostile feelings towards a fellow Christian."[27] This interpretation helps us to see the work of reconciliation called for in verse 24 as much more than apology for a harsh word. Taking up the work of reconciliation in the context of this passage requires disrupting behavior patterns. The text asks me to leave the altar to disrupt a pattern of simmering anger, of resentful murmuring, of belittling sideswipes, as well as the more overt verbal offense. It asks me to leave the altar to take ownership for the part I have played in separating myself from another. It calls me to do much more than apologize; it calls me to live differently.

This call is no small matter. It warrants one of the six antitheses in Matthew's version of the Sermon on the Mount: "You have heard that is was said to those of ancient times, 'You shall not murder'; and 'whoever murders shall be liable to judgment.' But I say to you that if you are angry with a brother or sister, you will be liable to judgment; and if you insult a brother or sister, you will be liable to the council; and if you say, 'You fool,' you will be liable to the hell of fire" (Matt. 5:21–22). The antitheses establish the "ethical demands of the Kingdom" in Matthew's Gospel.[28] This rhetorical device demonstrates Jesus' connection to the law and his argument for how to fulfill its intended meaning.[29] In this particular antithesis, Jesus insists that his hearers must not only refuse to murder but also refuse to let anger become a divisive force in the community.[30] When our anger fuels insults and belittling speech, we further rupture community. Thus, working through anger is the fulfillment of the law against murder. In Bailey's words, "Our failure to deal constructively with anger causes serious damage to ourselves and community."[31] Donald Hagner puts it more starkly: "Anger and insults spoken from anger are evil and corrupting, and they therefore call forth God's judgment, just as the act of murder itself does."[32] With this argument, Jesus draws attention to internal character and not only external deeds.

Matthew and Mark both record a story in which Jesus makes plain this connection between internal character and external deeds. The story finds Jesus in yet another dispute with scribes and Pharisees, who confront him because his disciples have been eating with unclean hands. In his rebuttal, Jesus quotes Isaiah: "This people honors me with their lips, but their heart is far from me; in vain do they worship me, teaching as doctrines the precepts of men" (Matt. 15:8–9 RSV, quoting Isa. 29:13). In a teaching moment, Jesus then turns to the crowd:

> And he called the people to him and said to them, "Hear and understand: not what goes into the mouth defiles a man, but what comes out of the mouth, this defiles a man." (Matt. 15:10–11, RSV)

> And he called the people to him again, and said to them, "Hear me, all of you, and understand: there is nothing outside a man which by going into him can defile him; but the things which come out of a man are what defile him." (Mark 7:14–16 RSV)

In both accounts, Jesus feels the need to offer an explanation to his disciples:

> "Do you not see that whatever goes into a man from outside cannot defile him, since it enters, not his heart but his stomach and so passes on?" (Thus he declared all foods clean.) And he said, "What comes out of a man is what defiles him. For from within, out of the heart of man, come evil thoughts, fornication, theft, murder, adultery, coveting, wickedness, deceit, licentiousness, envy, slander, pride, foolishness. All these evil things come from within, and they defile a man." (Mark 7:18–23 RSV)

We see here a connection to James's teaching about the power of the tongue (Jas. 3:5–6) and to Paul's teaching on righteous/godly living (Gal. 5:19–21). This similarity is not accidental. According to David Buttrick, this passage follows a "convention found in intertestamental Jewish literature and in the Pauline letters," including Galatians 5:19–21, discussed earlier.[33] Indeed, Buttrick suggests that the "list of human sins . . . is possibly a later addition to the story."[34] Buttrick continues a line of argument articulated by Rudolf Bultmann in the 1960s. Bultmann focused on the conflict-pronouncement patterns in the Gospels (such as this one concerning defilement from within) and argued that the arguments recorded in the Gospels as occurring between Jesus and the Pharisees were most likely ascribed to Jesus later. The substance of the pronouncements reflects controversial issues facing the Christian movement vis-à-vis its Jewish origins.[35] This thesis means that we need to be cautious about drawing conclusions from the conflict-pronouncement stories about Jesus' conflict style or positions on the various controversies. The moments were more likely constructed at a later time to address a controversy facing the community after Jesus' death rather than a conflict that Jesus addressed in person.

What most interests me in these texts is not the list of vices and whether they are original to Jesus or ascribed to him later; what intrigues me is that he seems to enact one of them in the very next scene with his rude treatment of the Syrophoenician woman (in Mark) or the Canaanite woman (in Matthew):

> But immediately a woman, whose little daughter was possessed by an unclean spirit, heard of him, and came and fell down at his feet. Now the woman was a Greek, a Syrophoenician by birth. And she begged him to cast the demon out of her daughter. And he said to her, "Let the children first be fed, for it is not right to take the children's bread and throw it to the dogs." But she answered him, "Yes, Lord; yet even the dogs under the table eat the children's crumbs." And he said to her, "For this saying you may go your way; the demon has left your daughter." And she went home, and found the child lying in bed, and the demon gone. (Mark 7:25–30 RSV)

> And behold, a Canaanite woman from that region came out and cried, "Have mercy on me, O Lord, Son of David; my daughter is severely possessed by a demon." But he did not answer her a word. And his disciples came and begged him, saying, "Send her away, for she is crying after us." He answered, "I was sent only to the lost sheep of the house of Israel." But she came and knelt before him, saying, "Lord, help me." And he answered, "It is not fair to take the children's bread and throw it to the dogs." She said, "Yes, Lord, yet even the dogs eat the crumbs that fall from their master's table." Then Jesus answered her, "O woman, great is your faith! Be it done for you as you desire." And her daughter was healed instantly. (Matt. 15:22–29 RSV)

The woman, though a Gentile, approaches Jesus with great faith, asking him to heal her daughter. In Mark's account, Jesus immediately calls her a dog (Mark 7:27). In Matthew's account, Jesus ignores her completely at first (Matt. 15:23) and then calls her a dog (Matt. 15:26). As Buttrick notes, "Here we seem to have words so starkly prejudicial that they run counter to everything else Jesus reputedly said."[36] Kathleen Corley notes various attempts to soften Jesus' language but insists that there is no getting around the harshness of the slur: "When used of a woman, [dog] is a term of reproach for her shameless behavior and audacity; it is not a term of endearment."[37] Like most modern interpreters, Buttrick and Corley understand the Syrophoenician woman to represent "non-Jewish supplicants," and they understand this encounter to reflect a larger debate over extension of the Christian mission to Gentiles.[38] Thus, Buttrick argues, "it is possible that the racial slur has been put on Jesus' lips to represent an argument animating some early Christian communities."[39] Corley focuses on the gender of this "non-Jewish" representative, arguing that Mark and Matthew use language that indicates that she was "no doubt a perfumed prostitute."[40] We have in this character a stark contrast to the Pharisees with their lack of faith and even the disciples with their lack of understanding. By contrast, she is clever enough in Mark and faithful enough in Matthew to change Jesus' mind. When explaining why he decides to heal her daughter, the Markan Jesus credits her clever rebuttal, and the Matthean Jesus credits her great faith.[41]

Read through a hermeneutic of conflict, we see here a woman who exhibits the kind of behavior for which Jesus has been calling. She speaks without slander and out of faith. Meanwhile, Jesus responds poorly, rudely, offensively. In effect, she responds as Jesus instructs in Matthew 5:38–42:

> "You have heard that it was said, 'An eye for an eye and a tooth for a tooth.' But I say to you, Do not resist one who is evil. But if any one strikes you on the right cheek, turn to him the other also; and if any one would sue you and take your coat, let him have your cloak as well; and if any one forces you to go one mile, go with him two miles. Give to him who begs from you, and do not refuse him who would borrow from you." (Matt. 5:38–42 RSV)

As Walter Wink has argued, this passage does not encourage passivity in the face of mistreatment.[42] Rather, Jesus is counseling subversive tactics that will shame the opponent. In his encounter with the Syrophoenician woman, Jesus, in effect, slaps her in the face, and she cleverly uses his own slur against him to reveal the injustice of his response. Using his own slur to undermine his position, she says, "Yes, Lord; yet even the dogs under the table eat the children's crumbs" (Mark 7:28

RSV). Jesus, thankfully, changes his tune: "For this saying you may go your way; the demon has left your daughter" (Mark 7:29 RSV). And as Jesus says in Matthew, "O woman, great is your faith! Be it done for you as you desire" (Matt. 15:28 RSV). This clever woman reminded Jesus of his disruptive mission at a moment when he slipped into the rut of traditional divisions and employed a despicable slur. Her clever response not only demonstrates her faith but also reminds Jesus that his healing ministry has no boundaries.

In this story, we also find a foil to the scribes, Pharisees, and Sadducees, with whom Jesus is in regular conflict through the Gospels. Whereas the Syrophoenician woman challenges Jesus from a position of no power but great faith in him, the others challenge Jesus from a position of power but no faith in him. Indeed, as recorded during one such interaction, "the scribes and Pharisees began to press him hard, and to provoke him to speak of many things lying in wait for him to catch at something he might say" (Luke 11:53–54 RSV). The woman argues (very carefully) to persuade; the scribes and Pharisees argue to provoke and trap. The power and intention of the opponent in conflict make a difference. It is worth noting that Mark and Matthew precede the story of the Syrophoenician/Canaanite woman with one of Jesus' interactions with the scribes and Pharisees. In this exchange, he responds to their charge of uncleanliness by calling them hypocrites and citing Isaiah: "This people honors me with their lips, but their hearts are far from me" (Mark 7:6). By contrast, though the woman leads an unclean life, her heart is close to God. And her faith in Jesus as the Messiah reminds him who he is.

The Syrophoenician/Canaanite woman brings to mind another tenacious female character, who appears in a parable that Jesus tells his disciples at a time when they are feeling discouraged:

> And he told them a parable, to the effect that they ought always to pray and not lose heart. He said, "In a certain city there was a judge who neither feared God nor regarded man; and there was a widow in that city who kept coming to him and saying, 'Vindicate me against my adversary.' For a while he refused; but afterward he said to himself, 'Though I neither fear God nor regard man, yet because this widow bothers me, I will vindicate her, or she will wear me out by her continual coming.'" (Luke 18:1–5 RSV)

Jesus points to the judge and tells the disciples to take courage: if this unrighteous judge finally responds in this way, even more so will God respond to their supplications. Jesus tells this parable after lengthy preaching about the separation and division in the end times, declarations that some will be taken and others will not. Here again, we have a pattern of Jesus preaching about divisions and separation and exclusion, followed by a character who effectively challenges a decision, this time through sheer persistence. The widow, who represents vulnerability, just keeps coming and bothering the judge. As the parable unfolds, we learn that this is a character to emulate. Through her persistence—her continual coming—she represents faithfulness. In a rhetorical question that has the effect of comparing the widow to his disciples, Jesus asks, "When the Son of man comes, will he find faith on earth?" (Luke 18:8 RSV). Will the people persist in faith or give up? In this parable, as in the story of the Syrophoenician/Canaanite woman, the moral exemplar is not the powerful man who changes his mind, but the woman who convinces him he was wrong.

These two women exhibit some of the behaviors denounced in the letters to Timothy and Titus. They do not accept the initial response of someone more powerful, but rather challenge that response until it changes. They are disobedient and, we might even say, quarrelsome. They are also advocating a personal interest—the health of a daughter and vindication against adversaries—yet they are not scolded in person or through narration for being motivated by jealousy or envy. In this sense, they demonstrate that conflictual behavior does not necessarily come from the vices that Paul and James identify. These women do not even exhibit the fruits of the spirit that Paul and James commend. They are persistent, not patient. They are tenacious, not meek. Yet Jesus commends the Syrophoenician woman for her thoughtful response and her faithfulness, and he offers the widow as an image of faithful persistence in the face of obstacles and discouragement. Jesus frames these conflictual behaviors as faithful. The Syrophoenician woman challenges Jesus to heal her daughter because she has faith in him. The widow's "continual coming" represents faithfulness in the parable. These women offer contrary evidence to the assumption that conflict reflects ungodly behavior and destroys the community. Indeed, their examples suggest that certain approaches to certain kinds of conflict might indeed be virtuous.

As I explained in the introduction, a virtue is a disposition that orients us toward a suitable goal. I suggested that the letters to Timothy and Titus are problematic today in part because they prioritize the goal of cohesion in the community and commend obedience and submission as virtues. By contrast, consider the Syrophoenician woman and the persistent widow again. Staying closely to the narratives, the Syrophoenician woman is working for the health of her daughter, and the persistent widow seeks vindication against her adversaries in a judicial proceeding. However, in a symbolic sense, both of these women point to the kingdom of God. The story of Jesus' encounter with the Syrophoenician woman reflects the broader debate over the reach of Jesus' mission. By healing the daughter of the Syrophoenician woman, Jesus symbolically extends invitations to the heavenly banquet. Similarly, the persistent widow represents people who remain faithful—and who act on that faith—while awaiting the coming kingdom. Both of these women spark conflict in our ongoing wrestling with these stories, but that conflict functions as a catalyst for learning and for remembering the deep connections between faith in what could be and resistance to what is.

These women provide space in Scripture to see conflictual behaviors as virtuous, as dispositions that orient us to a suitable end. I am reminded of an important argument from Katie Cannon, who identifies unctuousness as a virtue. Resisting the traditional view of suffering as virtuous, Cannon extolls "that which allows Black people to maintain a feistiness about life that nobody can wipe out, no matter how hard they try."[43] She finds unctuousness exemplified in the life and characters of writer Zora Neale Hurston. Lifting up Hurston as a moral exemplar, Cannon insists, "Creatively straining against the external restraints in one's life is virtuous living."[44] Cannon's writing has helped me to see the Syrophoenician woman and the persistent widow as more than minor characters in the stories of Jesus. I see them also as moral exemplars, figures who demonstrate that resistance and confrontation are also expressions of faith and virtuous living.

Conflict is everywhere in the Gospels, and it is everywhere in the Gospels because it is everywhere in life. It is not only that there are many conflicts, but that conflict is part of life. We are constantly interacting with others and with the world around us, and in that nexus of interaction there is tension, friction, striking together. In other words, we are constantly affecting other people, and they are affecting us. We also have material and conceptual differences that contribute to conflict. This constant striking together makes our behavior even more important. There are certainly conflict-related behaviors that are denounced in the Gospels. As we have seen, the Gospels discourage anger, jealousy, deceit, fear, anxiety, and judging others. And they commend patience, meekness, humility, forgiveness, faithfulness, and love. However, the Synoptic Gospels do not fix conflict squarely with the list of vices, juxtaposed against the list of virtues. Indeed, in his own actions and teaching, Jesus demonstrates how to exhibit virtuous behaviors in the midst of conflict. The virtues do not keep us from conflict; they indicate how we should behave in conflict.

This is what we see in the two passages of practical guidance from Matthew. Their value is not limited to the particular steps they describe; rather, their value extends to insights about communities in conflict more generally. These texts pass on traditions for dealing with offenses and transgressions in the community, and they convey wisdom about the disposition of love and an intention of care that must guide and ground our engagements with others. In other words, they call us to certain ways of being in conflict. These certain ways of being are the virtues, the dispositions that orient Christians toward the *summum bonum*, the kingdom of God.

CONCLUSION

Let us return now to the methodological dimension, picking up the concerns about selectivity and application that Gustafson articulated (and that I mentioned in the introduction to this chapter). Obviously, I did not cite every Scripture passage that has something to do with conflict. Rather, I selected passages in Galatians, James, and the Pastoral Letters that contain explicit admonishments against behavior that is translated as conflict. In the Gospels, I selected a few practical teachings about conflict, two stories about Jesus in conflict, and one parable. From this collection, I identified some instructions for behavior in the context of conflict and argued that conflict is neither avoidable nor necessarily bad. Indeed, it serves as a vehicle for change. Why did I select these passages and not others? Why do I derive rules for behavior from the Matthean texts and lift up the Syrophoenician woman as an ideal? These are questions of content. I also pair the Syrophoenician woman with the persistent widow in the parable and present them as analogous to vulnerable people who persist in challenging authorities. I lift up these women and their behaviors not only as moral exemplars for us, but also as moral correctives to the teachings on submission and obedience in the Pastoral Letters. These are questions of application as well as content. That is, I am suggesting that vulnerable, mistreated persons ought to resist in clever and persistent ways rather than be submissive or obedient. This is an issue of application: In what circumstances would I apply this guidance on behavior that I derive from Scripture? In a more general sense, how do I apply these teachings to life today, given the contextual chasm that exists between Jesus' time and our own?

Gustafson's overarching concern is about selectivity and weight. What do we select as authoritative? How much weight do we give it relative to other sources of knowledge and authority? And most pointedly, are we really learning from the texts, or are we seeking out confirmation of positions we hold and answers we want to receive? These concerns have merit, because turning to Scripture for moral authority is a highly subjective endeavor. We cannot avoid selectivity and interpretation as we strive to understand and apply Scripture to moral questions today. It is important, therefore, to be transparent and to have publicly defensible reasons for the selections, interpretations, and applications we offer. Here are mine.

I first selected passages that surface when one uses a concordance to look for "conflict" in the Bible. I focused on the five passages in Galatians, James, 1 Timothy, 2 Timothy, and Titus because they seem to most explicitly discourage followers of Christ from participating in conflict (contention, quarrels, strife). I then selected passages that Christians often employ to encourage (or equip) other Christians to engage conflict constructively (Matt. 5:23–24 and 18:15–17). As I considered the narrative surrounding these two pieces of practical instruction, a question emerged: Why is it so important to do more than follow procedure or law? With that question very much in my mind, I then focused on stories of Jesus in conflict himself. When I reached the argument about unclean hands, I found Jesus' teaching that we are defiled by what we give out, not by what we take in. This passage connects so quickly to the teachings in James and Paul—intentionally so according to commentaries—that it seemed important to investigate it further. As told by Matthew and Mark, Jesus abruptly leaves this lesson on good behaviors and immediately insults a foreign woman who is desperately seeking help for her daughter. Her response to his rudeness elicits from Jesus not only a compliment but a gift of healing for her daughter. Clearly, she does something right in an incredibly difficult situation of being grossly mistreated by one she needed and trusted. I lift her up as an ideal because her behavior brings a positive reaction from Jesus and also squares with many of his instructions in previous passages. Does Jesus lift up other desperate people begging those more powerful for help? Yes, he gives us the persistent widow in the parable and frames her annoying behavior toward the judge as faithfulness. Admittedly, my disagreement with the teachings on submission and obedience in the Pastoral Letters made me most interested in these insubordinate and disobedient women. It is possible that I give these two characters a more prominent position than the narratives actually warrant. However, it is also objectively true that Jesus praises them for their behavior, which gives us good cause to see it as commendable.

In keeping with the commitment to transparency—and also in an effort to illustrate further my methodology—it is important to note the other sources of knowledge and authority that influence my interpretation of these texts. As I interact with the text, I cannot escape my own experience that inevitably affects my reading and interpretation. I am also strongly influenced by the Wesleyan tradition with its emphasis on process, procedure, and behavior. The way in which we do something matters; dispositions matter. This formation no doubt influences my reception of the texts discussed here. My familiarity with peace and conflict studies has also shaped the way I understand these stories and teachings on conflict. Through study and experience with conflict, I am convinced that conflict is a feature of life and that it has the potential to be a catalyst for constructive change. There is an unavoidable interplay between what we read in Scripture and what we know from other sources of authority. Our persistent challenge, which is also an opportunity, is to bring these sources of knowledge together in ways that illuminate rather than obscure God's ongoing revelation and our discernment of the persons we are called to become.

In workshops and classes, I often ask participants to bring a passage of Scripture that guides them in times of conflict. I am always pleasantly surprised by the variety of texts that enter the room. People not only bring Scripture passages that help them know what to do in a conflict; they also bring passages that speak to them about the experience of being in conflict. As they talk about the experiences of conflict reflected in Scripture, I ask them to consider what God seems to be doing through conflict in this passage. This turn in our conversation reflects another approach to Scripture that James Gustafson calls "revealed reality." In this approach, we ask a different question: not "What should we do?" but "What is God doing?"[45] What does Scripture reveal to us about God? This approach to Scripture relies on a broader frame of reference and works with prominent lines or themes in Scripture. We zoom out from linguistic details of texts to think about the broader themes, and then we revisit the details of texts with the theme in mind.

In this study of conflict and virtue, we have already zoomed out a bit to consider the end connected to the virtues espoused. We saw that the virtues of obedience and the corresponding vice of conflict related to the goal of cohesion in the new community. And drawing on the Syrophoenician woman and the persistent widow, along with the writing of Katie Cannon, I suggested a way to read conflictual behaviors of persistence and resistance as virtues, orienting us in faith toward the kingdom of God. We see how virtue ethics connects with teleology, a form of ethics oriented toward a goal. The fifth chapter studies teleological ethics by examining the telos of reconciliation in contexts of conflict.

5

The Purpose and Process of Reconciliation

Considering Teleology and Narrative

I ended the last chapter by referencing James Gustafson's "revealed reality" alternative to the revealed morality approach to Scripture.[1] In this approach, one does not turn to Scripture primarily for moral instruction with the question "What should I do?" Rather, one turns to Scripture to understand what God is doing so that one might participate in God's work in the world.[2] Over and over again, written materials about conflict transformation and interviews with practitioners assert that God's activity in the midst of conflict has a particular direction to it: God moves in the direction of reconciliation.[3] Emmanuel Katongole and Chris Rice (founding directors of Duke Divinity School's Center for Reconciliation) describe reconciliation as a gift and a journey that we can understand only as part of God's story revealed through Scripture:

> Recovering reconciliation as God's story is an invitation to approach Scripture with a sense of adventure. We learn to live the question, what happens next? Scripture is neither a catalogue of spiritual insights nor a collection of moral guidelines and principles. It is a story. As a story, Scripture can be read through the central plot of Creation, Fall, Promise, and Restoration—a plot that is in essence the movement from old creation to new creation.[4]

This chapter explores both the *narrative* of "movement from old creation to new creation" and the *telos* (goal or purpose) of reconciliation. As we will see, those working in conflict transformation understand reconciliation to be a goal and also a journey, meaning that we cannot separate our considerations of teleology from discussion of the processes that move us from where we are to where God calls us to be. This chapter also considers the power of narrative as an interpretive lens for human experience. How does my interpretation of God's movement in history shape my interpretation of history? How does my sense of God's calling affect my perception of events and my response to them? If I believe that the telos is reconciliation and that God calls us on a journey to reconcile, how do I interpret and respond to intractable conflicts, disrupted processes, and individual decisions to separate? Even more to the heart of the tension explored in this chapter, how do I think theologically and ethically about struggles for justice and liberation? Where do these fit into the narrative of reconciliation? And, more pointedly, does the narrative of reconciliation constrict the ways that we understand and value the disruptive work of justice making?

In 1985, fifty black pastors in South Africa crafted *The Kairos Document: A Radical Challenge to the Church in South Africa*. Three times as many people (pastors and laypersons, white and black) signed the document as soon as it was released. The preface begins this way: "The Kairos document is a Christian, biblical and theological comment on the political crisis in South Africa today. It is an attempt by concerned Christians in South Africa to reflect on the situation of death in our country."[5] The document proceeds to describe and critique state theology and church theology and to articulate an alternative prophetic theology of liberation in the context of apartheid. In their discussion of church theology, the writers of the Kairos Document offer a critique of reconciliation that is absolutely central to this chapter:

> The fallacy here is that "reconciliation" has been made into an absolute principle that must be applied in all cases of conflict or dissension. But not all cases of conflict are the same. . . . There are conflicts where one side is a fully armed and violent oppressor while the other side is defenceless and oppressed. There are conflicts that can only be described as the struggle between justice and injustice, good and evil, God and the devil. To speak of reconciling these two is not only a mistaken application of the Christian idea of reconciliation, it is a total betrayal of all that Christian faith has ever meant. . . . In our situation in South Africa today it would be totally unchristian to plead for reconciliation and peace before the present injustices have been removed.[6]

In my view, it is irresponsible for Christian ethicists to begin a conversation about reconciliation without listening to these words from the Kairos Document. Our views on reconciliation need to be accountable to the victims of violence and injustice. To speak about reconciliation without attending to issues of justice is to say, "peace, peace when there is no peace" (Jer. 6:14).

The scholars and practitioners who appear in this chapter know these debates well. I am purposefully drawing on Christian theologians and ethicists who are profoundly and personally aware of the tension between justice and reconciliation and who come to different conclusions about where these two commitments are situated in "the movement from old creation to new creation."[7] While intrinsically important, of course, these arguments also function heuristically for us. That is, exploring the arguments helps us to discover some crucial dimensions of Christian ethics, and of teleology specifically.

In teleological approaches to ethics, we orient ourselves according to a goal. Clearly, our understanding of the substance of the goal (here, of what reconciliation means) has tremendous implications for our discernment about the process between what is and what ought to be. Moreover, our interpretation of the goal and the process also ascribes value to actions, behaviors, and events. The telos not only guides individual behavior but also functions evaluatively as we reflect on the events of history. We judge actions and behaviors according to whether they align with the goal or not. Alignment is not the only criterion, however. Our perception of possibility also impacts discernment and evaluation. Is the goal of reconciliation achievable in history, or is it a "horizon for another world"?[8] If we cannot actually experience reconciliation, then what? Do we value other things? Do we find value in more modest goals, appropriate to this broken existence? All of these considerations are in play here, underscoring once again contingency and dynamism in the study and practice of Christian ethics.

THE TELOS OF RECONCILIATION

In *The Journey toward Reconciliation* (revised and republished in 2014 under the title *Reconcile*), John Paul Lederach asserts that "God's mission is reconciliation."[9] He elaborates:

> I believe that the way God has chosen to be present and act throughout history demonstrates a methodology of reconciliation. *Our mission* is to align ourselves with God, who is working to bring all things together, to *reconcile* all of creation and particularly a broken, estranged humanity.[10]

Tom Porter and the organization he cofounded, JustPeace Center for Mediation and Conflict Transformation, share this two-part assertion: God reconciles, and we are called to a ministry of reconciliation.[11] Likewise, the Lombard Mennonite Peace Center draws its mission from 2 Corinthians 5:18: "All this is from God, who reconciled us to himself through Christ, and has given us the ministry of reconciliation."[12] And David Anderson Hooker, professor of the practice of conflict transformation and peacebuilding and an ordained minister in the United Church of Christ, explains, "Ultimately for me the central theme of the faith is about reconciliation. God through Jesus was reconciling Godself to the world and then gave each of us both a ministry and message of reconciliation."[13] Reconciliation constitutes more than a theological theme in this material. For these writers, practitioners, and trainers, reconciliation is the telos of God's work and of their own.

What does this say about them? Teleological moral agents orient themselves toward a goal, which guides their deliberation and discernment. Teleologists focus on consequences and try to discern processes for moral action that lead to the goal identified. In class once, I made a metaphorical point about the necessity of establishing sturdy foundations before constructing the building. After class, a student who was an architect told me that architects work the other way around: they design the top of the building first and then determine what foundation is required to support it. Architects work more like teleologists. They identify the desired end point or outcome and then discern how best to reach it or approximate it.

I have already referred to teleology a few times in this text because the ethical methodologies interact with one another. One of the dangers of teleological ethics is that the moral agent might use the end to justify any means, concluding that anything goes as long as we are pursuing a noble end. Therefore, it is important to keep deontology and teleology connected. Deontology sets parameters around the means, while teleology reminds us of their purpose. Or to paraphrase the political philosopher John Rawls, a principle "draws the limit," while the goal "shows the point."[14] We have also noted a connection between virtue ethics and teleology. Indeed, the very definition of a virtue includes reference to the goal: a virtue is a habit that disposes us to act well, in accordance with a suitable end. As we saw in the previous chapter, goals provide an orienting and evaluative function. We discern which action to take in light of a particular goal, and we also judge behavior (ours and that of others) according to whether it aligns with a particular goal.

We identify, orient ourselves, and evaluate our actions based on any number of goals. Within Christian ethics, however, the goals are not solely self-generated. Rather, they reflect the authority of Christian sources. On this point, again, we find variety within Christian ethics. For some people, it is crucial that the telos for the Christian comes directly from Scripture. Christians who hold this high view of Scripture might amend the previous sentence this way: Within Christian ethics, the goals are not self-generated but rather come from Scripture. Other Christians, however, assert that Scripture cannot be separated from other sources of knowledge (tradition, experience, and reason); thus, a unilateral movement from Scripture to human beings is not possible. Interpreting Scripture is a dynamic process that involves movement between these different sources of knowledge. A Christian telos must certainly be informed by Scripture, but it will also, necessarily, be interpreted in light of tradition, experience, and reason. I begin in the following pages with descriptions of reconciliation as a telos informed primarily by Scripture. We see very quickly, however, that reflections on the biblical call to reconciliation cannot be separated from experiences of ongoing conflict in the world.

According to *The Oxford Encyclopedia of Bible and Theology*, "The Greek words *katallassein* ('to reconcile') and *diallassein* ('to reconcile,' and their cognates and synonyms) have the fundamental meaning of 'exchange' and were used for a change from a relationship of conflict and enmity to one of peace and friendship."[15] Miroslav Volf describes reconciliation as the "restoration of communion" made possible by God who "has reached out in grace to the perpetrators in order to make friends out of enemies, and continues to do so despite their persisting sin and enmity."[16] In another essay, Volf describes reconciliation "as the creation of a community in which each recognizes and is recognized by all and in which all mutually give themselves to each other in love."[17] Emilie Townes describes an objective realm of reconciliation in which God "creates a new relationship with us" and gives the "gift of freedom." She also describes a subjective realm, which is the "restoration of harmony with groups and with individuals." And she asserts that the "subjective realm of reconciliation is what we do to remain faithful to God's gift of freedom in our lives."[18] These initial descriptions capture two essential features of reconciliation. First, there is a vertical dimension (referencing the relationship between God and humanity) and a horizontal dimension (the relationships we form between humans). Second, there is a shared conviction that reconciliation among ourselves is made possible by and called forth by God's invitation to us to reconcile with God. In other words, the horizontal work is made possible by the vertical work. Katongole and Rice write, "There are two movements in this story, and the order is important. The first movement is about God and what God has done in Christ. The second is about the transformation this first movement has enacted in the world and in the lives of people."[19] Remaining clear that it is God who initiates the vertical and the horizontal processes is crucial to Katongole and Rice and to many theologians and ethicists writing on reconciliation. This is not only motivated by piety and fidelity to the sovereignty of God; it also reflects the story of reconciliation as Paul relays it in Scripture.

When Paul uses *katallagé* ("reconciliation") to refer to a divine-human relationship, God remains the offended subject who extends reconciliation to human beings, the objects and the offenders.[20] Thus, Paul emphasizes that the invitation of reconciliation is an expression of grace. We do not earn this. This invitation occurs through Christ's atonement, God's invitation to human beings to be forgiven and to enter into right relationship with the divine. But according to Paul, we are not only invited into a reconciled relationship with God; we are also given the ministry of reconciliation (2 Cor. 5:18) and made "ambassadors for Christ" (2 Cor. 5:20). In many of the writings explored in this chapter, Dietrich Bonhoeffer surfaces as a reminder that the vertical reconciliation without the horizontal turn becomes a form of cheap grace. The reference comes from Bonhoeffer's text *The Cost of Discipleship*, in which he calls Christians to forms of costly grace: "Cheap grace is grace without discipleship, grace without the cross, grace without Jesus Christ living and incarnate."[21] In this conversation about reconciliation, cheap grace suggests that I accept God's invitation to me to reconcile to God through Christ, but I do not then participate in the ministry of reconciliation with my fellow human beings. We must not receive the gift of reconciliation and fail to respond.

This point—complete with the invocation of Bonhoeffer—surfaces clearly in the writings of Katongole and Rice, in which 2 Corinthians

5:17–18 functions as a central text. Their book, *Reconciling All Things*, is a rich example of reflection on reconciliation that is grounded primarily in Scripture. While they write explicitly about the experiences that inform them, they also insist that their ministry of reconciliation is a response to God's invitation through Scripture rather than the pursuit of their own goals and ideals. Katongole and Rice describe reconciliation as "God's language for a broken world" and "God's vision for our redemption."[22] They write:

> Reconciliation is not in the first place an activity or a set of attitudes but an invitation into a story. Reconciliation names God's story of creation, which is at the same time a promise of restoration. Restoration takes the form of a journey—God's journey to realize that promise in us.[23]

The language of gift and journey are central to this understanding of reconciliation. Through Christ, God extends this gift of reconciliation. With Christ, God calls us into ministries of reconciliation: "So if anyone is in Christ there is a new creation: everything old has passed away; see, everything has become new! All this is from God, who reconciled us to himself through Christ, and has given us the ministry of reconciliation" (2 Cor. 5:17–18).

In their work, Katongole and Rice criticize an exclusively vertical understanding of reconciliation that divorces personal salvation from social transformation. They call this "reconciliation as evacuation" because it evacuates or "abandons the past too quickly and confidently in search of a new future" away from a broken and divided world.[24] Katongole and Rice also identify an opposite error, namely, that of responding to the broken and divided world as a social service agency rather than as a church. They call this "reconciliation as firefighting." In this mode, Christians try to respond to the urgent needs of our time by developing better techniques and strategies, "pragmatically trying to 'put out' (or at least minimize) local and national fires of conflict, division, war, and brokenness. . . . If reconciliation as evacuation disconnects the gospel from social realities, reconciliation as firefighting transforms the church into a social agency."[25] Katongole and Rice are wary of projects that seem to be driven by human perception of need rather than the desire to respond to God's call.

Katongole and Rice assert that reconciliation, properly understood, avoids both of these errors. The activities of reconciliation do not begin as a human response to social division. Rather, God initiates reconciliation and invites human beings to respond. We respond to God by extending ministries of reconciliation into the world. The movement of reconciliation neither begins nor ends with us; it begins with God and moves through us to others: "Christians not only bear witness to the gift of reconciliation we have received from God; we also become ambassadors of God's new creation to a broken and divided world."[26]

In other words, the vertical dimension of reconciliation—the grace-filled invitation of reconciliation with God through Christ—also calls us to the horizontal processes of reconciliation with one another. In his influential text *Exclusion and Embrace* (1996), Croatian theologian Miroslav Volf describes this vertical dimension of reconciliation in terms of communion, emphasizing the self-giving act of God toward those who are and remain unworthy of the gift. Early in this text, he recognizes the theological work that others have done to connect the cross of Christ with solidarity with victims. And he clarifies that he is intentionally developing another point in his work, namely, "the theme of divine self-donation for the enemies and their reception into the eternal communion of God."[27] He then articulates the "social significance" of reconciliation: "As God does not abandon the godless to their evil but gives the divine self for them in order to receive them into divine communion through atonement, so also should we—whoever our enemies and whoever we may be."[28] Indeed, echoing Bonhoeffer again, Volf insists that the divine communion necessitates social reconciliation: "To claim the comfort of the Crucified while rejecting his way is to advocate not only cheap grace but a deceitful ideology."[29] For Volf, reconciliation not only has social significance; it should be at the center of Christian social responsibility just as it sits at the center of the faith.

Volf identifies two reasons why reconciliation has not occupied this central position, as prevalent as the language of reconciliation has been. First, in keeping with Katongole and Rice's criticism of reconciliation as evacuation, Volf criticizes an individual piety approach to reconciliation, one that employs the vertical dimension only but loses the social significance. Thus, Volf argues firmly against an individualistic, vertical understanding of reconciliation, insisting that reconciliation "has an inalienable social dimension."[30] Second, Volf argues that another reason why reconciliation has been sidelined is that justice and liberation have been placed at "the center of the Christian social agenda."[31] We will spend more time considering the second error because it takes us back to the Kairos Document and into debate with other contemporary Christian theologians and ethicists.

Volf argues against a dichotomous understanding of reconciliation and justice and also against a "first justice, then reconciliation" approach. Liberation and justice must not be understood as tasks distinct from and preceding reconciliation, but rather "as indispensable aspects of a more over-arching agenda of reconciliation."[32] Volf insists that the "struggle for justice [should] be understood *as a dimension of the pursuit of reconciliation whose ultimate goal is a community of love.*"[33] He identifies two practical reasons why establishing justice as a distinct and preliminary requirement is problematic. First, he argues that justice is not attainable in history and that strict justice (meaning here retributive justice) is not actually desirable. Therefore, if reconciliation is predicated on justice, we will never experience either one.

Like Volf, Katongole and Rice also resist a "first justice, then reconciliation" approach and offer an explicit critique of "justice without communion." They identify two motivations driving the demand for justice. The first is an effort to prevent an approach to reconciliation that fails to take seriously the connections between history, identity, and conflict.[34] Katongole and Rice recognize the tendency or possibility for reconciliation to be thin and soft, losing touch with the past and focusing solely on interpersonal dynamics without attention to the structural features of human life. A second argument for prioritizing justice is that the world is fallen. We cannot achieve "a perfect world where all hostilities are reconciled," but we can try to secure justice for some.[35]

However, Volf insists (and Katongole and Rice would concur) that this emphasis on justice jettisons the heart of the Christian faith, which he takes to be grace. The "restoration of communion" is not based on justice done but on God reaching out: "The restoration of communion rests fundamentally on the fact that God, the injured party who rightfully passes judgment on the injuring party, has reached out in grace to the perpetrators in order to make friends out of enemies, and continues to do so despite their persisting sin and enmity."[36] Thus, "grace has priority over justice (grace, again, that does not negate justice but that *affirms* justice in the act of transcending it)."[37] Volf also insists on grace precisely because justice is impossible. Grace is a "gift to you with the hope of a reciprocal response given in the face of the impossibility of justice."[38]

Volf locates an alternative to cheap reconciliation (vertical restoration without social responsibility) and to justice-first approaches

> at the heart of the Christian faith—in the narrative of the cross of Christ, which reveals the very character of God. On the cross, God is manifest as the God who, though in no way indifferent toward the distinction between good and evil, nonetheless lets the sun shine on both the good and the evil (cf. Matt. 5:45); as the God of indiscriminate love who died for the ungodly to bring them into the divine communion (cf. Rom. 5:8); as the God who offers grace—not cheap grace, but grace nonetheless—to the vilest evildoer.[39]

Volf's metaphor for reconciliation is embrace, which he understands to be modeled on "God's reception of hostile humanity into divine communion."[40] In what unfolds as some of the most provocative pages in contemporary literature on reconciliation and justice, Volf describes three features of the embrace: the repentance of the victim,[41] forgiveness of enemies,[42] and "a certain kind of forgetting."[43] These features emerge in part because of Volf's insistence on mirroring God's act of reconciliation: God in Christ is the victim who sacrifices himself, God extends forgiveness to those who have done wrong, and God's gracious welcome exhibits "a certain kind of forgetting." All of these things, Volf insists, are essential to prevent retribution and the ongoing cycle of violence in the name of pursuing justice. The victim must repent not of wrongs committed, but as an exercise of penance to gain a pure heart and then to forgive from a deep place of love and grace. Volf's proposal has met much resistance, and he anticipates and responds to criticism through the text. He also openly admits to ambivalence himself and doubt about his capacity to do what is required here. Yet he insists on the centrality and nonnegotiability of this interpretation: of God's self-emptying love through sacrifice of the victim who then transforms into the agent of forgiveness. That is the story that defines Christian life for Volf, and it is the story Christians must enact in the face of violence.

It is important at this point to take note of Volf's social location. Miroslav Volf comes from Croatia, a place devastated by violence in the 1990s. Croatia declared independence from Yugoslavia in 1991. The Yugoslav Army, which was dominated by Serbs, retaliated violently. When Croatia's neighbor, Bosnia, also tried to declare independence, Serbian resistance coalesced under the leadership of Radovan Karadžić and the Bosnian Serb Army. From 1992 until 1995, Serb forces attempted to create an ethnically pure state by forcing Croats and

Bosnian Muslims from their homes, interning them in camps, massacring them, and systematically raping women.[44] These experiences of violence generate the question at the heart of Volf's work: "How does one remain loyal both to the demand of the oppressed for justice and to the gift of forgiveness that the Crucified offered to the perpetrators?"[45] This question is not "an intriguing intellectual puzzle" for Volf, but a deeply personal, intellectual, and spiritual struggle.[46] He writes:

> I, a citizen of a world at war and a follower of Jesus Christ, could not hang up my commitments, desires, rebellions, resignations, and uncertainties like a coat on a coat rack before entering my study, to be taken up and put on when the work of the day was over. *My* people were being brutalized, and I needed to think through the response appropriate for *me*, a follower of the crucified Messiah.[47]

Emmanuel Katongole has also been shaped by political violence. Katongole is a Roman Catholic priest from Uganda. Katongole grew up under the rule of Idi Amin, the "butcher of Uganda," whose brutal regime murdered at least 300,000 people and tortured countless others. Amin claimed the presidency after a coup in 1971 and fled the country in 1979 after a failed attack on neighboring Tanzania.[48] Katongole's father died when he was twelve, and his mother fled their home in 1980 to escape military violence in the region. Katongole writes that his mother "walked fifty miles to Kampala and did not return until six years later."[49] He sums up his autobiographic reflection this way: "Here I am, with both my experience of growing up in Africa under the brutal regime of Idi Amin and my involvement in the dynamic and rich traditions of the African church."[50] As he brings this whole experience to the work of theology, he asks, "What does it mean for our conversations about God and peace never to be disconnected from the challenges of real, local places, from digging wells, organizing education and planting trees?"[51]

In their coauthored book, Chris Rice also describes his autobiographical journey through contexts of social and political conflict. Chris Rice is a white Protestant man who spent twelve years of his childhood and youth with missionary parents in South Korea during the "tumultuous post-Korean war years."[52] In 1981, he went to Jackson, Mississippi, where he stayed for seventeen years. There he became deeply engaged in racial reconciliation work through Voice of Calvary Ministries, where "Christians of different races worshiped, worked and lived side-by-side on the same streets, seven days a week."[53] The founder of

Voices of Calvary Ministries was an African American minister and activist named John Perkins. Over the years, Rice became friends with Perkins's son, Spencer Perkins, and together they started an intentional Christian community called Antioch. Rice concludes his autographical reflection: "The most important lesson of those seventeen Mississippi years was this: even in a deeply divided world, even in the most deeply divided relationship, *the way things are is not the way they have to be*."[54]

I include these autobiographical descriptions because they help students of ethics to see how personal experience shapes the questions we pose, the interpretations we offer, and the ongoing wrestling we feel as we think through deeply felt moral challenges. But I also cite them at this point to stave off the argument that these writers prioritize reconciliation and forgiveness over justice because they do not care about victims. Clearly, they care about victims. Indeed, their experiences of violence and conflict shape their work as theologians. But in their resistance to justice, we find adherence to an atonement-centered narrative of reconciliation that requires further sacrifice from victims as a repayment of God's sacrifice for them. And that is deeply troubling.

Again, Volf, Katongole, and Rice have deep commitments to justice, meaningful connections to places of violence, and profound relationships that continue to inform the ways they think and write about reconciliation. Their criticism of the justice-first approach is not a dismissal of the importance of justice, of the recognition of the wounds of victims, or of the need to hold perpetrators accountable for their actions. However, they do see pursuits of justice for some as fueling ongoing violence in cycles of retribution. In response to the "no reconciliation without justice" position, they ask, "Whose justice?" That is, what kind of justice is pursued, by whom, for whom, and to what end? As Katongole and Rice explain, "The definition of justice is not self-evident. If it is to make sense or to lead to a transformed vision of human relations, justice requires a story."[55] For them, the story connects human actions to identity rooted in relationship with God and to a future together through the reconciliation made possible in Christ. Without this narrative, our actions—even those in pursuit of justice—are disconnected from calling and purpose. Without a story, the justice approach includes "sophisticated initiatives that speak of redressing the structural results of historical injustices yet do not cast the vision of a new future of community and friendship between historic enemies."[56] For Katongole and Rice, a story roots human actions in relationship with God and binds them to a vision of reconciliation.

We can see in their writing how the narrative relates to character formation (discussed in chapter 4) and to teleology. The development of narrative ethics (which blends virtue ethics and teleology) arose in large part out of a concern about fragmented moral agents, people trying to do good in the world and to act well in the world through an assortment of actions loosely connected to an ad hoc collection of values.[57] Fragmented moral agents respond to circumstances as they arise with convictions that seem to apply and actions that seem effective, but they do not respond out of a story that reminds them who they are and where they are called to go. Katongole and Rice are pointing to a story in an effort to bring that kind of identity and purpose to the work of reconciliation. Like Volf, the story they point to and identify as God's story is "about God's costly embrace of an undeserving humanity."[58] Katongole and Rice point to the "justice of the Lord's table," which transcends the "tit for tat" justice that addresses wrongs without restoring relationship, "justice without communion." At the Lord's Table, we find "a far more radical form [of justice] pursued within a vision of costly communion to bring together what has been torn apart."[59] It is appropriate to ask, "Whose justice?" when references to justice lack a narrative to ground and guide them. But it is also appropriate to ask, "Whose cost?" when narratives claim to transcend justice. Katongole and Rice close this discussion of justice by referencing a "future of shared life with enemies," which may seem "unreasonably costly." They do not say who bears the cost. Instead, they reference Jesus' story to remind us "that we live not by the logic of cause and effect but rather by the mysterious order of death and resurrection."[60] Like Volf, Katongole and Rice articulate a particular interpretation of this narrative, one that culminates in death and resurrection and presents Jesus as the innocent victim who bears the cost of reconciliation. When that interpretation of the story functions as an analogy to guide our thinking about reconciliation between persons, then the victims of violence continue to bear the cost.

I make this point in this way to move us to two observations about Christian ethics and conflict. The first is that there is robust debate over the meaning of reconciliation and its relationship to justice, liberation, and forgiveness. We will look at one piece of this debate in a moment. The second observation concerns the power of narrative in ethics. We have seen how interpretations of a telos also illuminate a path. As illustrated here, Christians discern the telos and discern a path from where they are to where they are called to be. As we have explicitly heard from Katongole and Rice, the path from division to reconciliation is not marked simply by strategies and best practices, but also by deep spiritual awareness of God's gracious invitation to us and calling toward one another.

Let's think for a minute about the power of this calling toward one another. This is the horizontal dimension of reconciliation. Without this intentional movement toward one another, we cheapen the costly grace of God in Christ by refusing to give ourselves to others. In his work, Stanley Hauerwas has long argued that this story does not make sense in the world, nor does it need to. The narrative has meaning and authority only for those who believe it and know that they must then live as forgiven people.[61] Christians who root their identity in this story cannot but live according to it. On the opening page of *Exclusion and Embrace*, Miroslav Volf shares a question posed to him by Jürgen Moltmann after a lecture: "But can you embrace a cetnik [Serb fighter]?" Volf responds, "No, I cannot—but as a follower of Christ I think I should be able to."[62] Those who live according to the story of grace cannot but live as forgiven people who extend the embrace to others.

Clearly, this exchange (and much of the content of this chapter) provokes vigorous debate about forgiveness and, again, about the ordering of justice and reconciliation. Before we move into that, though, I want to use this provocation heuristically. The energy you feel as you consider this language of victims who must forgive offenders helps us to think about an important issue in Christian ethics, namely, accountability. Here, again, we find a divergence of views. Hauerwas and those who have been influenced by him insist that a Christian is accountable to God, to Christ, and to the community formed by the narrative that guides them. This does not mean that they do not care about the world or consider other sources of knowledge, but it does mean that they remain primarily accountable to the narrative even if living it out sets them at odds with cultural norms, with measures of effectiveness, and with realistic assessments of the way things are. The primary commitment is to live faithfully, which here means living out the narrative that forms them.

The other option is not living unfaithfully, though it is often presented that way. It is a way of living aware of compelling multiplicity. Christians who live this way perceive many stories in Scripture, not just one narrative. They understand God's story to involve many themes and purposes that sometimes seem to align and sometimes do not, but they feel somehow bound to them even in contradiction. Their identity is attached to many communities with guidance that sometimes aligns and sometimes does not, and they try to navigate between or hold in tension these various community traditions. These Christians live in the world aware that the way they live out their faith impacts those who do not share it. They are aware of a web of relationships in contexts of plurality. And they feel accountable to the telos and calling of their faith and also to the people impacted by the ways they enact their faith in the world. Living with this awareness of compelling multiplicity prompts dis-ease with Christian identity and purpose rooted in *the* narrative of *the* community.

The singular or monolithic assumption does not match the experience of multiplicity. In my view, the more concerning dimension of this singular narrative approach is that one prioritizes adherence to the narrative over concern for people affected by it. This point mirrors the caution about teleology mentioned earlier, namely, that the end might justify any means as necessary. The actions we take as we live out a narrative also make an impact on other people, and I think we must be accountable to them. After World War II, Jewish theologians articulated a criterion for theology, namely, "the presence of burning children."[63] These theologians made burning children the primary site of accountability, the test for the truthfulness of theological assertion—not doctrine, not Scripture, not logic, not even the narrative of the community that formed me, but burning children. I wholeheartedly affirm this approach. In our ongoing wrestling with the meaning and calling of reconciliation, I think we have to hold our ideas accountable to the victims. Can I really say to a twelve-year-old rape victim that she must forgive her rapist and reconcile with him? No; nor should I. Can I live according to a story that makes her forgiveness of the rapist the test of her discipleship? No way; nor should I. Can I affirm and share a story that says to this girl that God's loving gift to her comes with the expectation that she forgive the one who raped her? Absolutely not; nor should I. Can I say that God loves her, weeps with her, and desires her health and well-being? Yes—that I can say to this girl. And, thank God, that is also a story of Scripture.[64]

Throughout this book, I have underscored the dynamic nature of Christian ethics. When we experience conflict with other Christians or within ourselves, we should pause for examination. On one level, my resistance to atonement-centered narratives of reconciliation is that they condone the sacrifice of victims. The story not only identifies their suffering as Christlike, but it also calls them to forgive the undeserving offender as the Christlike response to suffering. This understanding of atonement applied to a process of reconciliation renders the victims of violence as the agents of forgiveness for the offenders, while sacrificing their own claims to justice.[65]

At another level, I am resisting the power of a single narrative to interpret, judge, and guide behavior. In the quest for integrity (rather than fragmentation) in the moral life, we allow a single narrative to dominate the moral imagination. In our commitment to live according to the narrative faithfully, we render its implications for others secondary. This observation about the power of the narrative echoes Jennifer Harvey's insightful critique of the reconciliation paradigm:

> Paradigms are powerful. A paradigm might be considered a framework that shapes how we understand a situation at its most fundamental level. A paradigm contains within it operative assumptions about how we see and comprehend the basic nature of a problem. As a result it necessarily informs the kind of solutions or responses we identify, as well as which responses we perceive to have the most urgency or even recognize as viable. In other words, a paradigm becomes itself an interpretation explaining what is going on and establishing the range of possibilities we might therefore engage.[66]

The singular narrative functions this way as well. It establishes parameters for the process and meaning of reconciliation. In doing so, it obscures from view a myriad of other stories and experiences that might also teach us and inspire us in contexts of ongoing conflict.

The second part of this chapter turns toward some of this variety. Here we find Christian conceptions of reconciliation that are not centered on atonement. We also find proposals for reconciliation that keep justice a part of the goal as well as the process. And we find practices of conflict transformation that unfold in circles and work constructively with nonlinearity. In these circles, there is not a singular narrative enacted but many stories shared.

STORIES AND PRACTICES OF RECONCILIATION

Within Christian ethics there is a vast amount of writing on reconciliation with a variety of theological-ethical resources in play.[67] For the purpose of this chapter, I lift up a perspective on reconciliation that privileges the health of bodies, prioritizes the needs of marginalized persons, and turns to marginalized persons as a resource for thinking about reconciliation.

In her writing on reconciliation, womanist theologian Stephanie Mitchem insists on a "socially grounded picture of reconciliation" in which "personal commitments are analyzed in light of social responsibility."[68] Utilizing womanist methodology, she situates her exploration of reconciliation in the experience of "black women in social contexts"[69] and draws on interviews with members of the Detroit Metropolitan Black Women's Health Project.[70] In this work, Mitchem argues that "African American women *enact* a theology of reconciliation" by linking health with healing and spirituality with wholeness.[71] Through her interviews, she identifies practices related to healing, defined by one interviewee as "the integration of the self."[72] The practices of reconciliation include "community building, anti-dissemblance, personal and social empowerment, self-discovery, and advocacy."[73] Mitchem then turns to theological and ethical writings from other womanist scholars and black theologians to assert, "Womanist reconciliation, then, aims toward personal and communal wholeness; it remains centered in, and informed by, spirituality."[74] This work of healing also requires challenging societal forces and cultural practices that threaten well-being. Thus, in her final paragraph, Mitchem offers this description of reconciliation informed by language of the Negro spiritual that also gives her essay its title: "In such a holistic view, reconciliation challenges all oppressive, dehumanizing systems, not merely restoring to former order, but rebalancing the old so that a new heaven and earth can begin."[75]

Mitchem's writing echoes the description of reconciliation from Emilie Townes cited in the beginning of this chapter. Townes writes, "It is my deep belief, from the particular perspective of the Black woman in the United States, that an ethic of justice is rooted in two concepts: liberation and reconciliation."[76] These concepts emerge from and respond to the particular experiences of African American women, and they reach "to the whole church and the whole society," according to Townes. In language very similar to Mitchem's description of healing, Townes writes that liberation aims "to restore a sense of self as a free person and as a spiritual being."[77] In Jesus' death and resurrection, Townes see "God's work of salvation" as the "promise of wholeness through our brokenness." As noted earlier, Townes describes objective reconciliation as "God's activity in our lives," giving us the gift of freedom through grace and love. We remain faithful to God's gift by living with respect toward and in harmony with others; this is subjective reconciliation.[78] Transformation requires both liberation and reconciliation, though Townes eschews a particular order for them. "Working together," she writes, "liberation and reconciliation, pointing toward the freedoms found in transformation, name the oppression of our lives and our institutions for what they are—sinful—and demand that we work with God for a new thing—the reign of God in all of life."[79]

In these words from Mitchem and Townes, we do not hear descriptions of reconciliation that are radically different from those in the first part of this chapter. Townes's description captures the vertical and horizontal dimensions, insisting that both are necessary. The difference I see is that self-assertion (antidissembling) and individual liberation do not threaten reconciliation, as Mitchem and Townes write about it. Recall that Volf, Katongole, and Rice discussed the ways in which justice is both important and a potential problem for reconciliation. It is a problem because it might be prioritized and thus delay the work on reconciliation. It is a problem because it means that one pursues the interests of one's group at the expense of reconciling with the other. It is a problem because it reflects an exercise of self-interest and human pursuit rather than a response to God's impartial love and universal grace. By contrast, what we see even in these brief excerpts from womanist scholars is the assertion that justice is nonnegotiable. It is not only that reconciliation cannot *proceed* without it, or that reconciliation must wait for justice. It is that reconciliation, true reconciliation, cannot *exist* without justice, without mutual flourishing of all people.

This is precisely what we heard from Jean Zaru in chapter 3: "Real reconciliation involves a fundamental repair to human lives, especially to those who have suffered. It requires restoring the dignity of the victims of violence."[80] And restoring human dignity requires dismantling structures of oppression and domination. While Zaru affirms "that of God" within her opponent, she still advocates nonviolent resistance in response to the structures of injustice and oppression. This work of resistance is not antithetical to reconciliation; it is part of it. We find a similar argument from the context of apartheid South Africa with the Kairos Document. Another well-known voice from that context is John de Gruchy, whose writing on reconciliation gives special attention to the concerns of the black liberation movement. "For the proponents of Black Consciousness," he writes, "any talk of reconciliation or social integration prior to achieving liberation was regarded as undermining liberation, hence the rhetoric of reconciliation was suspect."[81] De Gruchy also draws on the Kairos Document, which rejected "the liberal rhetoric of reconciliation" and called for "direct Christian participation in the [anti-apartheid] struggle."[82] "For the *Kairos* theologians," de Gruchy explains, "reconciliation was not a means to an end, that is, a process, but rather the goal for the liberation struggle. Justice and the ending of apartheid were preconditions for reconciliation."[83] Here we see clearly one line of argument that Volf, Katongole, and Rice challenge: the establishment of liberation and justice as a precondition for reconciliation. What we must see here, however, is that justice is not a step in a process toward something else, namely, reconciliation. It is that justice and liberation are constitutive features of reconciliation. Reconciliation cannot be realized without justice because reconciliation—as understood here—includes justice. Without justice, reconciliation is incomplete.

But the concern is even deeper than this. It is not just about "incomplete reconciliation"; it is that the focus on reconciliation thwarts the work of justice because justice making requires confrontation and disruption. Let's return to the work of Jennifer Harvey to see this clearly. Recall that Harvey is critiquing the reconciliation paradigm that frames approaches to racial justice in terms of restoring relationship. The reconciliation paradigm also tells a story in which separation is the problem—the thing to lament—and coming together is the hoped-for ending. Harvey writes, "The originating question is posed as 'Why are we still so divided?' The lament is 'Eleven o'clock is still the most segregated hour of the week.' Thus the overwhelming emphasis becomes the need to heal division, to come together in just and mutual ways across that divide."[84] This division reflects our brokenness while togetherness is the solution and our calling. In operating with the reconciliation paradigm or narrative, then, one values moments that seem to bring unity.

Harvey's proposal is a reparations paradigm in which separation is a symptom of a deeper problem, namely, "the extent to which our differences embody legacies of unjust material structures."[85] The journey toward the goal in this paradigm requires "justice-filled engagement with and responses to those very same structures that racialized our human bodies in the first place and continue to racialize us on a daily basis."[86] One of the things I appreciate about Harvey's work is its reminder that the work of justice making requires that those in positions of power reckon with their privilege and work toward the redistribution of unjust advantage. That reminder underscores how self-serving the rhetoric of togetherness can be for those in power. True reconciliation requires addressing the causes of separation, not just calling for togetherness. Addressing the causes of separation requires disruption, resistance, penance, and change. In my view, this also requires frameworks (paradigms and narratives) that help us to value the nonlinear process that such work requires.

Let me explain this a bit and then offer some examples. Harvey's analysis helps us to see that the narrative of reconciliation assigns values to experiences and occurrences according to this particular end. We value, affirm, and praise the event that seems to us to move us in the direction of reconciliation. The reconciliation paradigm prompts us to celebrate the handshake more than the raised fist. We affirm the movement toward an agreement more so than the decision to restart the boycott. But what if we keep justice a part of the goal as well as the means? What if we craft a narrative that integrates justice and reconciliation all along the way and can help us to find value in the raised fist and the boycott as part of the fits-and-starts process toward true reconciliation? What if we develop an understanding of justice and reconciliation as so integrated that we see defiance as Christlike too?

The writings of Mitchem, Townes, Zaru, and de Gruchy represent some of the myriad resources available to us. In these writings, we find a conception of justice, liberation, and reconciliation as means *and* ends, inextricably interrelated, all part of the process, and comprising the telos. We find this integrated notion of justice and reconciliation fully developed and practiced in the work of restorative justice. For forty years, restorative justice practitioners have been acting according to what Howard Zehr calls "an alternative framework for thinking about wrongdoing."[87] Of course, practices of restorative justice go back much further than that in indigenous communities around the world.[88] But since the 1970s, restorative practices have appeared with increased frequency in the justice system, in educational settings, and in community conflict transformation. Rather than focusing solely on punishing perpetrators, restorative justice pays attention to "the needs which crimes create."[89] And this assessment of needs is comprehensive, including the needs of victims, communities, and offenders.[90] At the heart of restorative justice is the conviction that all are interconnected and that this web of relationships creates obligations among us. In response to crime that tears the web of relationship, writes Zehr, "the central obligation is to put right the wrongs."[91] Putting right the wrongs entails holding offenders accountable, creating spaces where they hear the impact of their actions on others, and holding spaces where the victims are able to express their needs and have them addressed.

My engagement with restorative justice has primarily been through the use of circle process, a practice that has roots among First Nations communities in Canada, New Zealand, and Australia.[92] Circles can be used for a variety of purposes: to hear multiple perspectives on a question or issue, to discuss a contentious subject, to address a past harm and its continued effects on the community, and to restore relationship. These circles require a willingness among the participants to be vulnerable with one another, which constitutes a tremendous risk, especially when the relationships are fragile. Skilled circle facilitators take great pains to create a space and foster an interpersonal dynamic that is conducive to risk taking, vulnerability, and authentic listening. Christian practitioners working with a Christian group that is willing to incorporate elements of the faith into their process use liturgy, ritual, and images throughout a circle process to discern readiness to engage the process, to prepare participants for the circle, to ground them intentionally in a process of listening and mutuality, and to covenant with one another as they go forward.

For some earlier research, I interviewed Stephanie Hixon, a white, U.S. Protestant woman who facilitates circles and trains others to do so. Her words contain a rich description of the intentions of circle process and the theological convictions that undergird her work. For Hixon, the circle process brings to life a theological conception of the way God embraces people as they try to address harm and brokenness. Circles give her a way to imagine God holding people in an individual embrace and in a relationship or community. She opens every circle with this image: "God's embrace is wide enough and strong enough and also tender enough to carry all of us in this circle in whatever conversation, or silence, it is that we have to share with one another."[93] In Hixon's view, God is present in the circle and also maintains the circle. *When Blood and Bones Cry Out* by John Paul Lederach and Angela Jill Lederach provides striking reinforcement to this circle imagery. Interested in auditory metaphors for conflict and transformation, the Lederachs describe the role of containers in sound production and as rituals in trauma healing. They connect a Tibetan singing bowl to William Ury's metaphor of a "container that holds a conflict." The bowl and the container make interactions possible.[94] The Lederachs explain: "The container makes interaction possible to the degree that the vibrations are in a proximity that permits interaction and the rise of touchable sound."[95] Hixon has a similar view of circles; in her language, God's embrace, experienced in the circle, makes interaction possible.

Hixon does perceive a process unfolding as individuals move toward relationships that are "right, whole, just, nourishing, and life-giving." But the metaphors and imagery she uses also seem to leave the process itself a little more open-ended. Consider, for example, how she responded when asked to describe a moment of transformation. She focused on the affective change that comes over people. After interrupting herself to stress that circle process is not magical and incredibly difficult, she then described a moment when people in the circle "begin to breath more deeply and might begin to look at other persons in the circle, raise their eyes, and sometimes tears start to flow and that for me is becoming aware of the presence of God that is weaving those narratives and that story into something different."[96] God is weaving those stories into something different; this is a more open-ended way of describing a process of restoring justice and healing harm. And I find myself intrigued by the value of lingering on the moment of transformation itself, without placing it as a node on a journey. I find this intriguing primarily because conflicts do not unfold neatly through phases, and people do not move toward reconciliation along linear paths.

For example, in the introduction to their 2011 volume, Daniela Körppen and Norbert Ropers emphasize the multilayered and unpredictable nature of today's protracted conflicts and lament the persistence of dualistic and linear thinking that pervades the peacebuilding field.[97] They describe conflicts that become unmoored from their initial causes and develop their own dynamics, such that peacebuilding requires an ability to work constructively with ambiguity and contingency. Moreover, they argue that the multifaceted nature of conflicts requires a whole systems approach, attending to the social, economic, and political factors as well as historical narratives and interpersonal dynamics. Multifaceted problems and multilayered approaches obviously complicate sequencing.

In *When Blood and Bones Cry Out*, the Lederachs begin with a similar observation about the reality of nonlinear processes and the persistence of linear descriptions. They describe a kind of doublespeak in the literature, which insists that reconciliation is not a neat, linear process while still utilizing discernible, linear stages to describe peacebuilding. The Lederachs disrupt this tendency to fall back to linear forms of analysis and practice by using aural metaphors to "speak the unspeakable." In order to shift away from linearity, they focus on sound, particularly the sounds that give voice to people's pain, resistance, and healing. This practice of attending to sound draws one's attention to the moment, place, and people, and holds it there. The Lederachs then use the sounds and the metaphors related to them to talk about healing practices undertaken even while violence and injustice persist. This approach allows them to study and share practices of social healing that might be overlooked or misconstrued because they do not align with a "postconflict" phase.

John Paul Lederach's 2005 book *The Moral Imagination* has a similar sensibility: shifting away from technique-driven approaches to peacebuilding and toward more artistic metaphors and spiritual practices. He emphasizes mystery more than predictability, surprise more than probable outcomes, serendipity more than control, and humility more than expert knowledge. One can certainly argue that the Lederachs' texts contribute to an understanding of reconciliation that appropriately underscores the mystery of God's work and our humility in the face of it. One can draw on this same literature about nonlinearity to broaden our understanding of reconciliation. But I also think that this emphasis on nonlinearity and serendipity suggests the need for additional theological metaphors. Indeed, I think the reliance on a theology of reconciliation undermines the intention to break free from linear notions of progress and repair. Reconciliation, no matter how broadly we understand it, has a direction, a purpose, a narrative line. It continues to assert itself as the norm that determines the value of the changes that occur in a struggle or in a circle.

In the beginning of this chapter, I noted that practitioners of conflict transformation often say that reconciliation gives transformation its purpose. And we have seen that reconciliation as a purpose (telos) also comes with a narrative that interprets and evaluates the path between here and there. In my research, I asked conflict transformation practitioners how they reflect on a process that does not move forward, a mediation that falls apart, a conflict that remains intractable. Most often, the answer included a reference to the long horizon of reconciliation. I certainly appreciate this point and respect the patience and faithfulness reflected by those who articulate it. And I assert that we need to develop theological and ethical resources that help us to value the ambiguous moment, the protracted conflict, the highly contingent and unpredictable peacebuilding process. Is there a way to interpret failure or intractability other than by extending the horizon of reconciliation? Must we only heave the sigh of realism?

If we are going to live well in the midst of ongoing conflict, we must be able to find meaning and value in the things that do not seem to conform to our hopes. As long as we have a linear notion of the path to reconciliation, then we continue to frame things as either moving us forward or backward, or as diverting us from the goal. If we are going to live well in the midst of ongoing conflict, we need mechanisms for theological and ethical reflection that help us to also find meaning in the setbacks and surprises. We also need mechanisms for theological and ethical reflection that more truthfully reflect the contours of conflict and change, which are anything but linear.

CONCLUSION

What does all of this teach us about Christian ethics, especially teleology? First, it teaches us that the way Christians conceive of the telos matters. Our conception of the good shapes not only how we behave but also how we evaluate the events unfolding around us. In teleological ethics, we judge behavior and events as desirable or not depending on whether they move us toward the good. In these debates over reconciliation's relationship to forgiveness, liberation, and justice, we also see clearly that the way Christians conceive of the telos matters to our neighbors as well. It is not just a matter of one person identifying her goal and pursuing it. The way that I interpret the good—even the telos revealed in Scripture and formative in my community—impacts others because I work to make it a reality and because I assess the world around me in light of it.

The second thing we learn is that much of the excitement in Christian ethics comes out when we sort through the relationship between what we know and what we hope for. How do we interpret our current circumstance in light of the purpose we discern? How do we envision the movement from here to there? What resources help us to think about journeys from the real to the ideal? To whom and what do we remain accountable as we reflect on the relationship between the real and the ideal, and then judge and act accordingly? Our field of Christian ethics is filled with healthy debate over these crucial questions. And our ability as students to participate in these debates thoughtfully is essential to our development as moral agents and faithful people in contexts of ongoing conflict.

A third lesson from this chapter builds on the first two: Christian teleology is never an individualistic ethical practice. Unlike many forms of the "purpose-driven life," teleology is really not about "you and your goal." The Christian telos is not identified in isolation but is discerned in community. It is not enacted in private but is lived out among others. An awareness of conflict as an ongoing feature of our lives makes us even more aware of the relational dimension of ethics. My discernment and enactment of purpose affect other people. Teleology is not about "my goal and me" anymore than deontology is about "my principle and me" or virtue ethics is about "my virtue and me." This realization prompts us to embed rules, virtues, and goals more fully in contexts of ongoing interaction, which is the mode explored in chapter 6.

In this chapter, I have tried to do something that I ask of my students: to spend more time with the ideas that give me pause and work to represent them fairly. I have great appreciation for the work and writing of Miroslav Volf, Emmanuel Katongole, and Chris Rice. However, their reliance on an atonement-centered narrative of reconciliation gives me pause. Therefore, I turn to other conceptions of the telos and a more dynamic understanding of the relationship among its components. I also find that the context of ongoing conflict underscores the need for nonlinear conceptions of the relationship between what we know and what we hope for, and the need for theological resources to sustain us. This chapter has also emphasized accountability to others as a central criterion for ethics, and processes of dialogue have emerged as ways to embody that criterion. The next chapter turns to contexts of interpersonal conflict and the work of self-assessment and conflict analysis, which equip us most concretely to engage with others in circles of accountability and processes of meaningful, difficult conversation.

6
Need and Fear in Relationship
Considering Responsibility and Care

Chapter 3 explored references to the *imago Dei* in contexts of social conflict, such as police brutality, apartheid, and struggles for LGBTQ rights and fair labor laws. These contexts provided a place to think about deontology—an approach to ethics that focuses on principles, emphasizes intention, and privileges adherence to rules that transcend context and personal inclinations. In these contexts of social conflict (where we also see physical and structural forms of violence), we hear the clear mandate that, *no matter what,* all persons are created in the image of God and should be treated that way. In these contexts of resistance against violent persons and structures, we also considered the ways that the *imago Dei* confirms relationship as well as rights. Not only are we created in the image of God as individuals, but that affirmation of createdness pulls us into relationship with one another through a relational God. This theological doctrine connects to rights and to relationship (even with those to whom we stand in opposition). We considered the experiences of those who commit violent acts, particularly actions that run contrary to conscience. In the voices of soldiers relaying experiences of moral injury, we heard descriptions of a changing sense of self, which gave space to think about the way in which the image of God is a process of becoming more so than a state of being. This attention to contexts of conflict and violence prompted affirmation of the centrality of the image of God as a principle and also the need to think about the principle in light of relationships and changing experience.

Chapter 4 turned to Scripture to consider texts that teach us about conflict. We examined passages that categorize conflict as sinful or vicious and texts that present conflict as part of community life that one must engage in a particular way. This gave us an opportunity to think about virtue ethics, an approach that is focused primarily on cultivation of character—how we do things and in what spirit. We also considered the relationship between behaviors and the goals that guide them, such as unity and cohesion (which renders conflict vicious) and justice (which rendered the persistent widow faithful). In light of this engagement with the persistent widow of Luke's parable and also the Syrophoenician woman's clever challenge to Jesus, I underscored the importance of practicing a hermeneutic of suspicion toward the classification of certain behaviors as virtuous or not. Here, context and relationships matter significantly. It matters who commends which virtue to whom in what context. Moreover, throughout the Scriptures, the cultivation of character—whether the text discourages one from conflict, or guides one through it, or conveys subversive examples of it—also has implications for those with whom I am in relationship. Attention to character does not excuse me from attention to relationship.

Chapter 5 considered the telos, or end, of reconciliation in contexts of violent conflict (particularly political violence, including ethnic cleansing) as well as the connection between a goal and the narrative that illuminates our path toward it. Ends and means are intrinsically related; we cannot think about a goal without also thinking about the path toward it. And attention to the path is important if we are to avoid pursuing a goal at any cost. I articulated a concern about a path toward reconciliation that is dominated by a singular narrative, particularly an understanding of atonement that further sacrifices the victim. I strongly resisted this by referencing accountability to the victims of violence. This concern about accountability connects again to attention to relationships and to context. I argued that we should not hold to a narrative regardless of its implications for others. Rather, the implication of our narratives for other people in particular contexts should serve as a proving ground for the narrative itself. Is this narrative harmful to victims of violence? If so, I should reconsider my application of it in contexts of violence.

Each of these chapters raised a concern about relationships in response to the ethical methodology explored. In this chapter, relationship and context appear not in response to the methodology but as the methodology itself. In this chapter, we consider an ethic of care and an ethic of responsibility, both of which bring relationship and context into the center of ethics. In care ethics, relationship itself is the locus of ethical reflection. In responsibilist ethics, the question "What's going on?" is the beginning of ethical discernment. I explore these methods in the context of interpersonal conflict.

DAILY EXPERIENCES OF INTERPERSONAL CONFLICT

So far, this book has referenced all kinds of conflict but has focused most fully on rather high-profile, public, and dramatic forms of conflict (police brutality, social protest, nonviolent resistance, war, ethnic cleansing, transitional justice). Some readers may have personal experience with these forms of conflict. But I wager that each reader has experience with other kinds of conflict, namely, the daily interpersonal conflicts that are part of living life with other people. I am thinking here of the most mundane things: kitchen squabbles over cleaning the dishes, rude gestures on the freeway or even in the drop-off/pickup lane at the elementary school, disagreements between coaches and parents, arguments over returned items at a store, disputes about missed appointments, simmering tension about parenting styles, unspoken or murmured frustrations about behavior patterns. I am also thinking of microaggressions in the classroom, of miscommunication and misperception in the family, of unconscious bias in the workplace, of unchallenged racism, sexism, and homophobia at the dinner table. This is a sphere of conflict we all know well, and it is the sphere in which I most often engage with students and colleagues in our work on conflict transformation.

Our classes and workshops begin like this book did: with the assertion that conflict is a natural element of human life. We are in relationship and changing, and we cannot but strike together. Moreover, conflict can be a catalyst for constructive change in individual lives, in relationships, in institutions, organizations, and community. Our challenge then—and the purpose of our teaching and workshops—is to learn to engage conflict constructively. We aim for transformation through conflict. Without romanticizing conflict, this approach tries to do more than end something bad, that is, to resolve conflict. Informed by the work of Mennonites such as John Paul Lederach and Ron Kraybill, this approach to conflict tries also to begin something new and good. That requires a deep analysis of conflict to unearth its underlying causes and to address them fully. It also requires considerable self-awareness, to understand why each person responds to conflict as they do and to learn how to respond more constructively. And it requires some skills in communication that must be practiced and developed over time. The work of transformation through conflict also requires profound hope. We have to see in the messiness and hurt and frustrations of conflict some possibility for positive change.

In this chapter, I utilize these mundane conflicts and my low-profile work in classrooms and workshops as a locus for reflection on the moral life. I use feminist ethics and responsibility ethics to discuss moral considerations, and I use experiences of interpersonal conflict to illustrate some of the challenges to care ethics and responsibility ethics. In the end, I suggest that these real, mundane settings are really not mundane at all.

LEARNING ABOUT CONFLICT TRANSFORMATION

Think of a conflict that you have experienced. Who was involved? What happened? How did you respond? Why did you respond that way? What else might you have said or done? What underlying issues related to this conflict remain in place? What needs to happen to address those? What new or good thing could emerge from this conflict whether or not it is resolved? In a nutshell, this is the process we follow in conflict skills courses and workshops that I lead. When I work with Christians in theological schools or ecclesial contexts, we pursue one additional question: Where is God present in the midst of this conflict?

Understanding the conflict and one's response to it is essential, of course, and there are many resources for analysis. Self-assessment tools are most often some variation of the Thomas-Kilmann instrument, which indicates the individual's dominant conflict style to be either avoiding, forcing, accommodating, compromising, or collaborating. When I work with groups who have completed this instrument, we spend a good deal of time talking about the instrument itself and the ways in which our conflict styles vary depending on context.[1] We may also use other mechanisms for describing conflict styles beyond the Thomas-Kilmann instrument, such as metaphors for conflict behavior. We sometimes use a simple sentence-completion exercise: "I respond to conflict like a ______." Or we might identify conflict animals, which gives us a more lighthearted way to talk about these differences.[2] Depending on the group and the time we have, we might also work individually on a visual representation of the life experiences, family patterns, and cultural factors that seem to inform their responses to conflict.[3] The point of this is to demonstrate that we all have a default setting regarding conflict, a style that we are most likely to adopt. The default setting reflects culture, family history and behavior patterns, informal education related to gender and custom, and personality, among other things. However, the awareness that we behave differently in different contexts of conflict also shows that we have some flexibility across these conflict styles. This is a good thing, because different kinds of conflict require different kinds of behavior. In other words, all conflict styles (even avoidance) have their place and time. The challenge is determining which one to employ in which circumstance and then adopting it. Or as H. Richard Niebuhr would say, the task is determining the fitting response. More on that connection in a bit.

While the specifics of each context and its match to a conflict style are difficult to capture in a workshop, let alone in a book chapter, we can identify certain features of conflict that help us to determine the match to a conflict style. These are the value of the relationship and the importance of the issue. A simple graph captures these factors and their relationship to different conflict styles. This version of the graph comes from *Peacebuilding: A Caritas Training Manual.*[4] (I have added "Avoiding" and "Accommodating," which were absent from the graphic in the manual.)

As the graph indicates, we tend to behave more forcibly when the issue in contention is of great importance to us but preserving the quality of relationship with our opponent is not. When we are in a dispute over something that matters greatly to us with someone whose relationship is also of great value to us, collaboration is appropriate. (Collaboration is also most appropriate when the opponent in the conflict is trustworthy.) Accommodation is more appropriate if we value the relationship more than getting our way. When the relationship and the issue are both of low concern, it is appropriate to avoid the conflict altogether. Two other dimensions of conflict feature here, though they are not represented on this particular graph. One is time. Collaboration is a time-intensive endeavor, whereas competition and compromise are more time-efficient responses. The second dimension that is not pictured here is power. We avoid and accommodate when we lack the power to secure the outcome

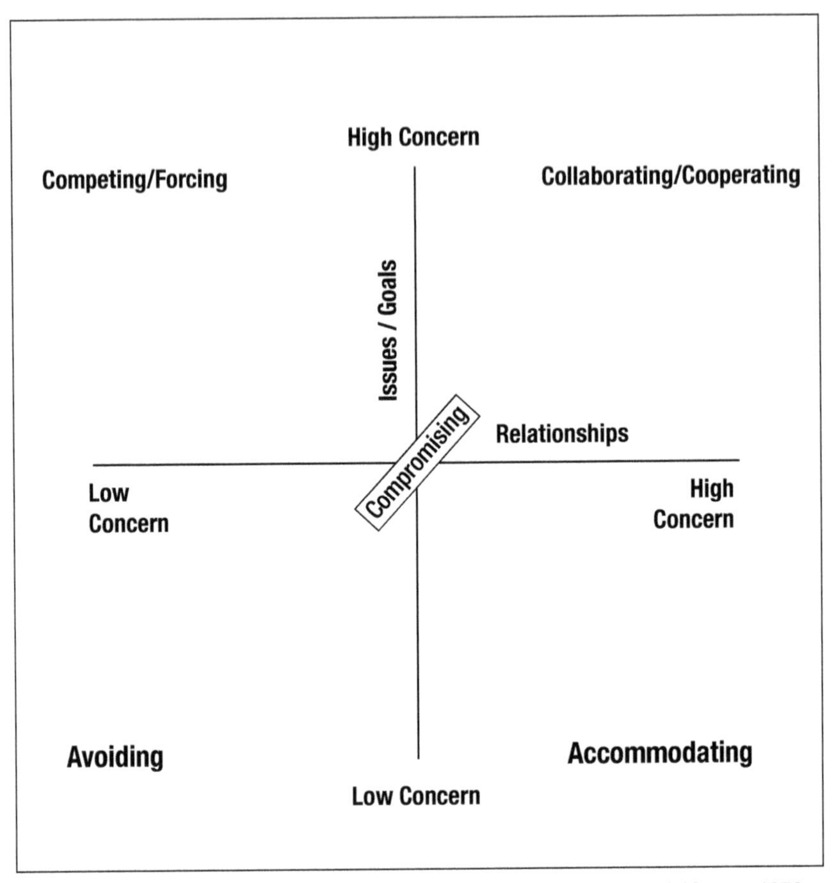

Peacebuilding: A Caritas Training Manual, 112 Adapted from Blake & Mouton, 1979

we desire. We force the situation when we have the power to get our way. We collaborate and compromise when we have power we are willing to share or can garner enough power to negotiate.

Clearly, graphs and descriptions of behavior and context do not capture the dynamic nature of our lives, the individual dimensions of personality and relationship, and the subtle and sometimes surprising details of disputes. But this basic orientation serves to make the point that our behavior in conflict not only depends on context and circumstance in a passive sense but can also respond to the nature of conflict in an active sense. We can adopt a style that is better suited to the dispute, even if that style is not our default setting, once we are attuned to the nature of the conflict and can see clearly what the circumstance demands of us.

H. RICHARD NIEBUHR AND THE ETHICS OF RESPONSIBILITY

When I lead groups through this work of self-assessment and conflict analysis, I always have H. Richard Niebuhr in my mind, because Niebuhr's first question was, "What's going on?" When the deontologist asks, "What should I do?" and the teleologist asks, "What is my goal?" and the virtue ethicist asks, "Who am I becoming?" the responsibilist begins with a question about context: What is going on? H. Richard Niebuhr was a Christian ethicist, moral philosopher, and theologian, but he also had a master's degree in history and worked as a journalist. Throughout his life, he was preoccupied with accurate description of the world and faithful interpretation of God's relationship to it. Unlike the other methods of ethics explored in this text, responsibility ethics is really attached to one person, though many have since adopted it and critiqued it. So to understand the responsibilist approach, we need to spend a little more time with the younger Niebuhr.

H. Richard Niebuhr (1894–1962) was the youngest of four children, another of whom was Reinhold Niebuhr, one of the great public theologians of the twentieth century. H. Richard Niebuhr was more of a theologian's theologian[5] or an ethicist's ethicist. While Reinhold was a master of making powerful points, H. Richard Niebuhr was more interested in how we make points. He was intrigued by processes of moral discernment and argument, occupied by matters of interpretation and historicity, and concerned about human propensity to misinterpret and to align God's will with our own. He was also the son and grandson of clergy in the German Evangelical Synod. He attended his denominational college (Elmhurst College) and seminary (Eden Theological Seminary), worked as a journalist, and pursued a master's degree in history. He pastored Walnut Park Evangelical Church in St. Louis and taught theology and ethics at Eden Seminary, all before going to Yale University for his PhD. After completing his doctoral program, he returned to Elmhurst College as president and shepherded his alma mater through the accreditation process. In 1927, he took a faculty position at Eden until 1931, when he finally accepted Yale's third invitation to join the faculty. Niebuhr remained on the faculty at Yale until his death from a heart attack at age sixty-seven in 1962.[6]

H. Richard Niebuhr wrote his dissertation on Ernst Troeltsch, introduced in the first chapter of this book. Like Troeltsch, Niebuhr took a historical approach to the Christian tradition and focused on the ways in which Christians understood the claims of their faith differently over time. The interaction between theology and history both fascinated him and raised significant questions for him. As historical beings, how do we speak faithfully about the transcendent God? Our perspective is necessarily limited. What we see depends on where we stand, Niebuhr insisted in *The Meaning of Revelation* (1941). From our limited perspective, we are prone to interpret God's activity in the world in ways that align with our own point of view. From our historical location, we also tend to confuse that which is relative with that which is absolute. We fail to keep God as the center of value and rely on other goals and sources to guide us and give us hope. In other words, as historical beings we are prone to various kinds of idolatry. We reify our perspective as the only one, or the complete one, or the godly one. We place our ultimate faith and hope in the worldly things we can see and achieve, orient our lives around them, and perceive God in relation to them instead of the other way around. (Example: I am striving for this goal, and I know that God is with me.)

The Responsible Self: An Essay in Christian Moral Philosophy, published posthumously in 1963, represents thirty years of teaching Christian ethics and introduces an alternative metaphor for the moral agent. Niebuhr describes the deontologist using the metaphor of citizen, meaning one who acts according to rules, laws, or principles, asking, "What should I do?" He describes the teleologist using the metaphor of fashioner or maker, one who fashions the future in the direction of a purpose by asking the question "What is my goal?" However, Niebuhr suggested that a different symbol might more fully capture our experience as beings in relationship to other beings and matter being acted upon by matter: "man-the-answerer." For the citizen, actions respond to rules. For the maker, actions move us toward goals. For the answerer, actions are responses to other actions upon us.[7] Niebuhr proposed responsibility as a symbol for moral agency, a way to "think of all our actions as having the pattern of what we do when we answer another who addresses us."[8] When someone addresses us, we interpret their comment and reply with expectation of another response from them. In the course of a dialogue, I try to respond in a way that is appropriate to what is asked of me or shared with me. To respond appropriately, I must interpret well and wait to see how my response is received. Thus, H. Richard Niebuhr described a pattern of moral action using the symbol of dialogue: I find myself on the receiving end of an action, which I must interpret and to which

I must respond. My primary question, then, is "What's going on?" I interpret the action upon me, aim to respond in a way that is fitting, and anticipate a response to my response. Niebuhr's responsible self is accountable to the persons with whom they interact, the persons with whom one remains in community. Niebuhr then summarizes the four features of responsibility (response, interpretation, accountability, and social solidarity) this way:

> The idea or pattern of responsibility, then, may summarily and abstractly be defined as the idea of an agent's action as response to an action upon him in accordance with his interpretation of the latter action and with his expectation of response to his response; and all of this is in a continuing community of agents.[9]

The work we do with interpersonal conflict connects naturally with Niebuhr's responsibilist approach. I propose that we live well in the midst of ongoing conflict as responsible selves—aware of our actions as a response to actions upon us, striving to determine the fitting response, and remaining accountable for the impact of our actions on others. The responsible self provides a formal structure into which we can place our intentions for and our process of conflict transformation. But the connections remain formal and procedural, not helpful in a more concrete and substantive way.

A brief engagement with one of Niebuhr's critics will make this point clear. In his book *Voices of the Silenced*, Darryl Trimiew argues that Niebuhr assumes an empowered moral agent, one who is in position to respond and has the power to do so. According to Trimiew, Niebuhr perceived marginalized persons as those in need, but not as responsible selves. Marginalized persons are the ones to whom the responsible self answers. This is not a terrible thing. Responsible selves should be accountable to those on the margins! Trimiew's point, however, is that it does not seem to occur to Niebuhr that the marginalized person is also a responsible self. He does not locate examples of moral agency in marginalized communities. In Trimiew's words, Niebuhr "did not see the members of a debased community as sources of moral insight or possible ethical dialogue partners."[10]

Trimiew's argument helps me to see that Niebuhr did not truly describe real dialogue at all, or real dialogue partners. His work remained at the formal or abstract level, intentionally. The "fitting" is a category for the response but not a substantive description of one. (By contrast, Trimiew provides a substantive description when he argues that responsible selves in marginalized communities would quickly insist that the fitting response must at least include meeting basic needs.[11] But Niebuhr does not fill in the category with a description of what constitutes fitting.) Responsibility has four features (response, interpretation, accountability, and social solidarity), but those who might actually participate in this ongoing dialogue and what they might say are not part of Niebuhr's work. This is, as I say, intentional. He did not propose a substantive notion of responsibility because it must be contextually determined, but also because he was deeply concerned about imposing human patterns of interpretation on events. Thus, he left the responsible self intentionally formal and abstract, a compelling metaphor for moral agency but not a describable, lived ethic.

While we can connect H. Richard Niebuhr's starting point with the groundwork of self and conflict analysis, we cannot carry his approach further into the conflict in a substantive way. I argue that we can and should retain responsibility as a metaphor for a moral agent who takes context seriously and who attempts to respond in the form of ongoing dialogue with those affected by our actions. And I think we can meaningfully see self and context analysis as a mechanism for addressing Niebuhr's first question: "What's going on?" But if we are going to dive more deeply into the details of conflict between persons as a site for moral reflection and action, we need to turn to feminist methodology and an ethic of care.

FEMINIST METHODOLOGY AND THE ETHICS OF CARE

In chapter 2, I mentioned the work of feminist philosopher Margaret Urban Walker, specifically her argument for contextually attentive moral theory. For Walker, theory that fails to attend to context is bad theory. By bad theory, she means "theory that does not connect with life; theory that distorts, rather than reveals and clarifies its subject matter; theory that becomes a pastime and even a competitive game for theory-makers independently of whether the theory enhances our understanding of its subject matter."[12] Walker's point reflects a methodological shift in ethics and moral philosophy to insist on attention to the real, lived experiences of people; to the particulars of circumstance and relationship; to the emotions, perceptions, and internal narratives that occupy daily life. Whatever we say or write about the moral life writ large must actually connect with real life, or it is bad theory.

Walker's argument, which is perhaps more common today, was a radical move initially because it challenged a dominant perception about the places worthy of ethical reflection and the modes of reflection deemed appropriate to ethics. Feminist ethics does not have a monopoly on attention to the everyday context, but it is one place in the history of ethics where such attention has been advanced and defended. The term *feminist ethics* came into general usage in the late 1970s to denote two kinds of projects: ethical analysis of so-called women's issues and critique and reconstruction of ethical theory. Both of these projects, topical and theoretical, were born from the realization that traditional moral philosophy assumed a male moral agent and prescribed only a certain sphere of life as relevant for moral inquiry. Philosopher Alison Jaggar writes about her experience of sitting alongside male students gaining doctorates in philosophy in the 1960s with no discussion of gender differences. She almost never encountered mention of sex or gender and did not even think about its absence. These topics were simply not morally relevant in the classroom. In her words, "If I had thought about this omission at all, I would have assumed it indicated that sex and gender were nonessential human attributes and therefore irrelevant to philosophical concern with the supposedly ultimate issues of truth, beauty, and goodness."[13] However, for the female students who were also part of the rising feminist consciousness of the 1960s and '70s, this was an increasingly frustrating situation. In response, they began to push academics to take up certain issues such as abortion, equal opportunity, wage justice, compulsory heterosexuality, rape, and surrogate motherhood. What became increasingly apparent to feminists was that the tradition needed not only an infusion of topics but also a critique of the cultural context of the canon. The underlying problem with the Western moral tradition was that

> its fundamental understanding of moral competence was masculine. . . . Feminist ethics, then, in the newly emerging view, was no longer a matter of simply applying traditional ethical theory to contemporary issues, much less of seeking to show that women were as capable as men of moral agency. In other words, feminist ethics was not simply a matter of adding women and stirring them into existing theory. Instead, the new view held that feminist ethics must be dedicated to rethinking the deepest issues in ethical theory—what counted as moral issues and by what means they might properly be resolved—in light of a moral sensibility perceived as distinctively feminine.[14]

At this point in the history of feminist ethics, references to "women's issues" and a "distinctively feminine" moral sensibility raise concerns about essentialism, and rightly so. It is inaccurate to present the varied experiences, concerns, and thoughts of women as monolithic and somehow determined by gender and sexual identity. The charge of essentialism also alerts us to the tendency to simply assume a new norm for the moral agent, this time as a white, heterosexual, middle-class, cisgender woman.[15]

Like all healthy schools of thought, feminist ethics continues to develop. Amidst its current vibrancy and variety, one finds a few shared commitments. One of these is the commitment to resist the subjugation of persons through policies and practices and also through modes of thought and study.[16] This commitment to nonsubjugating forms of moral reasoning compels feminists to listen carefully to lived experience in all its fullness and to remain accountable to that experience in their work. We considered this briefly in chapter 1 through the work of Karen Lebacqz (who says that what is logic to the birds might mean death to the fish) and Kelly Brown Douglas (who uses the language of epistemological privilege to grant authority of knowledge to those who experience the problems we study). In this chapter, we will take up these points again through a broader consideration of feminist methodology and, particularly, the ethics of care.

From this set of philosophical and political commitments, Margaret Urban Walker describes three features of feminist moral reasoning. First, it practices attention to "particular others in actual contexts." Second, it offers a "way of constructing morally relevant understandings which is 'contextual and narrative' rather than 'formal and abstract.'" And, third, it represents a form of thinking that values the "ability to communicate among persons involved or affected."[17] She then contrasts this approach to the justice orientation discussed in chapter 3:

> A view consistent with this [alternative epistemology] will not be one of individuals standing singly before the impersonal dicta of Morality, but one of human beings connected in various ways and at various depths responding *to each other* by engaging together in a search for shareable interpretations of their responsibilities, and/or bearable resolutions to their moral binds.[18]

In other words, the reference for a moral decision is not an objective standard or a transcendent principle to which all parties refer. Rather, Walker envisions ethics as the shared, dialogical work of human beings in relationship thinking together about responsibilities and their obligations. These practices of moral reasoning are embedded in relationship and embodied in persons such that experiences and emotions become a part of the ethical endeavor. This is significant, because for much of the tradition of Western moral philosophy, it was assumed that in order to deliberate well, the moral agent needed to detach from context, relationship, and emotion. Underlying this argument was the insistence that we reason best from a distance, objectively. We cannot do our best moral thinking when we are embedded in a context, affected by our relationships, caught up in our own emotions and attachments. But feminist ethics has developed an alternative method of moral reasoning, one that values relationship, experience, and even emotion as partners in a process of ethical reflection.

There is clear and striking overlap between feminist ethical methodology and theory, and the practice of conflict transformation; yet these two literatures do not resource one another as often as they could. There is some connection between gender analysis and peacebuilding, but still not a great deal.[19] And there is little connection at this level of methods and approaches.[20] In the field of Christian ethics, this gap has been addressed recently by essays from Debbie Roberts, Marcia Riggs, and Liz Bounds. Roberts forges connections to truth and reconciliation processes using the work of Sallie McFague and Beverly Wildung Harrison.[21] Marcia Riggs connects womanist ethics to transformative mediation to craft a pedagogical approach.[22] And Liz Bounds uses the microcosm of teaching conflict skills courses in a women's prison and a theological school to capture insights about self and social structures.[23] All three of these scholars contribute to the development of theoretical approaches that utilize concrete experiences, particularly of conflict and pedagogy. In their writing, they demonstrate the difference that attentiveness to context can make to ethics. Their essays also convey two points that I hope to communicate in this chapter: (1) Our interaction with these concrete sites of reflection does not diminish but rather enhances our abilities to reason well about them; and (2) in the seemingly private sphere of interpersonal conflict, justice is also at stake.

We cannot understand a dispute, let alone address it, from a distance or in general terms. Echoing the three features named by Walker, mediators practice a kind of ethical reasoning that attends to particular persons in actual contexts, is contextual and narrative, and utilizes dialogue among parties to discern a way forward. The mediator literally sits with the disputants (and often between them), actively listens while they tell their story, and facilitates discussion between them to generate options and come to their own agreement. Key to a successful mediation is the moment when participants are able to articulate and hear the needs initially buried beneath the noise of stated positions.

Within the variety of feminist methodologies, one approach is an ethic of care. Care ethics stems primarily, but not solely, from the work of Carol Gilligan, a psychologist whose research with women uncovered a different form of moral reasoning in the 1980s.[24] Instead of preoccupations with fairness and equality, Gilligan's interviewees expressed concerns related to detachment and abandonment. Instead of construing the moral agent as one who adheres to a principle of justice, Gilligan perceived these women to be moral agents who were responding to "perception of need."[25] Gilligan's colleague Lawrence Kohlberg placed moral postures like these on a hierarchy of ethical maturity, with the justice orientation at the top. In her work, Gilligan challenged that hierarchy, reframing this relational, care ethic as a different moral voice rather than an immature one.

Care ethics frames the moral task around perception of need and orients the moral agent to respond to the needs of others. The moral agent derives necessary information from context and from relationship, and acts in response to it. In Jaggar's words, "Care thinking emphasizes its responsiveness to particular situations whose morally salient features are perceived with an acuteness thought to be made possible by the carer's emotional posture of empathy, openness, and receptiveness."[26] The very things believed to muddy ethical thinking in a justice orientation—experiential engagement, relationship, attention to context and particulars, emotions, attachment—are perceived to be valuable sources of ethical insight in the care orientation.

However, care also has its critics. For the purpose of this discussion, I note two criticisms of care ethics that seem particularly salient in a discussion of interpersonal conflict. The first concerns the unilateral direction of care. There is the one caring and the one cared for. The flow of interaction is unidirectional, which exacerbates power inequities and raises the specter of paternalism. As Sarah Lucia Hoagland writes, the model of caring for another "suggests that it is appropriate for us to take over another's situation and try to control it, try to make it all right."[27] We face here the related danger of misconstruing a need and acting inappropriately altogether. Certainly interpersonal conflict situations are filled with examples of persons intending to care but misconstruing or miscommunicating and causing harm instead. We know well the effects of unidirectional care. But the context of mediation not only provides testimony to this concern raised about care; it also offers a discipline that might help to counteract the tendency to take over when we try to care.

In my experience, the mediator role is often frustrating and difficult for the "do-ers," the people who like to just get things done. In classes and workshops, these are the participants who cannot help but make suggestions to the disputants about what they should do to solve the problem. But this is not the job of the mediator. The mediator does not solve other people's problems for them; rather, the mediator facilitates a process through which the parties come to their own understanding of the issues and generate their own solutions and agreements. In the words of Bernard Mayer, "A mediator does not make a decision or impose a solution but rather assists the disputants as they attempt to find their own way through the conflict."[28] For all of its variety—and it can be considerable—mediation is at base a tool for empowering other people. One of the field-shaping books in mediation is *The Promise of Mediation* by Robert A. Baruch Bush and Joseph Folger. The title refers to two effects of mediation, namely, empowerment and recognition. Bush and Folger define those terms this way:

> In simplest terms, *empowerment* means the restoration to individuals of a sense of their value and strength and their own capacity to make decisions and handle life's problems. *Recognition* means the evocation in individuals of acknowledgment, understanding, or empathy for the situation and the views of the other.[29]

Recognition is clearly essential to care, but so is empowerment. That is, empowerment—or, I would say instead, sharing power—interrupts the move toward unidirectional care and opens space for mutuality and collaboration.

A second important concern about ethics of care is that it remains in the sphere of private interaction and fails to address structural issues. As voiced by Alison Jaggar, "Care's reliance on individual efforts to meet individual needs disregards the social structures that make this virtually impossible in many cases. Care thinking seems unable to focus on the social causes of many individual problems."[30] Jaggar is not alone in raising this concern about care's inattention to structural issues. But I appreciate her formulation in particular because she does not assume that the individual issues that care might address are void of structural dimensions. This is important because some argue that an ethic of care is appropriate to the private sphere *because* it does not address structural dimensions. Jaggar reminds us that individual issues always have a structural, public dimension. In a similar vein, Jaggar argues that care's focus on the individual inhibits the one caring from fostering care across social groups. In contexts of structural opposition between groups, acts of care between representative individuals are ineffectual, even if they are possible or desirable.

Mediation has also been on the receiving end of this criticism. It too has the potential to focus solely on interpersonal dynamics without attending to structural dimensions of relationships. Some mediators recognize this fact and determine to facilitate the best process they can for two people in a dispute, believing that the larger structural issues—though relevant—are beyond the scope of their work. However, other mediators reject as insufficient the attempt to resolve an interpersonal dispute without attending to the systemic and structural issues related to it. This is, in fact, one of the arguments that gave rise to conflict transformation itself. As discussed in chapter 1, conflict transformation started as a resistance to attempts to resolve disputes without attending to their underlying causes, no matter how vast they were. Conflict, in this approach, is not just a problem to solve in a narrow or superficial sense; conflict is both a symptom of deeper issues and the opportunity to address them.

When one attempts to address all underlying causes of conflict and to engage conflict itself constructively for purposes of social change, then the work quickly becomes far-reaching and multifaceted. Indeed, this concern about structural dimensions of conflict moves us beyond the scope of interpersonal conflict and to the recognition of conflict as an ongoing dimension of life. But it is also crucial to see that the structural dimensions of conflict were present in the scope of interpersonal conflict all along. We are not isolated individuals, but members of social groups in a society that immediately attaches various kinds of power and stigma to our bodies. When we walk into a room, we bring all of that privilege and bias along with us.

This is, perhaps ironically, why we need to bring H. Richard Niebuhr back into the conversation. The empowered self that Niebuhr assumes (and that care ethics assumes as well)—that is, the one in position to care—also continues to ask, "What's going on?" and to critically examine patterns of interpretation that we place onto our experience. As we attempt to care or to mediate or to resist or to transform, we need to keep asking whether we are perceiving the situation accurately. In the rest of this chapter, I want to add another set of voices to this conversation, voices that can help us to consider more fully the role that fear plays in contexts of conflict. And for those of us (myself included) who are already empowered to respond and to care, we need to consider very carefully the way that fear obstructs our view. Living a good life in the midst of ongoing conflict requires that we respond to need rather than react to fear.

This book has indirectly explored a range of fears related to conflict. Chapter 3, on the *imago Dei*, included references to fear of violent attack on self and loved ones, as well as the way that construal of "the guilty" body fuels fear that justifies violent action in response to a perceived threat. In this sense, the perception of the other as created in the image of God directly challenges the construal of that person as enemy and threat. This, again, is the power and challenge of affirming every person as created in the image of God. Chapter 4, on Scripture, named the fear of disunity that motivated admonitions against conflict in the newly formed community of Jesus followers. Fear of division certainly persists as a motivating factor in Christian communities today. And among Christians who already feel divided, the fear of "losing their church" looms large. I hear this in congregational disputes over everything from worship styles to human sexuality. Chapter 5, on reconciliation, explored fear of retaliation and cycles of revenge that are part of the story of violent political conflict. The call for forgiveness and reconciliation is, in part, an effort to resist the power of that fear to continue cycles of violence. On the other hand, we considered the concern that the language of reconciliation compromises justice and sacrifices the needs of victims. And in the face of persistent calls for justice, we see also the fear of those who anticipate the loss of power. Clearly, living a good life in the midst of ongoing conflict requires that we address fear.

In contexts of interpersonal conflict, these and many other fears come to the surface. Fear fuels the positions that people adopt as they try to defend themselves, justify their actions, and guard their resources. As parties in the dispute begin to tell their perspectives on the conflict, fear often appears as a character in their stories. It shapes perception, informs decisions, motivates action, affects speech and body language, and delimits perceived choices. When I welcome people into a difficult conversation, I always begin by commending them for their courage. And throughout the conversation, I listen particularly closely to the way that fear presents itself in the history of this interaction and the way it threatens to shape the future.

My work in conflict transformation is primarily in educational and congregational contexts. I am not mediating disputes in settings of political violence or large-scale community conflict. Rather, I work with congregations concerned about political or social division, with faculty trying to navigate contentious conversations in their classrooms, and with students who feel silenced or unheard. Attention to these particular sites of conflict is not in any way a turn away from the larger social and political issues or the work of resistance and struggle for social justice and violence reduction. It is also more than a resignation to simply do what I can in my small piece of the universe. Rather, attention to interpersonal conflict recognizes that these massive social and historical patterns of fear and violence manifest themselves in our daily interactions in classrooms, congregations, and civic associations (and disassociations!). When we address interpersonal conflict, we are also addressing social and political conflict. Moreover, I have come to believe that we cannot fully address social and political conflict if we fail to attend to our daily interactions with one another.

In the remainder of this chapter, I am going to advance a very small-scale argument focused on friendship and interpersonal acts of care. I make this turn because of the role that fear plays in human relationships and in social systems and because fear is both unconscious and formed. Educators are fond of the idea that fear is a result of ignorance or a lack of understanding. If we can learn more, and teach more, we will fear less. There is some truth to this. But we also learn to fear. And this process of education for fear is, by and large, unconscious.

FORMED TO FEAR

Sarah Perry's novel *The Essex Serpent* takes place on the Essex coast of England in 1893. The recently widowed protagonist, Cora, leaves her highbrow London life to sink her feet into the muddy marshes and explore. She quickly finds herself surrounded by a growing hysteria along the coast as people become convinced that a serpent spotted in 1669 has returned to the area. An atheist and a woman of science, Cora befriends the local clergyman who—with different resources—is trying to calm his flock.

One day, Cora visits the local school to offer a short science class on fossils; instead, she finds herself peppered by questions about the serpent and her sense of the danger it poses. At first, she responds with recognition of the fact that there is so much of the world that remains a mystery: "There are places in the world no one's ever walked, and water so deep they've never found the bottom: who knows what we might've missed." When the teacher gestures nervously toward the younger members of the class, Cora offers a different response: "There is nothing to be afraid of . . . except ignorance. What seems frightening is just waiting for you to shine a light on it. . . . I don't know if there's anything out in the Blackwater but I do know this: if it came up on the banks and let us see it, we wouldn't see a monster, just an animal as solid and real as you and me." The narrator then describes the girl who asked the question: "The girl in the yellow dress, plainly preferring to be afraid than to be instructed, yawned delicately into the palm of her hand."[31]

It is a powerful line and a familiar sentiment—that we prefer to be afraid rather than to be instructed. We get caught up in the drama of fear and the scramble for security, and the slow, rational processes of clarification, attention, listening, reading, and understanding don't quite hold our attention. In a radio interview about the book, Sarah Perry discussed that scene. She admitted that she was more hopeful when she wrote the book. At the time of the interview, however, she considered the treatment of refugees seeking safe haven in Europe, and she described awakening to "a fermenting of ill will and a fermenting of willful ignorance." It is not just that we don't know or don't understand, she suggests. Fear is not simply a result of these passive realities. Rather, Perry perceives an intention to incite fear, an intention to disseminate hatred and to purposefully mischaracterize the other. She says, "I had my eye fixed on other monsters," and now I "have been confronted with the possibility that there are monsters that can't be vanquished."[32]

I believe there is an important lesson here, though I remain more hopeful than Sarah Perry. Fear is not a result of passive ignorance; it is not only a result of lack of knowledge. We are in a much more dire situation than that: we are being formed to fear. Being formed to fear is, of course, not a new phenomenon. In his powerful book *Faces of the Enemy*, psychologist Sam Keen documented enemy creation through rhetoric and images. By examining political cartoons across generations of violent conflict and from different political perspectives, he showed how propaganda crafts a psychology of enmity, even recycling images across time.[33] We can see this dynamic in play in current rhetoric about Muslims and immigrants in the United States. They are construed as a threat using the same language and images employed against Irish Catholics in the nineteenth century, for example. Nativists who were trying to restrict the immigration of foreigners into their land framed Irish Catholics as responsible for the negative social effects of urbanization and for any and every social problem: "pauperism, disease, criminality, rowdyism, alcoholism and indolence."[34] Syracuse University historian David Bennett quotes and paraphrases one of the prominent conspiracy theorists (Christopher Morse) this way:

> "We are the dupes of our hospitality. The evil of immigration brings to these shores illiterate Roman Catholics, the tools of reckless and unprincipled politicians, the obedient instruments of their more knowing priestly leaders." In this way, "our very institutions are at the mercy of a body of foreigners," people who might boast of being Americans but who talk of Ireland as home, people who bring mob violence to our cities.[35]

Do you hear the echoes of fear formation today? We hear today the ideas that immigrants are not only bringing economic burdens but also social ills—even more than that, we hear that they are actually loyal to foreign powers and threatening violence in our cities. The other piece that we can see so clearly from a distance was the appalling way in which nativist propaganda intentionally fueled fear of Catholicism itself. Catholics were loyal to Rome, not to Washington. Clearly, that is a sentiment that took firm root in our history.

One of the most blatant examples of this nativist practice was a book titled *The Awful Disclosures of Maria Monk*, which was published in 1836. As described by David Bennett, the book told of Maria Monk's experiences in a nunnery, where she went "to be educated, only to be abused by both nuns and priests." *Maria* opened the door to a new genre of literature detailing the perverse lives of priests and nuns behind convent walls. In these dark, hedonistic places, young girls were "beaten and stomped to death by superiors and priests," "branded with hot irons" and "whipped . . . with rods before private altars."[36] Such books were read widely in the mid-1830s and served to bolster the image of Catholic degeneracy. Irish Catholics living outside of the convent walls were also cast as the source of other social ills, including pauperism, disease, and crime. And nativists, many of whom were pro-temperance Protestants, sharply criticized the Irish newcomers for their drunken rowdiness.

I come from a line of pro-temperance Protestants. My people were Methodist. Coffee was their social drink. They were reserved and stoic folk who didn't dance or play cards. My Protestant family was formed in different ways to fear Catholics (or at least not to trust them), to be skeptical and resistant to their sources of authority, to cast a wary and dismissive glance at Catholic ritual, to voice offense when Catholic practices interfered with our life in some way. When I look to my own upbringing in southern Indiana—aware now of some of those social forces in play—I am incredibly grateful that my best friend was Catholic. She lived two doors down. Her parents worked at the Whirlpool factory; they smoked cigarettes, were in a bowling league, drank beer, and played cards. I did not stay in touch with my friend after high school, and I do not know what became of her family. But given the anti-Catholic formation still present in my Protestant culture, that relationship was one of the most important of my life.

One of my son's best friends is a Muslim boy whose family is from India. During the presidential campaigns of 2016, Steve began to worry about this friend and his family. The day after President Trump was elected, Steve's first question was whether they would have to leave the United States. His second question was whether his friend's grandmother could come visit him. Even at eight years old, Steve was listening. He was listening to language about Muslim immigrants, and he was worrying for his friend. But it was more than that. Steve was becoming increasingly clear that what he heard about Muslims and about Islam did not square with what he knew about his friend and what he had learned from the family he knows so well.

One night last spring as Steve was climbing into bed, he said, "Mom, today I told [my friend] that I believe in his religion." Steve said this in a way that suggested he was a little nervous about having said it. So I asked what he meant by that and how his friend responded. As we talked it through, it became clear that Steve was not announcing a conversion to Islam. Rather, he was trying to say that he believed in his friend's religion as something other than the violent and threatening force that was repeatedly presented to him. Steve meant, "I don't believe what others say about your religion. I believe in your religion."

There is something significant here. It goes even beyond the sheer beauty of friendships that cross boundaries. There is a lesson here about formation. Steve is growing up in a society that is trying very hard to form him to fear Islam. He sees Islamic extremists committing violence on the news, he hears references to Muslim terrorists, he knows that people are afraid to have a mosque in their neighborhood, he hears that Muslims want to impose sharia law all over our country, he hears that Muslims hate America and are attacking Christians. The list goes on and on. With speech, images, and behavior, Steve's society is communicating fear of Muslims. And still he says to his friend, "I believe in your religion." He is communicating trust in something that his society is forming him to fear. Is that because he understands Islam? No. It is because he knows his friend and his family.

In her essay "Fear and Muslim-Christian Conflict Transformation," Evelyne Reisacher draws on a distinction in neuroscience between grounded and ungrounded fears. Grounded fears are realistic and appropriate fears; ungrounded fears refer to "anxiety about potential outcomes and situations that can never exist."[37] Add to this distinction the point that fears can be acquired and that the association in our brain that triggers fear often occurs without our awareness—that is, we are not consciously becoming afraid. We simply feel fear. "Harmless individuals, objects, or events can become fearful through fear conditioning," writes Reisacher.[38] In other words, our brain is forming associations of which we are not fully aware. This is referred to as implicit or unconscious bias.[39] Reisacher, who is an associate professor of Islamic studies and intercultural relations, shares an experience of her own to underscore this point:

> Not too long ago, I was sitting in the Los Angeles Airport on my way to Chicago, when a group of about twenty Muslims, going on pilgrimage, made their way to the plane I was about to board. At their view the crowds around me froze. The face of several passengers displayed a flushed pallor. To my utter surprise, I started to resonate with the fear of the crowd. My body got tense, my palms sweated, my mouth got dry, and my stomach churned. How could it be? I have hundreds of friends in the Muslim world whom I have known for years and enjoy being with. I suddenly realized what was happening to me. I was nonconsciously associating the view of Muslims to internal images of violence and danger that my mind had stored after watching threatening events on television in which some Muslims were involved.[40]

Later in her essay, Reisacher names several types of fear that Christians have about Islam and Muslims. We have historical fears passed down from generations; we also have a fear of losing land or space (we see this particularly in reaction to demographic data), a fear of different beliefs, and a fear of death or persecution. It is important to name the fears we have; we cannot work with them in healthy ways if we allow them to remain buried under the surface. Once we name them and examine them, we might be able to regulate them a bit—to distinguish between grounded and ungrounded fears, among other things. Still, no matter how much we understand them, no matter even if we debunk them entirely, the associations will remain there, triggered in a moment before we can fully process what is happening.

One thing that has become apparent to me as I connect the conflict transformation literature with the literature on implicit bias is that we cannot get rid of our fears. We can work with them; we can articulate them and process them with others who can help us to regulate them. However, the fears and the associations that trigger them remain with us. Moreover, unconscious bias is something that we all experience, regardless of social location. Our brains may forge associations between things differently, but they are all forging associations. We cannot prevent negative associations, a reality that gives power to enemy-creating and fear-inducing propaganda. But we can continue to supplement negative associations with positive ones.

In peace and conflict studies, there are plenty of suggestions for "trust building" between parties: be consistent, reliable, predictable; communicate regularly and with transparency; share control; create shared goals and joint projects; show concern for and about the other. However, we do not respond to fear with a tool kit alone. We need to develop capacities and habits for living differently together, such as learning to see each other as interrelated, cultivating curiosity and a willingness to listen, practicing humility and comfort with ambiguity, and fostering a willingness to risk and to open ourselves to relationship. More than learning tools and strategies, we need to counter the formation to fear by cultivating different ways of being together. We need formation in mutuality and openness, we need to develop friendships, and we need to turn to one another. One particularly striking element in Reisacher's essay is her recommendation for Christians and Muslims to address fear by articulating their fears to one another. Sharing vulnerability is one way to build a sense of mutuality, but it also requires a mutual commitment to risk openness with one another.

Without dismissing the impact of relationship and friendship in the midst of fear, I want to return to a point articulated by Alison Jaggar, namely, that our interpersonal, relational work must never lose sight of the social realities each party experiences. The intensity and groundedness of our fears varies. One year, I led a monthly book discussion with third-graders at my kids' elementary school. During one visit, we read a folk tale about a brave boy who determines that the huge monster on the hill above the village only seems big from a distance. He courageously climbs the hill to find that what seemed like a huge monster is actually quite small. As we moved into the discussion, I asked the students if they had any fears, any "what ifs," which is the name that the villagers gave to the monster. Steve's Muslim friend was in this group, and he said that he was worried about being shot. Our book group met just a few days after two Indian-born men had been shot by someone in Kansas who said he thought they were Arabs. We all have fears. Some are grounded. Some are not.

I position myself squarely as an empowered self—a white, relatively affluent, well-educated, straight, cisgender woman. Although I certainly have experiences of marginality as a woman in sexist contexts, I live most of my life in positions of privilege.[41] I close this chapter with some recommendations for the way in which empowered selves like me should live a good life in the midst of conflict. I suggest that we (privileged moral agents) live a good life in the midst of ongoing conflict by responding to need rather than reacting to fear.

RESPONDING TO NEED RATHER THAN REACTING TO FEAR

Above the altar in the Church of All Nations in Jerusalem, there is a powerful painting of Jesus in Gethsemane. The church itself sits at the base of the Mount of Olives, next to the small garden of olive trees we call Gethsemane. This church is also called the Basilica of Agony, and the painting above the altar shows why. Jesus looks exhausted, his body heavy against the rock. I like this painting because it seems to me to be an honest rendering of Jesus. At least, it is an honest rendering of the Jesus whom Matthew and Mark describe. Gathering up the adjectives from several different translations, we read that Jesus was sorrowful, troubled, and deeply distressed, sad and anxious, grieved and agitated. Even more so than Matthew, Mark describes Jesus as deeply troubled and even distraught.[42] The Gospel of Luke gives a briefer and less dramatic portrayal of Gethsemane, but it mentions the "strengthening angel" sent by God. The Gospel of John presents Gethsemane as the place across the Kidron Valley where Judas brings the soldiers to Jesus. But he does not find a distraught Jesus there. Earlier in John, Jesus articulates a moment of feeling troubled, but the reassurance comes immediately: "for this purpose I have come." These contrasting descriptions of Jesus' emotional state continue to fuel debates about his human and divine nature, but I will not enter those debates here.

For the purpose of this chapter on responsibility, care, conflict, and fear, I take us to Gethsemane to reflect on this moment when Jesus articulates needs that no one meets:

> Then Jesus went with them to a place called Gethsemane; and he said to his disciples, "Sit here while I go over there and pray." He took with him Peter and the two sons of Zebedee, and began to be grieved and agitated. Then he said to them, "I am deeply grieved, even to death; remain here, and stay awake with me." And going a little farther, he threw himself on the ground and prayed, "My Father, if it is possible, let this cup pass from me; yet not what I want but what you want." Then he came to the disciples and found them sleeping; and he said to Peter, "So, could you not stay awake with me one hour? Stay awake and pray that you may not come into the time of trial; the spirit indeed is willing, but the flesh is weak." Again he went away for the second time and prayed, "My Father, if this cannot pass unless I drink it, your will be done." Again he came and found them sleeping, for their eyes were heavy. So leaving them again, he went away and prayed for the third time, saying the same words. Then he came to the disciples and said to them, "Are you still sleeping and taking your rest? See, the hour is at hand, and the Son of Man is betrayed into the hands of sinners. Get up, let us be going. See, my betrayer is at hand." (Matt. 26:36–46)

Peter and the sons of Zebedee, James and John, are three of the first four disciples whom Jesus called from the Sea of Galilee. And they have climbed a hill with Jesus before.[43] That time, Jesus "was transformed in front of them. His face shone like the sun, and his clothes became as white as light. Moses and Elijah appeared to them, talking with Jesus. . . . [And then] a voice from the cloud said, 'This is my Son whom I dearly love. I am very pleased with him. Listen to him!'" (Matt. 17:1–8 CEB). These are the same three disciples who witnessed the transfiguration. You would think they might respond to Jesus' invitation this time with a little more energy. Given what they have witnessed before, given the obvious needs clearly articulated by the *Messiah*, you would think they would at least stay awake.

As with the adjectives above describing Jesus' mood, I find it enriching to hear Jesus' words through the language of several translations: "I'm very sad. It's as if I'm dying. Stay here with me and keep alert" (CEB). "I am deeply grieved, even to death; remain here and stay awake with me" (NRSV). "My soul is overwhelmed with sorrow to the point of death. Stay here and keep watch with me" (New International Version). Scholars name several different reasons for Jesus' plea here. Some frame this as an imperative appropriate to the night watch of Passover. Some suggest that Jesus encourages watchfulness as a form of protection against surprise visits from his enemies. Some assert that Jesus wants the disciples to witness his prayer and his suffering. Others suggest that he simply wants their companionship. Still others describe the call for watchfulness as fitting the "eschatological context of [his] death."[44] I am partial to the argument that he wanted witnesses and companions, because I see no indication that their presence with him would have changed what unfolded. Their wakefulness would not have prevented his arrest and crucifixion. This trial would not have passed over him. To the eschatological interpretation, I do see the connection to parables in which staying awake is a theme and the kingdom of God is the point. But I also want to preserve the familiar humanity of Jesus in the garden. He is the Messiah fulfilling his purpose, and he is also a person in sorrow who needs his friends.

But they fall asleep—three times, according to Matthew and Mark. It is true that they probably had to walk a relatively long distance from the place where we think the Last Supper took place to the garden named Gethsemane. The terrain was hilly, and their days were obviously long and stressful. In the Gospel of Luke, the narrator reports that they slept because they were overcome with grief. Maybe so, but still it is hard to justify such obvious irresponsibility, such lack of care.

When Jesus finds them sleeping the first time, he says, "Stay alert and pray so that you won't give in to temptation. The spirit is eager, but the flesh is weak" (Matt. 26:42). No matter how physically and emotionally tired they might have been that night, it is difficult to hear Jesus' response as pertaining only to the temptation to sleep. What other temptations might he have had in mind?

In Matthew's chapter surrounding the story in Gethsemane, we find a variety of disciples succumbing to a variety of temptations. Judas plots and then enacts betrayal. Peter, one who was invited into a special closeness with Jesus so many times and pledges his loyalty, denies Jesus entirely. After Jesus is arrested, another follower grabs a sword and cuts off the ear of the high priest's slave. Jesus admonishes him for this act of violent resistance. Betrayal, denial, violent resistance: these are some things we are tempted to do in our fear.

Earlier in chapter 26, there is another story that grabs my attention even more. This is the response of the disciples to the woman who anoints Jesus' head with oil. When she pours this expensive oil or perfume over Jesus, the disciples become indignant: "Why this waste? This perfume could have been sold for a lot of money and given to the poor" (Matt. 26:8–9). The disciples are right about that, of course. She uses precious resources for one person that might have served the needs of many. She gives abundantly in a situation of scarcity. But Jesus reprimands the disciples for scolding her. Jesus knows that she sees the whole situation differently. She sees what is precious and what can and should be spent. She is preparing Jesus for burial. She is using a precious resource to demonstrate care for someone who is facing his most difficult hour. She sees what is happening. She is awake. In the midst of fear and anxiety, she remembers to care for the one who is targeted.

In Gethsemane, we not only meet Jesus heavy and alone; we also meet the disciples as people who (for now anyway) are not directly targeted but who experience a kind of fear by proximity. In that fear, they are tempted to betray, to deny, to close their eyes. Because they are not the direct targets of violence, they can betray the one who is. They can deny their relationship, their loyalty, their convictions. They can close their eyes. I think that this passage raises a profound and challenging question for those of us who are not the direct targets of violence but who claim to stand in solidarity with those who are. What are we tempted to do in our fear? Those who are targeted by violence and hate entreat the rest of us, "Stay with me," "Keep watch with me," "Remain with me." What are we tempted to do in our fear? Straight, white people like me, what are we tempted to do in our fear? Blend in with the mainstream and betray? Deny our companions and deny our complicity? Or do we simply close our eyes and rest because *we* are so tired or so sad or so discouraged?

I think another reason why the three close their eyes in the garden is that they cannot stand to watch what they cannot stop. This I understand completely. When the foolishness of some costs the lives and livelihoods of others, when greed and selfishness continue to overrun the common good and care for the vulnerable, when hatred and killing are all around us unashamed and on full display, I want to close my eyes too. However, the targets of all of this awfulness cannot close their eyes. And they need us not only to resist but to be witnesses and companions—in these interim days—if and when resistance fails. This is not a call to resignation or for acts of care minus the work of justice. We absolutely need to continue every form of resistance and justice work we can. And if the change we seek does not come today, we who could exit the struggle must continue to stand beside those who suffer most. We must lavish our care and attention and love on those who bear the burden of the things that do not change.

Last summer, my kids put a beautiful little novel in my hands called *The Tiger Rising* by Kate DiCamillo. What they thought was an exciting and kind of sad story quickly swept me away. The main character is Rob, a boy whose mother has died and whose father cannot deal with his grief and has fallen on hard times financially. They live in a motel, and every night Rob's dad coats Rob's legs with an ointment that fails to treat a severe skin condition. Into this sad space marches a girl named Sistine. Sistine's father has abandoned her family, and she is angry—really angry. Willie May is the story's wise woman. (DiCamillo's novels always include a wise woman.) When Willie May sees Rob and Sistine together for the first time, she says, "'Ain't that just like God, throwing the two of you together? This boy full of sorry, keeping it down low in his legs. And you,'—she pointed her cigarette at Sistine—'you all full of anger, got it snapping out of you like lightning. You some pair, that's the truth.'"[45] The first time Sistine sits next to Rob, she touches the sores on his legs, hoping to get the condition that he has so that she can miss school like he does. Near the end of the story, she holds his hand, and DiCamillo writes, "He marveled at what a small hand it was and how much comfort there was in holding on to it."[46]

I would place feisty little Sistine in Gethsemane if I could. She would keep watch. And the woman at Bethany could come with her oil. In the midst of this watchful and caring company, I would place every person whose body is targeted by violence and meanness. And I would have them know God's love and presence deep in their bones. And I would have them feel hope for a better world, energy for resistance and transformation, and a breathtaking, loving embrace in the meantime. I would add this image to the mosaic of behaviors and actions necessary for living a good life in the midst of ongoing conflict.

7
Christian Ethics through Conflict

I have been writing this book during a particularly contentious time in my country. There is certainly nothing new about the conflicts that erupted during the course of the U.S. presidential campaigns and the election of 2016. Nor is it surprising that the eruptions persisted and even increased after the election. There is nothing new about division based on identity and ideology. There is nothing new about political rhetoric that exacerbates divisions while simultaneously calling for unity. There is nothing new about the rage of those who experience mistreatment and the fear of those who experience a loss of control. Underneath the eruption there is material inequity rooted in historical injustice, and there are persistent practices of unfair treatment rooted in disrespect for persons. In other words, we have concrete wrongs to address, and it is good that this period of volatility makes those wrongs more visible to people who have not felt them before.

However, making wrongs visible does not mean that we actually right them. We regularly respond to moments like this in a variety of unhelpful ways. We deny the depth of wrongdoing and our complicity in it. We conclude that things will never change, and so we stop fighting. We determine to protect our own and let the rest of society do what it will. We compete with others who are in pain, claiming that our pain is worse. We redirect our fear into hatred and blame of others. We escape through self-absorption, drugs, and delusions. We exercise the most spiritualized, otherworldly dimensions of our faith and direct our attention away from the world that needs us. We exhaust ourselves, burn out, and give up. In other words, we fail to live a good life in the midst of conflict.

But what does it look like to live a good life in the midst of conflict? In this final chapter, I suggest four things:

1. We live a good life in the midst of ongoing conflict by taking responsibility for the impact of our actions on others.
2. We live a good life in the midst of ongoing conflict by refusing to be afraid.
3. We live a good life in the midst of ongoing conflict by maintaining an awareness of relatedness.
4. We live a good life in the midst of ongoing conflict by discerning possibility.

Many resources inform these suggestions, and I will share those in the coming pages. But the foundation for these proposals is an understanding of baptism that provides my definition of "a good life." As someone baptized into the Christian tradition and formed in Methodist churches, and who now regularly attends an Episcopal church with my family, my understanding of the good life finds expression in this prayer, found at the end of the baptism liturgy in the *Book of Common Prayer*:

> Heavenly Father, we thank you that by water and the Holy Spirit you have bestowed upon *these* your *servants* the forgiveness of sin, and have raised *them* to the new life of grace. Sustain *them,* O Lord, in your Holy Spirit. Give *them* an inquiring and discerning heart, the courage to will and to persevere, a spirit to know and to love you, and the gift of joy and wonder in all your works. *Amen.*[1]

AN INQUIRING AND DISCERNING HEART

One of the most frustrating dynamics in conflict is that we stop asking real questions, if we ask questions at all. When we are in attack mode in a conflict, we tend to ask questions for which we already know an answer in hopes of securing the "gotcha moment." When we feel under attack, we often pose the "But what about . . . ?" question as a way to deflect or distract.[2] Again, you can imagine (and have likely enacted) any number of inauthentic questions in the heat of conflict. My point is that the questions we pose—if we actually pose any—are not serving the purpose of questions. They are not intended to elicit new information or insight. This is precisely why mediators and circle facilitators put so much effort into crafting careful questions. The parties to a dispute need someone to prompt them to engage one another in a different mode of discourse and to create a space between them where they can actually learn something new. Good questions carefully posed prompt the parties in a dispute to share their perspectives and identify misperception and miscommunication as well as material differences that might be contributing to the conflict. Mediators and circle facilitators use questions not only to share information and perspectives but also to make sure that the parties are actually hearing one another. "Zoe, can you tell me what you heard Katherine say?" Think about the kind of recognition that Katherine experiences when she knows that Zoe has heard her. More soberly, think about the important work that questions like this continue to perform while Zoe and Katherine struggle to hear one another fully.

Living a good life in the midst of ongoing conflict means that we must practice asking good questions of ourselves and others. Good questions in the context of conflict have an open quality to them. They elicit information rather than prompting a response to information offered. They ask, "What do you think about that idea?" rather than "Didn't you find that idea a little naive?" Like the first example, open questions do not convey judgment. Of course, we can ask perfectly open questions and still have an agenda that drives us to hear the answers the way we want to hear them. So I would add another criterion, namely, that good questions help us learn something new. The questions we need in the context of ongoing conflict move us into patterns of dialogue rather than debate. As Lisa Schirch and David Campt explain, "Dialogue is a unique communication process because it focuses participants' attention on listening for understanding."[3] We are listening for the other person's best insights, not their weakest argument; we are listening for clarity about similarities and differences; we are listening for common concerns and shared hopes. But we are also listening for truths that are hard to receive. We are listening with an inquiring and discerning heart. This kind of listening requires discipline to create in ourselves space to receive what the other shares with us, even if it is something we do not want to hear.[4]

In his preface to *The Meaning of Revelation*, H. Richard Niebuhr argues that "self-defense is the most prevalent source of error in all thinking and perhaps especially in theology and ethics."[5] Our impulse to defend our perspective, justify our position, rationalize our actions, or assert our own point of view leads us to erroneous understanding. We simply cannot see well when we are insisting we are right. H. Richard Niebuhr has only appeared on a few pages of this text, but his influence runs throughout. Niebuhr raised an important challenge to deontology and teleology when he described the moral agent not as a citizen responding to laws or as a maker fashioning the future, but as an answerer, responding to actions upon him.[6] In a responsibilist approach to ethics, he wrote, "we think of all our actions as having the pattern of what we do when we answer another who addresses us."[7] Niebuhr conceived of the moral life as dialogue, an ongoing interaction between actions upon me, my interpretation of them, my response, and the response to my response. As a social self, I am always responding to actions upon me and accountable for the responses of other people to my actions.[8] Self-defense interrupts the dialogue, impairs my interpretation of events, and shifts the focus from accountability to self-justification.

Living a good life in the midst of ongoing conflict requires that I participate in dialogue literally, by asking open questions that facilitate learning. It also requires that I conceive of the moral life as ongoing dialogue with others. I must see myself within a web of relationships in which I carefully interpret actions upon me and remain accountable to others for the impact of my actions on them. As noted in chapter 3, deontologists value adherence to rules and principles that transcend context and relationships. But we have seen how our adherence to principles has implications for those with whom we stand in relationship. Positively, they establish important parameters for our behavior toward the other in the midst of conflict, but they can also have harmful effects, whether intended or not. I am not suggesting that we jettison rules and principles, of course. But I insist that in contexts of ongoing conflict, rules must remain part of an ongoing dialogue rather than the final word.

While I appreciate Niebuhr's description of the social self and his dynamic and dialogic understanding of responsibility, I am struck by the clinical nature of his descriptions. He describes the features and mechanics of responsibility without communicating the feeling of relationship.[9] Similarly, the careful descriptions of dialogue strategies and facilitator guidelines are incredibly helpful and consistently fail to capture the emotionally charged nature of dialogue as we actually experience it. Accountability stinks. It's awful to be told that you have done something and someone wrong, to feel flooded with guilt and humiliation, to try to find words strong enough to acknowledge fully the hurt and to seek forgiveness. It is also emotionally draining to confront someone who has wronged you. It takes tremendous courage to speak up and fortitude to keep speaking up until you are actually heard and taken seriously. This dialogue about responsibility is both awful and essential. And living a good life in the midst of conflict means that we must do more than think through the mechanics of responsibility; we must do the emotional work as well.

THE COURAGE TO WILL AND TO PERSEVERE

In chapter 4, we considered virtue ethics and scriptural teaching related to conflict and conflictual behaviors. I pointed to the Syrophoenician woman and the persistent widow as examples of conflictual behavior that Jesus appreciated. He recognized the cleverness and faithfulness of the Syrophoenician woman and healed her daughter. And he lifted up the widow as a model of faithfulness to his disciples at a time when they were discouraged. These biblical characters function as important correctives to the idea that conflict is sinful. They remind us that engaging conflict for purposes of constructive change is also virtuous behavior. Thus, these women stand as crucial figures for theological reflection about resistance and persistence in the face of mistreatment and injustice. In the midst of ongoing conflict, the good life requires courage and a willingness to persevere.

But I want to write now from another perspective I hold, that of a white person in a racist society. I find it easier to write about engaging conflict in Christian ethics when we can stand alongside the persistent widow and bother the unrighteous judge. But as a white person in a racist society, I see the persistent widow continually coming toward me.[10] If I still affirm accountability and want to live into dialogue as a space of learning, I need to acknowledge that as a white person in a racist society, the widow is still trying to get my attention. And if I'm honest about the intensity and urgency of her approach, I must say that she sounds more and more like Woman Wisdom in Proverbs 1:

How long, O simple ones, will you love being simple?
How long will scoffers delight in their scoffing
and fools hate knowledge?
Give heed to my reproof;
I will pour out my thoughts to you;
I will make my words known to you.
Because I have called and you refused,
have stretched out my hand and no one heeded,
and because you have ignored all my counsel
and would have none of my reproof,
I also will laugh at your calamity;
I will mock when panic strikes you,
when panic strikes you like a storm,
and your calamity comes like a whirlwind,
when distress and anguish come upon you.

Woman Wisdom is no nonchalant teacher. She implores us; she entreats us. As one commentary puts it, she grabs us by the shirt and shouts in our faces.[11] She is intense: "I will pour out my thoughts to you; I will make my words known to you."

Have you been on the receiving end of that kind of intensity and urgency? I have. I heard that level of intensity and urgency in the convocation address of my colleague Robert Franklin not long ago. In a particularly powerful moment in his address, he implored white people to teach our kids about racial hatred. As the African American guests and colleagues around me greeted his call with affirmation and enthusiasm, I admit that I felt uncomfortable. A part of me wanted to say, "Hey, wait, I talk to my kids about racism." Self-defense kicked in, and self-justification interrupted my listening. I also felt implicated, acknowledging to myself, "I don't talk about this very much, really. Occasionally—you know, when there is something in the news . . . when something happens at school. But my kids know racism exists and it's bad, they know. They know, right? . . ." Dr. Franklin called with intensity and urgency. Wisdom stretched out her hand. And my internal two-step of defensiveness and guilt was a sorry response.

Chapter 3, on the *imago Dei*, began in the context of the movement for black lives and concluded with experiences of moral injury. That combination of material is instructive for white people in our society. Living a good life as a white person in contexts of ongoing racial conflict means that we must do more than affirm the image of God in persons of color. We must also recognize that our participation in racist structures diminishes the image of God in ourselves. We are not reflecting the image of God in the world as long as we benefit from the unearned privileges attached to whiteness. We do bear the image of God, but we are not reflecting it in the world. This warrants confession, repentance, and change.[12]

In contexts of conflict, parties who fear a loss of power find a variety of ways to secure themselves. We create or reinforce barriers between ourselves and those who threaten us. We craft and tell stories about the threats we feel and the wrongs we have experienced. We cast the others as violent and unreasonable. And, of course, we rely on mechanisms of physical and structural violence to keep the threat under control. In our fear and anxiety, we turn away from Woman Wisdom and appeal to Aaron instead. In Exodus 32:1, the people have been waiting at the base of Mount Sinai for forty days and forty nights for Moses to return from receiving instructions and tablets from God. Finally, in their anxiety and impatience, they turn to Aaron: "Come, make gods for us, who shall go before us; as for this Moses, the man who brought us up out of the land of Egypt, we do not know what has become of him" (Exod. 32:1). Aaron obliges them, apparently without hesitation, taking their gold to fashion a calf. Biblical scholars debate the precise intention of the calf: Was the golden calf itself a god or a representation of God, or was it intended as an image to stand in place of the absent Moses, or was it to serve as a pedestal for the invisible presence of the divine? Whatever the precise intention, creating the calf—or more properly, the bull—was indeed problematic.[13]

This story about anxious people who secure themselves to an idol has some universal truth to it. But I am suggesting an analogy here: in contexts of conflict, people who fear the loss of power reach for policies, practices, and perceptions to secure them. In our fear and anxiety, we turn to Aaron: "Keep us safe; secure us." And Aaron obliges us: Here is a new interrogation technique. Here, drop these bombs and use this drone. Here, close this border, build this wall, ban these people. Remember that this land is yours. Profile these people and screen for this. Buy a gun; conceal it and carry it. Stand your ground.

This analogy connects with a dominant narrative about the human condition, that we are inherently anxious beings always searching for ways to make ourselves feel more secure. The golden calf is a powerful metaphor for the idols we worship in an attempt to avoid awareness of vulnerability and to resist a loss of power. But the making of the golden calf is actually an interruption in another story, and I think that contexts of ongoing conflict require that we put the interruption back in its place and remember the story interrupted by it. The preceding chapters of Exodus are filled with instructions for the tabernacle (Exod. 25–31). God instructs Moses to gather an offering of all kinds of materials. "And have them make me a sanctuary," God says, "that I may dwell among them" (Exod. 25:8). Finally, after every detail of the dwelling is addressed, God admonishes Moses to keep the Sabbath and gives him the tablets of stone. But instead of the next scene opening on construction, the narrators take us to the anxious and impatient people who have been waiting at the base of Mount Sinai all this time. Instead of implementation, we have idolatry. The story of the golden calf is a familiar one not only because we have heard it before, but also because we live it. We know the interruption of idolatry in a journey from instruction to implementation. We know how it feels to grow anxious and impatient; we know how it feels to reach for something to secure ourselves; we know how the interruption becomes the story.

I think we are helped in contexts of conflict by putting the interruption back in its place and remembering the story disrupted by it. God says to Moses, "Have them make me a sanctuary that I may dwell among them." Hebrew Bible scholar Carol Meyers emphasizes that the wilderness shrine described here is more like a tent than a temple. It is designed to be portable, movable, so that God may dwell among the people. God intends to stay with the people, to journey with them. And so (three chapters later) Moses gathers the Israelites and instructs them on God's commandments, including the offerings they should bring for the tabernacle (Exod. 35). They get to work, collecting and offering up all of the materials and constructing the tabernacle: "When Moses saw that they had done all the work just as the Lord had commanded, he blessed them" (Exod. 39:43). This is a story we need to remember and enact—the construction of the tent, not the crafting of an idol. It is a story of a people who make a place for God to dwell among them. In contexts of ongoing conflict, we must refuse to be afraid by remembering God's presence among us. We must resist the temptation to secure ourselves with idols and rather build a place for God to dwell among us, present in the midst of conflict.

A SPIRIT TO KNOW AND TO LOVE YOU

In chapter 5, we examined the atonement-centered narrative of reconciliation, and I expressed concern about its dominant place in the work of addressing wrongdoing and wounds. Looking to other writings on reconciliation and restorative justice, as well as the experiences within circle practices, we heard other stories and other ways of thinking about the relationship between justice, liberation, forgiveness, and reconciliation. I encouraged a nonlinear conception, drawing on writings that emphasize containers of conflict that create a space where people can hear one another. In these spaces, we also hear about goals and journeys. But the space itself is marked by an awareness of deep interrelatedness already present. The journey is not necessarily from here (a place of division) to there (a place of reunion), but a journey in and through conflict that helps us to see what already exists—relatedness. The journey is not from separation to reunion, but from harmful forms of relatedness to healthy forms of relatedness. To stay with my earlier example: instead of reaching out to reconcile with persons of color, I need to see the ways that my relationship to them is harmful. We are already in relationship, and my behavior in the relationship is causing harm. These insights come from writing and the practices of restorative justice and conflict transformation, but they also resonate with the Christian liturgical practice of Eucharist.

The eucharistic table creates a space where we can risk revealing our whole selves, knowing that we are loved and remain in relationship with God and one another. It is a space where we are heard and forgiven, and it is a space we return to again and again. It is a space that grounds us for life in the midst of ongoing conflict. The eucharistic table is not a place where an easy road is forecast. It is not a place where success is promised. And even those who have faith that God is ultimately working for good know that this table does not promise a future without loss. The Eucharist does something much more powerful and beautiful than that: It reminds us that we are not alone. It prepares us to live well in the midst of ongoing conflict not by telling us we are good or right, but by reminding us that we are loved.

Kate DiCamillo's beautiful novel *Because of Winn-Dixie* tells the story of ten-year-old India Opal Buloni, who has recently moved to a small Florida town with her father, a preacher. Opal's mother left them when Opal was three, and the move from Watley to Naomi caused Opal to leave all her friends behind. In the opening scene of the book, she rescues a big, ugly dog from the Winn-Dixie grocery store, which gives him his name. She spends the rest of the novel developing relationships with an odd cast of characters, to whom she eventually offers communion through a Littmus Lozenge. (That is how I read the scenes anyway.) A Littmus Lozenge is a candy that was created by Littmus W. Block after he returned from the Civil War to find his entire family dead and his house burned down. As Opal explains to her dad, Littmus returned from the war wanting something sweet. "So he built a candy factory and made Littmus Lozenges, and he put all the sad he was feeling into the candy."[14]

When Opal's dad tastes the candy, he describes it as melancholy and says it makes him think of Opal's mother.[15] When Opal gives the candy to Ms. Gloria Dump, she recognizes the flavor and says, "It taste sweet. But it also taste like people leaving."[16] When Opal gives a Littmus Lozenge to the young man at the pet store, he says, "It tastes good, but it also tastes a little bit like being in jail."[17] Finally, she gives one to a little girl named Sweetie Pie, who spits it out because it tastes "like not having a dog."[18] Opal continues this sweet and sad work of connecting with people in their pain, and eventually she is able to gather everyone together for a party in the yard of Ms. Gloria Dump. When all of the beautiful, wounded people are gathered with their odd assortment of food and nonfood items, Ms. Dump asks the preacher to offer a blessing. He thanks God for summer nights, candlelight, and good food, and then he says, "But thank you most of all for friends. We appreciate the complicated and wonderful gifts you give us in each other. And we appreciate the task you put down before us, of loving each other the best we can, even as you love us."[19]

Every time that we participate in the Eucharist, we acknowledge that we fall short on this task: "We have not loved you with our whole heart; we have not loved our neighbors as ourselves."[20] And every time we participate in the Eucharist, we pray that God will "send us into the world in peace, and grant us strength and courage to love and serve [God] with gladness and singleness of heart."[21] I believe that the Eucharist forms us to live well in the midst of ongoing conflict, to remember that we are loved, to acknowledge that we hurt one another, to give us strength and courage to change, and to call us back again to the table. In spite of all the ways we deny our relationship to one another and refuse to do right by each other, the Eucharist extends to us a kind of grace that is radically inclusive and binding. We leave the Eucharist (and return and leave again) knowing that "here, together in the grace of God, go we."[22]

THE GIFT OF JOY AND WONDER IN ALL YOUR WORKS

It seems appropriate to pause for a moment to note that my proposal above may seem either discouraging or idealistic. I am suggesting that we will not escape conflict and that within contexts of ongoing conflict we can still love one another. Again, I am inviting you to see conflict as ongoing and also a site of constructive possibility. To assert that conflict is ongoing is not a statement of despair but a recognition that conflict is a natural and necessary element of life. We are created within a world that is interrelated and changing; conflict is an essential part of that process. We cannot choose whether or not to exist in conflict, but we can choose how to respond to conflict. And that is what this book is about. We need principles that set parameters around our behavior in contexts of conflict, and we need practices of accountability to one another as we try to live faithfully to rules and to relationships. In Christian ethics, this means that we respond to and reflect the image of God in the world. We need to interrogate a preoccupation with unity that yokes conflict to sin, and we need to cultivate habits of engaging conflict well for purposes of constructive change in the world. We need to think differently about the telos and its relationship to what we know. I certainly see the beloved community as one without violence, but not necessarily without conflict. If we throw conflict out of the eschatological vision, then we envision life without vitality. What I hope for and orient myself toward is not an ahistorical, transcendent vision of peace without conflict. I orient myself toward a hope for spaces within history where people in conflict can live well together. This hope is rooted in a faith in creation, in the good bones of creation.

"Good Bones" is a poem by Maggie Smith that went viral during the summer of 2016, in the weeks following the shooting massacre at the Pulse nightclub in Orlando, Florida. Smith reflects on a world that is full of sadness and violence and grief. She writes that "life is short" and "at least half terrible." Yet her poem communicates her desperate work to sell this world to her children the way a real estate agent tries to sell a house to a doubtful buyer. "This place could be beautiful, right? You could make this place beautiful."[23] Like this poet, I desperately want my children to believe in this world. I want them to see possibility here.

Maggie Smith's poem has something profound in common with Psalm 90, at least the way that H. Richard Niebuhr hears the psalmist. We tend to read Psalm 90 at funerals, but Niebuhr urges us to hear the psalm "as a song of work, a prayer to be said as we go about our business in school and church and nation."[24] He focuses on the last few verses, translating them this way:

> Let thy work appear unto thy servants,
> And thy glory upon their children.
> And let the favor of the Lord our God be upon us;
> And establish thou the work of our hands
> Yea, the work of our hands establish thou it.

I think Niebuhr would also like the translation in the Common English Bible:

> Let your acts be seen by your servants;
> let your glory be seen by their children.
> Let the kindness of the Lord our God be over us.
> Make the work of our hands last.
> Make the work of our hands last!

Niebuhr interprets the text this way: "Show us [Lord] what you are doing with all that we are doing. Show us what it is that we are working on. . . . Build this particular thing that we are doing *into the permanent structure*."[25] This is not a plea for attention or fame; it is not a prayer of vanity or pride. It is a prayer for guidance, for clarity, and for help—in effect, "Lord, help me to see your work and to see the connection between your work and mine."

I'm quite taken with Niebuhr's interpretation of the psalm. Our pain and sadness are not only due to loss of life. Our sadness is not only a response to the fragility and brevity of life. It is also a response to this sense that things don't seem to be getting better. Part of the heaviness I feel when I reflect on the world comes from the awareness that people are indeed trying. Buried beneath the headlines of awfulness are individuals who are truly trying to make things better. There are doctors and nurses who give up their personal safety to work in hospitals in war zones. When the bombs fell on the maternity hospital in Syria that summer of 2016, tremendous sadness at this senseless violence was compounded by the awareness that the hard work and courageous risks taken by good people had come to naught. There are countless variations on this theme. The Pulse nightclub was a place where the LGBTQ community in Orlando could come to relax, to have fun without fear of ostracism, ridicule, or violence. People had labored to create that place. Some of the most painful stories coming out about gun violence in Chicago feature people who had worked so hard to build a good, honest life and were in the wrong place at the wrong time. And for every story about extremist violence, my mind goes immediately to the members of the community whose good work is derailed or diverted by the need to once again explain the difference between Islam and ISIS or between the Black Lives Matter movement and the targeting of police officers. I think about how many people are working to end sex trafficking in Atlanta, the city in which I live, and how the statistics just get worse. In every arena of life, it seems our good work is not somehow sticking in history. And, like Maggie Smith, I want my kids to see possibility here. Like the psalmist, I find myself pleading, "Lord, make the work of our hands last. Help me to root my work in yours, to build this particular thing I am doing into the permanent structure. Into the good bones. Into the sure foundation."

This prayer is possible because there are good bones here. This is not a kind of wishing, but a way of seeing. It is a way of seeing the world—or at least a determination to keep trying to see the world in a certain way—not in a simplistic "glass half-full" kind of way. This is not a way of seeing that glosses over the real losses and limits of life. Rather, this is a way of seeing beneath them to the bones, to the foundation, to the dwelling place, to the work of God. We are living in the world like the poet does, or at least like Mary Oliver does. In a lovely poem titled "The World I Live In," Oliver insists on living in a world that is wider than "reasons and proofs." "What's wrong with Maybe?" she asks.[26] Poets such as Oliver, Smith, and the psalmist invite us into a different way of seeing the world, insisting on the possibilities within it, and teaching us to discern them.

One summer, my family had the great opportunity to spend a week at Ghost Ranch in New Mexico. Ghost Ranch is a 20,000-acre ranch in the high desert that functions as a retreat and conference center, a multigenerational family vacation place, and a home for any kind of workshop you can imagine related to spirituality and the arts. One of the top-ten paleontology sites in the world, this place also was Georgia O'Keeffe's home and the subject of many of her paintings. My family happened to attend during the "festival of the arts." So we spent the week surrounded by artists of all kinds—painters, potters, sculptors, poets, musicians, quilters, and jewelry makers. Even from the very edge of their world and work, we quickly picked up on the sense that they were particularly capable of doing creative work in this land where they felt so closely connected to God. It is a magical place, majestic and mysterious. It is the kind of place where you feel utterly small and remarkably grateful at the same time. In the layers of rock, you must reckon with the reality of your brief existence compared with the history of the planet. In the paths through the mountains, you become aware of all the people who worked this land, struggled on it, fought over it, claimed it, told stories about it, and connected to it for thousands of years.

I found myself thinking about this mountain again, thanks to a line from Walter Rauschenbusch's *Theology for the Social Gospel*, of all things. Hardly a desert mystic, Rauschenbusch was grappling with plurality and divisiveness among people when he asserted, "Our human personalities may seem distinct, but their roots run down into the eternal life of God."[27] Our roots run down into the eternal life of God. We are connected to other people and to the whole of creation through a common root system. Our roots run down into the eternal life of God. That connectedness to God makes creativity in the midst of destruction possible. It makes relationship in the midst of division possible. It makes faithfulness in the midst of fear possible. The challenge is to live out that story of connectedness in contexts that defy it, ridicule it, trivialize it, and trash it. In those very contexts, we must create the space for God to dwell among us, to be manifest in our actions, words, and ways of being together. Our roots run down into the eternal life of God, and we must be bold enough to live that way. That is what living a good life in the midst of ongoing conflict looks like.

CONCLUSION

This final chapter puts forth a constructive response to the question driving this book: How do we live a good life in the midst of ongoing conflict? In truth, however, the whole book is my response to this question, or at least the response I offer through my vocation as a Christian ethics professor. Like some readers, perhaps, I often hesitate to explain what I do, especially on airplanes, where a getaway is impossible. When my attempts at evasion fail and I am forced to say out loud to a stranger, "I teach Christian ethics," I receive a range of responses. Most people offer a courteous smile and quickly return to their mobile device. I once had a woman apologize for cursing as she was cramming her belongings into the overhead bin. Another woman responded effusively, "Oh, good for you! We need to send you to Washington!" Once, a man replied with a smirk, "Christian ethics? That's an oxymoron, isn't it?" In some sense, all of these people have a point. Christian ethics does include strong normative claims about behavior and about social structures. Of course, neither of the first two women knew the content of my particular normative claims. The first assumed that I would issue moral judgments against cursing, and the second assumed I would advance an agreeable political platform. The cynic, too, has a point. He knows Christians who pray on Sunday, lie on Monday, cheat on Tuesday, abuse on Wednesday, exploit situations to their own advantage on Thursday, do violence to the most vulnerable on Friday, and rest on Saturday by ignoring those in need. To him, "Christian ethics" sounds like a self-righteous lie.

However, all of these interlocutors are also wrong about what I teach. They assume that I lecture my students about what they should and should not do, that I carry across time the dogmatic mandates of my faith and apply them in unidirectional fashion to these changing times. I do not teach that way because I do not understand my vocation or my field that way. As a Christian ethicist, I participate in the dynamic and ongoing work of holding the tenets of a faith tradition in relationship to a changing world. This relationship is not unilateral in nature; rather, I understand my faith differently because of things I learn in and about the world. My faith should be accountable to the world and the sources of knowledge that reside in spaces beyond my own Christian tradition. I also see the world through the lens of my faith tradition, which sometimes sets me at odds with cultural norms, political arguments, or even sober assessments about the way things really are. In this dynamic interaction, I am constantly in conflict. I disagree with colleagues in my field and members of my church. I find myself struggling between competing commitments both of which I hold dear. I wrestle with conflicting views of a text or tension between text and experience. I struggle against claims about my tradition that are unfair or misrepresentative, and sometimes I struggle with claims about my tradition that are true and troubling. I am writing in the first person here to make this as concrete as possible, but nothing here is unique to me. To study, teach, and practice Christian ethics is to engage conflict.

This book puts forth a view of Christian ethics that is informed by this awareness of conflict as ever present and also potentially good. As in every arena of life, conflict in Christian ethics offers an opportunity for learning and for growing. Thus, each chapter of this book offers some insights and lessons about methods of ethics learned through contexts of conflict and texts about conflict. Chapter 2 discussed method itself (and Methodists!) to make clear the particular approach and the building blocks of ethics that shape this book. Chapter 3 considered the parameters we place around the treatment of persons in contexts of conflict. It also argued that we need to keep these universal principles in conversation with contextual realities so that they contribute to relationship and formation of persons. Chapter 4 reckoned with texts that discourage conflict as ungodly. We examined the motivations behind the texts and critiqued them. And we searched out other models of behavior, ways of engaging conflict that reflect faithfulness and also embody love. Bringing the lens of conflict transformation to the Scriptures helps us to locate virtues for behaving well in the midst of ongoing conflict. Chapter 5 suggested that we attend to the movement of God in the midst of conflict and examined the telos of reconciliation. I also suggested that we respond to the call of reconciliation by creating space for different narratives and remaining accountable to the experiences shared there. Chapter 6 took us into the mundane, daily work of dealing with conflict in interpersonal contexts and emphasized practices of care that still attend to justice by refusing the power of fear, among other things.

This final chapter has used liturgical language from the *Book of Common Prayer* to organize four suggestions for living a good life in the midst of conflict. Drawing on sources from Scripture, tradition, reason, and experience, I suggest that we take responsibility for the impact of our actions on others, refuse to be afraid, maintain an awareness of relatedness, and discern possibility. However, clearly, nothing is resolved here. Nor could it be, if we take the foundational assertion seriously: conflict is ongoing. Yet within the ongoing dynamics of conflict, we find opportunities to understand more fully, to relate more honestly, to love more carefully, and to live faith more courageously.

Notes

Chapter 1

1. For further discussion of the emergence and practice of conflict transformation, see Ellen Ott Marshall, "Learning through Conflict, Working for Transformation," in *Conflict Transformation and Religion*, ed. Ellen Ott Marshall (New York: Palgrave Macmillan 2016).

2. See Hugh Miall, "Conflict Transformation: A Multi-Dimensional Task," in *Berghof Handbook for Conflict Transformation* (Berghof Foundation, 2004), 4, accessed December 5, 2016, at http://www.berghof-foundation.org/fileadmin/redaktion/Publications/Handbook/Articles/miall_handbook.pdf.

3. Ronald S. Kraybill, Robert A. Evans, and Alice Frazer Evans, *Peace Skills: Manual for Community Mediators* (San Francisco: Jossey-Bass, 2001), 5.

4. John Paul Lederach, *The Journey toward Reconciliation* (Scottdale, PA: Herald Press, 1999), 100.

5. Stephanie Hixon, personal interview, October 9, 2013.

6. JustPeace Center for Mediation and Conflict Transformation, *Engage Conflict Well: A Guide to Prepare Yourself and Engage Others in Conflict Transformation* (Washington, DC: JustPeace, 2011), 3.

7. Lederach, *Journey toward Reconciliation*, 117.

8. Lederach, 116.

9. Hixon, personal interview.

10. Martin Luther King, *Why We Can't Wait* (New York: Penguin Books, 1964), 86.

11. Douglas F. Ottati, *Jesus Christ and Christian Vision* (Louisville, KY: Westminster John Knox Press, 1996), 5.

12. James M. Gustafson retired from Emory University in 1998 after teaching at the University of Chicago and Yale Divinity School. He received the Lifetime Achievement Award from the Society of Christian Ethics in 2011 because of his influence in and contributions to the field of Christian ethics. One of Gustafson's gifts to our field has been his capacity to make sense of variety in Christian ethics, particularly the various implications of methodological differences (such as how one approaches Scripture). James M. Gustafson, "Ways of Using Scripture," in *From Christ to the World: Introductory Readings in Christian Ethics*, ed. Wayne Boulton, Thomas D. Kennedy, and Allen Verhey (Grand Rapids: Eerdmans, 1994), 21–26. "Ways of Using Scripture" is a portion of a longer essay by Gustafson,

"The Place of Scripture in Christian Ethics: A Methodological Study," *Theology and Christian Ethics* (Philadelphia: Pilgrim Press, 1974), 121–46.

13. Richard Mouw, for example, suggests that not all divine commands are in the imperative form. Richard J. Mouw, *The God Who Commands* (Notre Dame, IN: University of Notre Dame Press, 1990), 9–10.

14. Gustafson, "Ways of Using Scripture," 22.

15. Gustafson, 23.

16. Gustafson, 24. The other approaches are law, ideal, and analogy.

17. Gustafson places these four approaches—law, ideal, analogy, and reflective discourse—under the heading of revealed morality, which he contrasts to revealed reality. Revealed reality approaches Scripture with a different question: rather than asking first what we ought to do, revealed reality turns to Scripture to ask what God is doing (Gustafson, 24). I will come back to this approach and its implications for conflict later in the book.

18. Adolf von Harnack, *What Is Christianity?* (Philadelphia: Fortress Press, 1957), 13–14.

19. Harnack, *What Is Christianity?* 298.

20. Ernst Troeltsch, "What Does 'Essence of Christianity' Mean?" in *Writings on Theology and Religions*, trans. and ed. Robert Morgan and Michael Pye (Atlanta: John Knox Press, 1977), 128.

21. Troeltsch, "What Does 'Essence of Christianity' Mean?" 166.

22. Ernst Troeltsch, *The Social Teaching of the Christian Churches*, trans. Olive Wyon (London: George Allen & Unwin, 1931; repr., Library of Theological Ethics, Louisville, KY: Westminster/John Knox Press, 1992), 999–1000 (page citations are to reprint edition). H. Richard Niebuhr, who wrote his dissertation on Troeltsch, exhibited a similar approach to the study of Christian ethics through his typology of Christ and culture in *Christ and Culture* (New York: Harper & Row, 1951) and in a more narrative way in *The Kingdom of God in America* (New York: Harper & Row, 1959). Later, Peter J. Paris addressed a lacuna in the work of Troeltsch and Niebuhr with his text *The Social Teaching of the Black Churches* (Minneapolis: Fortress Press, 1985). These three scholars and their students have secured a place for a historical and sociological approach to the study of Christian ethics. Because they focus on the interactions that give shape to the ongoing tradition, they also offer methods for studying Christian ethics as conflict. I will return to this point later in this chapter.

23. Karen Lebacqz, *Justice in an Unjust World: Foundations for a Christian Approach to Justice* (Minneapolis: Fortress Press, 2007), 52.

24. Kelly Brown Douglas, "Twenty Years a Womanist," in *Deeper Shades of Purple: Womanism in Religion and Society* (New York: New York University Press, 2006), 147–49.

25. I am drawing on an image used by Glen Stassen to describe the dimensions of his collaboration on just peace. Stassen brought together twenty-three scholars in the early 1990s to articulate a set of practices for reducing the severity and propensity of war. During a ten-year reflection on just peace at the Society

of Christian Ethics, Stassen described the work of this group with reference to a double-axis in order to describe how their focus on practice supplemented a preoccupation with moral debate. Glen Stassen, "The Unity, Realism, and Obligatoriness of Just Peacemaking," *Journal of the Society of Christian Ethics* 23, no. 1 (2003): 176. See also Glen Stassen, ed., *Just Peacemaking: Ten Practices for Abolishing War* (Cleveland: Pilgrim Press, 1998).

26. *The Book of Common Prayer and Administration of the Sacraments and Other Rites and Ceremonies of the Church* (New York: Church Publishing, 1979), 308.

Chapter 2

1. Ellen Ott Marshall, *Christians in the Public Square: Faith That Transforms Politics*, reissue ed. (Eugene, OR: Wipf & Stock, 2015).

2. I present feminist ethical methodology in chapter 6 as background to an ethic of care. However, feminist commitments also appear as I critically engage the other methodologies in chapters 3–5.

3. Aristotle, *Nicomachean Ethics*, trans. Martin Ostwald (Englewood Cliffs, NJ: Prentice Hall, 1962), 1.1.1094a.0-5.

4. Aristotle, *Nicomachean Ethics*, 1.7.1098a.15.

5. Aristotle, 1.8.1098b.20.

6. Aristotle, 10.7.1178a.5. See also Sir David Ross, *Aristotle*, 6th ed. (London: Routledge, 1995), 195–243.

7. Margaret Urban Walker, *Moral Contexts* (Lanham, MD: Rowman & Littlefield, 2003), xi.

8. Walker, *Moral Contexts*, xiii.

9. Walker, xii.

10. Walker, xii–xiii.

11. Although the concept of a moral agent that is detached from context does not only belong to Thomas Nagel, this language comes from the title of his book *The View from Nowhere* (Oxford: Oxford University Press, 1986).

12. Gary Dorrien, *Social Ethics in the Making: Interpreting an American Tradition* (Chichester, UK: Wiley-Blackwell, 2011), 1.

13. Rebecca Todd Peters and Elizabeth Hinson-Hasty, *To Do Justice: A Guide for Progressive Christians* (Louisville, KY: Westminster John Knox Press, 2008), xv–xvii.

14. Peters and Hinson-Hasty, *To Do Justice*, xix.

15. Traci C. West, *Disruptive Christian Ethics: When Racism and Women's Lives Matter* (Louisville, KY: Westminster John Knox Press, 2006), xiv.

16. West, *Disruptive Christian Ethics*, xv.

17. Marshall, *Christians in the Public Square: Faith That Transforms Politics*, reissue ed. (Eugene, OR: Wipf and Stock, 2015), 75–80.

18. Mark Thiessen Nation, "Toward a Theology for Conflict Transformation: Learnings from John Howard Yoder," *Mennonite Quarterly Review* 80 (January 2006): 43–60. John Howard Yoder is a formative figure in Mennonite theology

and in conflict transformation. We also know now that he sexually harassed women throughout his career in the church and the academy. Out of respect for these women, I state that. For more information, see Karen V. Guth, "Doing Justice to the Complex Legacy of John Howard Yoder: Restorative Justice Resources in Witness and Feminist Ethics," *Journal of the Society of Christian Ethics* 35, no. 2 (fall–winter 2015): 119–39.

19. Nation, "Toward a Theology for Conflict Transformation," 44–45.

20. I wrote about this in chapter 3 of *Christians in the Public Square.*

21. See, for example, the work of James Cone, who articulates a principle of interpretation based on the "revelation of God in Christ as the liberator of the oppressed from social oppression and to social struggle" (439). From this perspective, he insists that "any starting point that ignores God in Christ as the liberator of the oppressed or that makes salvation as liberation secondary is *ipso facto* invalid and thus heretical" (439). James H. Cone, "Biblical Revelation and Social Existence," *Interpretation* 28, no. 4 (October 1974): 422–40. For a feminist liberationist argument about the authority of passages that violate core convictions of freedom and mutuality, see Margaret A. Farley, "Feminist Consciousness and the Moral Authority of Scripture," in *Feminist Interpretation of the Bible*, ed. Letty M. Russell (Philadelphia: Westminster Press, 1985): 41–51.

22. *The Book of Common Prayer and Administration of the Sacraments and Other Rites and Ceremonies of the Church* (New York: Church Publishing, 1979), 308.

23. H. Richard Niebuhr, "The Grace of Doing Nothing," in *War in the Twentieth Century: Sources in Theological Ethics,* ed. Richard B. Miller (Louisville, KY: Westminster/John Knox Press, 1992), 6.

24. H. Richard Niebuhr, "Grace," 9.

25. H. Richard Niebuhr, "Grace," 11.

26. Reinhold Niebuhr, "Must We Do Nothing?" in *War in the Twentieth Century: Sources in Theological Ethics,* ed. Richard B. Miller (Louisville, KY: Westminster/John Knox Press, 1992), 13.

27. Reinhold Niebuhr, "Do Nothing?," 17.

28. H. Richard Niebuhr, "The Only Way into the Kingdom of God," in *War in the Twentieth Century: Sources in Theological Ethics,* ed. Richard B. Miller (Louisville, KY: Westminster/John Knox Press, 1992), 20–21.

29. Richard P. Heitzenrater, *Wesley and the People Called Methodists* (Nashville: Abingdon Press, 1995), 129.

30. John Wesley, *The Nature, Design, and General Rules of the United Societies in London, Bristol, Kingswood, Newcastle upon Tyne, &c.*, 17th ed. (London: J. Paramore, 1782), 4.

31. Wesley, *Nature, Design, and General Rules*, 5.

32. Heitzenrater, *Wesley and the People Called Methodists*, 138.

33. Heitzenrater.

34. John B. Cobb Jr. used this language to title and shape his book on contemporary Wesleyan theology: *Grace and Theology: A Wesleyan Theology for Today* (Nashville: Abingdon Press, 1995).

35. Theodore Runyon, *The New Creation: John Wesley's Theology Today* (Nashville: Abingdon Press, 1998), 29.

36. Wesley, *Nature, Design, and General Rules*, 5–8.

37. John Wesley, "On Working Out Our Own Salvation," in *The Works of John Wesley*, vol. 3, ed. Albert C. Outler (Nashville: Abingdon Press, 1986), 199–209.

38. Wesley, "Our Own Salvation," 203.

39. Wesley, 204.

40. Wesley, 205.

41. Wesley.

42. My thinking on risk and control, reflected here, is strongly influenced by Sharon Welch, *Feminist Ethic of Risk* (Minneapolis: Fortress Press, 1990).

43. I develop this understanding of hope as a practice of ongoing negotiation between the promising and sobering elements of faith and history in *Though the Fig Tree Does Not Blossom: Toward a Responsible Theology of Christian Hope*, reissue ed. (Eugene, OR: Wipf & Stock Publishers, 2015).

Chapter 3

1. Synclaire Cruel, "Boko Haram Has Used 83 Children as Human Bombs So Far This Year," *PBS Newshour*, August 23, 2017, https://www.pbs.org/newshour/world/boko-haram-used-83-children-human-bombs-far-year, accessed December 18, 2017.

2. "Deontological Ethics," *Stanford Encyclopedia of Philosophy*, https://plato.stanford.edu/entries/ethics-deontological, accessed March 20, 2017.

3. H. Richard Niebuhr, *The Responsible Self: An Essay in Christian Moral Philosophy* (San Francisco: Harper & Row, 1963), 51.

4. Carol Gilligan, "Moral Orientation and Development," in *Justice and Care: Essential Readings in Feminist Ethics*, ed. Virginia Held (Boulder, CO: Westview Press, 1995), 34–35.

5. Ian A. McFarland, *The Divine Image: Envisioning the Invisible God* (Minneapolis: Fortress Press, 2005), 1.

6. McFarland, *Divine Image*.

7. Noting that the *imago Dei* is "far from a straightforward or uncontroversial theological doctrine," theologian Jeremy Waldron writes that "it is surely worth pausing to ask whether we should be associating human rights with this degree of theological controversy. And this is to say nothing about whether we should expect the theologians to be happy about having the waters of controversy which lap around the doctrine of *imago Dei* muddied by the opportunistic enthusiasm of human rights advocates, casting around for something that can serve as a religious foundation" (219–20). Jeremy Waldron, "The Image of God: Rights, Reason, and Order" (2010), *New York University Public Law and Legal Theory Working Papers*, paper 246, https://core.ac.uk/download/pdf/13534034.pdf, accessed March 8, 2017.

8. Leah Gunning Francis, *Ferguson and Faith: Sparking Leadership and Awakening Community* (St. Louis, MO: Chalice Press, 2015), 18.

9. Francis, *Ferguson and Faith*, 23.

10. It is important to note that the Black Lives Matter movement did not begin in churches. Alicia Garza, Patrisse Cullors, and Opal Tometi created #BlackLives Matter in 2013 after Trayvon Martin was shot and killed by George Zimmerman. The hashtag became a social movement as people in local communities organized to resist violence against black and brown bodies and to affirm the "humanization of Black lives." Alicia Garza, "A Herstory of the #BlackLivesMatter Movement," *The Feminist Wire*, October 7, 2014, http://www.thefeministwire.com/2014/10/blacklivesmatter-2/, accessed July 23, 2018.

11. Kelly Brown Douglas, *Stand Your Ground: Black Bodies and the Justice of God* (Maryknoll, NY: Orbis Books, 2015), 50.

12. Douglas, *Stand Your Ground*, 151.

13. Brian Batnum, "Black Lives Matter: Seven Writers Assess the Movement," *Christian Century* 133, no. 6 (March 16, 2016): 27.

14. Desmond Tutu, "The First Word: To Be Human Is to Be Free," in *Christianity and Human Rights: An Introduction,* ed. John Witte Jr. and Frank S. Alexander (Cambridge: Cambridge University Press, 2011), 3.

15. Tutu, "First Word," 1, 2.

16. Tutu, 2.

17. Federal Council of Churches, "The Social Creed of the Churches," adopted December 4, 1908, http://nationalcouncilofchurches.us/common-witness/1908/social-creed.php, accessed May 25, 2016.

18. National Council of Churches, "A Social Creed for the 21st Century," approved by the General Assembly of the National Council of Churches on November 7, 2007, http://www.ncccusa.org/news/ga2007.socialcreed.html, accessed May 25, 2016.

19. National Conference of Catholic Bishops, *Economic Justice for All: Pastoral Letter on Catholic Social Teaching and the U.S. Economy* (Washington, DC: National Conference of Catholic Bishops, 1986), ix.

20. "A Pronouncement: Civil Liberties without Discrimination Related to Affectional or Sexual Preference," https://openandaffirming.org/wp-content/uploads/2013/09/1975-A-PRONOUNCEMENT-CIVIL-LIBERTIES-WITHOUT-DISCRIMINATION.pdf, accessed March 14, 2017.

21. "Equal Marriage Rights for All," http://uccfiles.com/pdf/2005-equal-marriage-rights-for-all-1.pdf, accessed March 14, 2017.

22. Toni Morrison, *Beloved: A Novel* (New York: Vintage Books, 2004), 103.

23. John Paul Lederach, "Spirituality and Religious Peacebuilding," in *The Oxford Handbook of Religion, Conflict, and Peacebuilding*, ed. Atalia Omer, R. Scott Appleby, and David Little (Oxford: Oxford University Press, 2015), 552.

24. Lederach, "Spirituality and Religious Peacebuilding."

25. Jean Zaru, *Occupied with Nonviolence: A Palestinian Woman Speaks* (Minneapolis: Fortress Press, 2008), 74.

26. Zaru, *Occupied with Nonviolence*, 75.
27. Zaru, 75–76.
28. Zaru, 74.
29. Martin Luther King Jr., *Why We Can't Wait* (New York: Mentor, 1963), 64.
30. Zaru, *Occupied with Nonviolence*, 76.
31. Zaru.
32. Zaru.
33. Richard Amesbury and George M. Newlands, *Faith and Human Rights: Christianity and the Global Struggle for Human Dignity* (Minneapolis: Fortress Press, 2008), 25–27.
34. Gilligan, "Moral Orientation," 35.
35. Theodore Runyon, *The New Creation: John Wesley's Theology Today* (Nashville: Abingdon Press, 1998), 5 (emphasis in original).
36. Runyon, *New Creation*, 13.
37. Runyon, 17 (emphasis in original).
38. Runyon, 18.
39. Jonathan Shay, "Moral Injury," *Psychoanalytic Psychology* 31, no. 2 (2014): 183.
40. Tyler Boudreau, "The Morally Injured," *Massachusetts Review* 52, nos. 3–4 (September 2011): 751.
41. Boudreau, "Morally Injured," 752.
42. Michael Yandell, "Hope in the Void: How Veterans with Moral Injury Can Help Us Face Reality," *Plough Quarterly* no. 8 (spring 2016), https://www.plough.com/en/topics/justice/nonviolence/hope-in-the-void, accessed May 29, 2016.
43. Yandell, "Hope in the Void."
44. Boudreau, "Morally Injured," 753.
45. Boudreau, 749.
46. Rita Nakashima Brock and Gabriella Lettini, *Soul Repair: Recovering from Moral Injury after War* (Boston: Beacon Press, 2013), xv.
47. Brock and Lettini, *Soul Repair*, xv–xvi.
48. Brock and Lettini, 75.
49. Brock and Lettini, 89.

Chapter 4

1. James M. Gustafson, "The Place of Scripture in Christian Ethics: A Methodological Study," *Theology and Christian Ethics* (Philadelphia: Pilgrim Press, 1974), 121–46. Page numbers refer to the essay as published with the title "Ways of Using Scripture" in *From Christ to the World: Introductory Readings in Christian Ethics*, ed. Wayne Boulton, Thomas D. Kennedy, and Allen Verhey (Grand Rapids: Wm. B. Eerdmans Publishing Co., 1994), 21.
2. Gustafson, "Ways of Using Scripture," 21–23.
3. Gustafson, 21–24.

4. James Strong, *Strong's Exhaustive Concordance*, accessed through http://biblehub.com/hebrew/4066.htm.

5. Philip Esler, *Conflict and Identity in Romans: The Social Setting of Paul's Letter* (Minneapolis: Fortress Press, 2003), 20–21.

6. David E. Aune, "The Pastoral Letters: 1 and 2 Timothy and Titus," in *Blackwell Companion to the New Testament*, ed. David E. Aune (Malden, MA: Blackwell Publishing, 2010), 552–55.

7. David Ackerman, *1 and 2 Timothy, Titus*, New Beacon Bible Commentary (Kansas City, MO: Beacon Hill Press, 2016), 46.

8. Ackerman notes three theological themes in Timothy and Titus: God as savior, sound doctrine, and the ethic of godliness (Ackerman, *1 and 2 Timothy, Titus,* 50–51). One of the primary purposes of the letters was to offer "polemical defenses against various false teachers" whose "heretical teachings were leading churches astray" (Ackerman, 46).

9. I am grateful to my colleague Susan Hylen for this insight. See chapter 5 of her book, *Women in the New Testament World* (New York: Oxford University Press, 2018).

10. Christian ethics hosts a rich debate on this matter. See, for example, contrasting perspectives in Margaret Farley, "Feminist Consciousness and the Interpretation of Scripture," in *Feminist Interpretation of the Bible*, ed. Letty Russell (Philadelphia: Westminster Press, 1985), 41–51; Stanley Hauerwas, "The Moral Authority of Scripture: The Politics and Ethics of Remembering," in *Community of Character: Toward a Constructive Christian Ethic* (Notre Dame, IN: University of Notre Dame Press, 1981), 53–74; and James Cone, "Biblical Revelation and Social Existence," *Interpretation* 28, no. 4 (October 1974): 422–40.

11. See, for example, David Buttrick, *Speaking Conflict: Stories of a Controversial Jesus* (Louisville, KY: Westminster John Knox Press, 2007); and Richard A. Horsley, *Jesus and the Powers: Conflict, Covenant, and the Hope of the Poor* (Minneapolis: Fortress Press, 2011).

12. Matthew goes on to use "sword" another three times in 26:52. Robert Horton Gundry, *Matthew, A Commentary on His Literary and Theological Art* (Grand Rapids: Wm. B. Eerdmans Publishing Co., 1982), 199.

13. John Paul Lederach, *Reconcile: Conflict Transformation for Ordinary Christians* (Harrisonburg, VA: Herald Press, 2014), 97–107.

14. Lederach, *Reconcile*, 95.

15. Lederach, 95–97.

16. Lederach, 106–7.

17. Lederach, 107.

18. Bridget Illian, "Church Discipline and Forgiveness in Matthew 18:15–35," *Currents in Theology and Mission* 37, no. 6 (December 2010): 446.

19. Illian, "Church Discipline and Forgiveness," 447.

20. Illian, 448.

21. Illian, 449.

22. Illian, 446, 450.

23. Jeffrey A. Gibbs and Jeffrey J. Kloha, "'Following' Matthew 18: Interpreting Matthew 18:15–20 in Its Context," *Concordia Journal* 29, no. 1 (2003): 19.

24. Gibbs and Kloha, "'Following' Matthew 18," 10–11.

25. James Bailey, "The Sermon on the Mount: Invitation to New Life," *Currents in Theology and Mission* 40, no. 6 (December 2013): 401.

26. Bailey, "Sermon on the Mount," 401.

27. Bailey, 400.

28. Donald A. Hagner, *Matthew 1–13*, Word Biblical Commentary, vol. 33A (Dallas: Word Books, 1993), 111.

29. Hagner, *Matthew 1–13*, 111.

30. I am purposefully refusing the interpretation that Jesus calls his followers not to be angry.

31. Bailey, "Sermon on the Mount," 402.

32. Hagner, *Matthew 1–13*, 118.

33. Buttrick, *Speaking Conflict*, 91.

34. Buttrick, 92.

35. Buttrick, 11.

36. Buttrick, 99.

37. Kathleen E. Corley, *Private Women, Public Meals: Social Conflict in the Synoptic Tradition* (Peabody, MA: Hendrickson Publishers, 1993), 99.

38. Corley, *Private Women, Public Meals*, 97.

39. Buttrick, 100.

40. Corley, *Private Women, Public Meals*, 98.

41. Corley, 101, 167–69.

42. See Walter Wink, *Jesus and Nonviolence: A Third Way* (Minneapolis: Fortress Press, 2003).

43. Katie Geneva Cannon, *Katie's Canon: Womanism and the Soul of the Black Community* (New York: Continuum, 1996), 91.

44. Cannon, *Katie's Canon*, 92.

45. Gustafson, "Ways of Using Scripture," 21.

Chapter 5

1. James M. Gustafson, "The Place of Scripture in Christian Ethics: A Methodological Study," in *Theology and Christian Ethics* (Philadelphia: Pilgrim Press, 1974), 121–46. Page numbers refer to the essay published as "Ways of Using Scripture" in the anthology *From Christ to the World: Introductory Readings in Christian Ethics*, ed. Wayne Boulton, Thomas D. Kennedy, and Allen Verhey (Grand Rapids: Wm. B. Eerdmans Publishing Co., 1994), 21.

2. Gustafson, "Ways of Using Scripture," 24.

3. This research did not capture all of the religious diversity that now informs the work of conflict transformation, but it did draw from a diversity of Christian

writers and practitioners. The workshop materials came from Anabaptist, Roman Catholic, United Methodist, and American Baptist churches and organizations. The interviewees were Mennonite, United Methodist, Christian Methodist Episcopal, and United Church of Christ. The authors of the texts were Mennonite and United Methodist.

4. Emmanuel Katongole and Chris Rice, *Reconciling All Things: A Christian Vision for Justice, Peace, and Healing* (Downers Grove, IL: InterVarsity Press, 2008), 63.

5. *The Kairos Document: Challenge to the Church: A Theological Comment on the Political Crisis in South Africa* (Grand Rapids: Wm. B. Eerdmans Publishing Co., 1985), 11.

6. *Kairos Document,* 26–27.

7. Katongole and Rice, *Reconciling All Things*, 63.

8. Robert J. Schreiter, "A Practical Theology of Healing, Forgiveness, and Reconciliation," in *Peacebuilding: Catholic Theology, Ethics, and Praxis* (Maryknoll, NY: Orbis Books, 2010), 367.

9. John Paul Lederach, *Reconcile: Conflict Transformation for Ordinary Christians* (Harrisonburg, VA: Herald Press, 2014), 162.

10. Lederach, *Reconcile*, 160.

11. Tom Porter, *The Spirit and Art of Conflict Transformation* (Nashville: Upper Room Books, 2010), 27–29.

12. See the organization's webpage: http://www.lmpeacecenter.org/about.

13. Interview with David Anderson Hooker, October 9, 2013, in Ellen Ott Marshall, "Conflict, God, and Constructive Change: Exploring Prominent Christian Convictions in the Work of Conflict Transformation," *Brethren Life and Thought* 61, no. 2 (fall 2016): 9.

14. John Rawls, "The Priority of Right and the Ideas of the Good," *Philosophy and Public Affairs* 17 (1988): 252.

15. "Reconciliation," in *The Oxford Encyclopedia of the Bible and Theology* http://www.oxfordbiblicalstudies.com.proxy.library.emory.edu/article/opr/t467/e192, accessed December 5, 2017.

16. Miroslav Volf, "The Social Meaning of Reconciliation," *Interpretation* 2, no. 54 (April 2000): 167.

17. Miroslav Volf, "Forgiveness, Reconciliation, and Justice: A Christian Contribution to a More Peaceful Social Environment," in *Forgiveness and Reconciliation: Religion, Public Policy, and Conflict Transformation*, ed. Raymond G. Helmick, S.J., and Rodney L. Peterson (Philadelphia: Templeton Foundation Press, 2001), 44–45.

18. Emilie M. Townes, "Ethics as an Art of Doing the Work Our Souls Must Have," in *Womanist Theological Ethics: A Reader*, ed. Katie Geneva Cannon, Emilie M. Townes, and Angela D. Sims (Louisville, KY: Westminster John Knox Press, 2011), 41.

19. Katongole and Rice, *Reconciling All Things*, 43.
20. Townes, "Ethics as an Art," 41.
21. Dietrich Bonhoeffer, *The Cost of Discipleship* (New York: Macmillan, 1963), 47.
22. Katongole and Rice, *Reconciling All Things*, 39, 41.
23. Katongole and Rice, 74.
24. Katongole and Rice, 28.
25. Katongole and Rice, 33–34.
26. Katongole and Rice, 72.
27. Miroslav Volf, *Exclusion and Embrace: A Theological Exploration of Identity, Otherness, and Reconciliation* (Nashville: Abingdon Press, 1996), 23.
28. Volf, *Exclusion and Embrace*, 23.
29. Volf, 24.
30. Volf, "Social Meaning of Reconciliation," 163.
31. Volf, 162.
32. Volf.
33. Volf, 163, emphasis in original.
34. Katongole and Rice, *Reconciling All Things*, 31.
35. Katongole and Rice, 32.
36. Volf, "Social Meaning of Reconciliation," 167.
37. Volf, 169.
38. Volf, 171.
39. Volf, "Forgiveness, Reconciliation, and Justice," 41.
40. Volf, *Exclusion and Embrace*, 100.
41. Volf, 114–19.
42. Volf, 123.
43. Volf, 131.
44. "Balkans War: A Brief Guide," *BBC News*, March 18, 2016, http://www.bbc.com/news/world-europe-17632399, accessed December 13, 2017; "Ratko Mladic: The 'Butcher of Bosnia,'" *BBC News*, November 22, 2017, http://www.bbc.com/news/world-europe-13559597, accessed December 13, 2017.
45. Volf, *Exclusion and Embrace*, 10.
46. Volf, 9–10.
47. Volf, 10.
48. "Idi Amin," *Encyclopedia Britannica*, September 29, 2017, https://www.britannica.com/biography/Idi-Amin, accessed December 13, 2017.
49. Katongole and Rice, *Reconciling All Things*, 14.
50. Katongole and Rice.
51. Katongole and Rice, 15.
52. Katongole and Rice, 12.
53. Katongole and Rice.
54. Katongole and Rice, 13 (emphasis in original).

55. Katongole and Rice, 32.

56. Katongole and Rice, 33

57. See Alasdair MacIntyre, *After Virtue* (Notre Dame, IN: University of Notre Dame Press, 1981); and Stanley Hauerwas, *A Community of Character: Toward a Constructive Christian Social Ethic* (Notre Dame, IN: University of Notre Dame Press, 1981).

58. Katongole and Rice, *Reconciling All Things,* 32.

59. Katongole and Rice, 32.

60. Katongole and Rice, 33.

61. Stanley Hauerwas, *The Peaceable Kingdom: A Primer in Christian Ethics* (Notre Dame, IN: University of Notre Dame Press, 1983), 89.

62. Volf, *Exclusion and Embrace*, 9.

63. Irving Greenberg, "Cloud of Smoke, Pillar of Fire: Judaism, Christianity, and Modernity after the Holocaust," *Auschwitz: Beginning of a New Era? Reflections on the Holocaust,* ed. Eva Fleischner (New York: Jewish Life Network, 1977), 26.

64. Marjorie Suchocki, *Fall to Violence: Original Sin in Relational Theology* (New York: Continuum, 1995), provides an important argument for forgiveness from the perspective of the victim.

65. Like Volf, Katongole, and Rice, Robert J. Schreiter encourages us to connect "our narratives of suffering" and our "experience[s] of violence and violation" to the passion, death, and resurrection of Christ. The story of God's work in Christ "organizes our chaotic and painful experience of violence into a narrative that will carry us, too, from death to life" (Robert J. Schreiter, *The Ministry of Reconciliation: Spirituality and Strategies* [Maryknoll, NY: Orbis Books, 1998], 19). This divine process restores the humanity of the victim. This is the heart of reconciliation for Schreiter: "the restoration of one's damaged humanity in a life-giving relationship with God" (*Ministry of Reconciliation*, 15). Schreiter understands reconciliation—this restoration of dignity that transforms both victim and offender—to be the precondition for repentance and forgiveness. I include Schreiter briefly here simply to note another kind of variety: that Christian theologians and ethicists might draw on the atonement with equal authority and conceptualize the steps of a reconciliation process differently. But also, Schreiter represents the perspective that connecting a victim with the suffering Christ restores the humanity of the victim rather than condones suffering.

66. Jennifer Harvey, *Dear White Christians: For Those Still Longing for Racial Reconciliation* (Grand Rapids: Wm. B. Eerdmans Publishing Co., 2014), 19–20.

67. For example, William Danaher draws on the resurrection, James McCarty works with the Trinity, and Amy Levad turns to the Eucharist. William J. Danaher Jr., "Music That Will Bring Back the Dead? Resurrection, Reconciliation, and Restorative Justice in Post-Apartheid South Africa," *Journal of Religious Ethics* 38, no. 1 (2010): 115–41; James W. McCarty III, "The Embrace of Justice: The Greensboro Truth and Reconciliation Commission, Miroslav Volf, and the Ethics of Reconciliation," *Journal of the Society of Christian Ethics* 22, no. 2 (2013):

111–29; Amy Levad, *Redeeming a Prison Society: A Liturgical and Sacramental Response to Mass Incarceration* (Minneapolis: Fortress Press, 2014).

68. Stephanie Mitchem, "To Make the Wounded Whole: Womanist Explorations of Reconciliation," in *Gender, Ethnicity, and Religion: Views from the Other Side*, ed. Rosemary Radford Ruether (Minneapolis: Fortress Press, 2002), 249–50.

69. Mitchem, "To Make the Wounded Whole," 251.

70. Mitchem, 245–62.

71. Mitchem, 247.

72. Mitchem, 251.

73. Mitchem. Dissembling means to hide or conceal. Mitchem's interviewees describe dissemblance as a strategy of protection that ends up destroying or erasing the self (250).

74. Mitchem, 258.

75. Mitchem, 258–59.

76. Emilie Townes, "Ethics as an Art," 39.

77. Townes, 39.

78. Townes, 41.

79. Townes, 42.

80. Jean Zaru, *Occupied with Nonviolence: A Palestinian Woman Speaks* (Minneapolis: Fortress Press, 2008), 77.

81. John W. de Gruchy, *Reconciliation: Restoring Justice* (Minneapolis: Fortress Press, 2002), 34.

82. De Gruchy, *Reconciliation,* 36.

83. De Gruchy, 35.

84. Harvey, *Dear White Christians*, 20.

85. Harvey, 60–61.

86. Harvey, 61.

87. Howard Zehr, *The Little Book of Restorative Justice* (Intercourse, PA: Good Books, 2002), 5.

88. See Rupert Ross, *Returning to the Teachings: Exploring Aboriginal Justice* (Toronto: Penguin, 2006); and Paul Christoph Bornkamm, *Rwanda's Gacaca Courts: Between Retribution and Reparation* (Oxford: Oxford University Press, 2012).

89. Zehr, *Little Book of Restorative Justice,* 13.

90. Zehr, 18.

91. Zehr, 19–20.

92. Zehr, 4. See also Kay Pranis, *The Little Book of Circle Process: A New/Old Approach to Peacemaking* (Intercourse, PA: Good Books, 2005).

93. Stephanie Hixon, personal interview, October 9, 2013, in Marshall, "Conflict, God, and Constructive Change," 11.

94. John Paul Lederach and Angela Jill Lederach, *When Blood and Bones Cry Out: Journeys through the Soundscape of Healing and Reconciliation* (Oxford: Oxford University Press, 2010), 101.

95. Lederach and Lederach, *When Blood and Bones Cry Out,* 101–2.

96. Hixon, interview.

97. Daniela Körppen and Norbert Ropers, "Introduction: Addressing Complex Dynamics of Conflict Transformation," in Daniela Körppen, Norbert Ropers, and Hans J. Giessmann, eds., *The Non-Linearity of Peace Processes: Theory and Practice in Systemic Conflict Transformation* (Opladen and Farmington Hills, MI: Verlag Barbara Budrich, 2011), 11.

Chapter 6

1. See, for example, "Discover Your Conflict Management Style," in *Mediating Interpersonal Conflict*, ed. Bob Gross and Angenetta Briner (North Manchester, IN: Education for Conflict Resolution, 2007), 15–20.

2. See "Animal Conflict Styles," in *Peacebuilding: A Caritas Training Manual* (Vatican City: Caritas Internationalis, 2002), 123.

3. See "Maps of 'Conflict History,'" in *Peace Skills Leaders' Guide*, by Alice Frazer Evans and Robert A. Evans with Ronald S. Kraybill (San Francisco: Jossey-Bass, 2001), 71.

4. "Module 5: Skills for the Peacebuilder—Communication and Conflict Handling," in *Peacebuilding: A Caritas Training Manual* (Vatican City: Caritas Internationalis, 2002), 112.

5. H. Richard Niebuhr is regularly referred to this way. See, for example, James Livingston and Francis Schüssler Fiorenza, *Modern Christian Thought: The Twentieth Century,* vol. 2 (Minneapolis: Fortress Press, 2006), 174.

6. James W. Fowler, *To See the Kingdom: The Theological Vision of H. Richard Niebuhr* (Eugene, OR: Wipf & Stock, 2001), 1–7.

7. H. Richard Niebuhr, *The Responsible Self: An Essay in Christian Moral Philosophy* (San Francisco: Harper & Row, 1963), 49–56.

8. Niebuhr, *Responsible Self,* 56.

9. Niebuhr, 65.

10. Darryl M. Trimiew, *Voices of the Silenced: The Responsible Self in a Marginalized Community* (Cleveland: Pilgrim Press, 1993), 90.

11. Trimiew, *Voices of the Silenced,* 85.

12. Margaret Urban Walker, *Moral Contexts* (Lanham, MD: Rowman & Littlefield, 2003), xiii.

13. Alison Jaggar, "Feminist Ethics: Projects, Problems, Prospects," in *Feminist Ethics*, ed. Claudia Card (Lawrence: University Press of Kansas, 1991), 80.

14. Jaggar. "Feminist Ethics," 82.

15. See Elizabeth Spelman, *Inessential Woman: Problems of Exclusion in Feminist Thought* (Boston: Beacon Press, 1988).

16. Jaggar, "Feminist Ethics," 95, 98–99.

17. Walker, *Moral Contexts*, 72–75.

18. Walker, 76.

19. There is a growing literature on women peacebuilders, but gender analysis itself remains rather thin. On this point, see Atalia Omer, "Religious Peacebuilding: The Exotic, the Good, and the Theatrical," in *The Oxford Handbook of Religion, Conflict, and Peacebuilding*, ed. Atalia Omer, R. Scott Appleby, and David Little (Oxford: Oxford University Press, 2015), 19.

20. Debbie Roberts, a mediator and professor of reconciliation studies, noted this in her dissertation from the Claremont Graduate University and addressed it admirably. Debbie Roberts, "Toward a Feminist Vision: A Critical Appraisal of Conflict Resolution Theory and Method" (doctoral dissertation, Claremont Graduate University, 2007).

21. Debbie Roberts, "'I Am Because We Are': A Relational Foundation for Transformation of Conflicts and Classrooms," in *Conflict Transformation and Religion: Essays on Faith, Power, and Relationship*, ed. Ellen Ott Marshall (New York: Palgrave Macmillan, 2016), 97–110.

22. Marcia Y. Riggs, "'Loves the Spirit': Transformation Mediation as Pedagogical Practice," in Marshall, *Conflict Transformation and Religion*, 111–24.

23. Elizabeth M. Bounds, "The Conflict Skills Classroom as Social Microcosm," in Marshall, *Conflict Transformation and Religion*, 125–38.

24. See Carol Gilligan, *In a Different Voice: Psychological Theory and Women's Development* (Cambridge, MA: Harvard University Press, 1993).

25. Carol Gilligan, "Moral Orientation and Moral Development," in *Justice and Care: Essential Readings in Feminist Ethics*, ed. Virginia Held (Boulder, CO: Westview Press, 1995), 35.

26. Alison Jaggar, "Caring as a Feminist Practice of Moral Reasoning," in Held, *Justice and Care*, 180.

27. Sarah Lucia Hoagland, "Some Thoughts about 'Caring,'" in Card, *Feminist Ethics*, 254.

28. Bernard Mayer, *The Dynamics of Conflict: A Guide to Engagement and Intervention*, 2nd ed. (San Francisco: Jossey-Bass, 2012), 271.

29. Robert A. Baruch Bush and Joseph P. Folger, *The Promise of Mediation: The Transformative Approach to Conflict*, new and rev. ed. (San Francisco: Jossey-Bass, 2005), 22.

30. Jaggar, "Caring as a Feminist Practice," 197.

31. Sarah Perry, *The Essex Serpent* (New York: Custom House, 2016), 191.

32. Ari Shapiro, "Confronting the Possibility of Monsters in *The Essex Serpent*," *All Things Considered*, June 14, 2017, https://www.npr.org/2017/06/14/532818864/confronting-the-possibility-of-monsters-in-the-essex-serpent, accessed March 17, 2018.

33. Sam Keen, *Faces of the Enemy: Reflections on the Hostile Imagination* (San Francisco: Harper & Row, 1986).

34. Ira M. Leonard and Robert D. Parmet, *American Nativism, 1830–1860* (New York: Van Nostrand Reinhold, 1971), 51.

35. David H. Bennett, *The Party of Fear: From Nativist Movements to the New Right in American History* (Chapel Hill: University of North Carolina Press, 1988), 40.

36. Bennett, *Party of Fear*, 42–43.

37. Louis Cozonlino, *The Neuroscience of Psychotherapy: Building and Rebuilding the Human Brain* (New York: Norton, 2002), 237, quoted in Evelyne A. Reisacher, "Fear and Muslim-Christian Conflict Transformation, in *Peace-Building by, between, and beyond Muslims and Evangelical Christians*, ed. Mohammed Abu-Nimer and David Augsburger (Lanham, MD: Lexington Books, 2009), 161.

38. Reisacher, "Fear and Muslim-Christian Conflict Transformation," 161.

39. For more on these insights from neuroscience, see Mahzarin Banaji and Anthony Greenwald, *BlindSpot: Hidden Biases of Good People* (New York: Delacorte Press, 2013). Also, visit https://implicit.harvard.edu/implicit to take an "Implicit Association Test." This is an instrument that tests the associations our brain makes between different groups of people and good or bad qualities.

40. Reisacher, "Fear and Muslim-Christian Conflict Transformation," 157.

41. I am grateful for the wonderful work of Sarah MacDonald, who has explored the "paradox of privilege" at Emory, "The Paradox of Privilege: Responsibility Solidarity for Faith-Based Activism," unpublished dissertation, Emory University, 2018.

42. Raymond E. Brown, *The Death of the Messiah: From Gethsemane to the Grave: A Commentary on the Passion Narratives in the Four Gospels*, vol. 1 (New York: Doubleday, 1998), 153.

43. Jesus also singles them out to follow him when he raises from death the daughter in Mark 5:37–43.

44. Brown, *Death of the Messiah*, 156.

45. Kate DiCamillo, *The Tiger Rising* (Somerville, MA: Candlewick Press, 2001), 83.

46. DiCamillo, *Tiger Rising*, 117.

Chapter 7

1. *The Book of Common Prayer and Administration of the Sacraments and Other Rites and Ceremonies of the Church* (New York: Church Publishing, 1979), 308.

2. I am drawing here on descriptions of conflict styles and conflict dynamics. See, for example, Bernard Mayer, *Dynamics of Conflict: A Guide to Engagement and Intervention*, 2nd ed. (San Francisco: Jossey-Bass, 2012), 33–66.

3. Lisa Schirch and David Campt, *The Little Book of Dialogue for Difficult Subjects* (Intercourse, PA: Good Books, 2007), 7.

4. Kori Leaman-Miller, "Listening," *Making Peace with Conflict: Practical Skills for Conflict Transformation*, ed. Carolyn Schrock-Shenk and Lawrence Ressler (Scottdale, PA: Herald Press, 1999), 64. See also John Paul Lederach, "Keeping Silent and Listening," in *The Journey toward Reconciliation* (Scottdale,

PA: Herald Press, 1999), 141–56; and Ronald Kraybill, Robert Evans, and Alice Frazer Evans, "Listening Skills," in *Peace Skills: Manual for Community Mediators* (San Francisco: Jossey-Bass, 2001), 87–93.

5. H. Richard Niebuhr, *The Meaning of Revelation* (New York: Macmillan, 1941), x.

6. H. Richard Niebuhr, *The Responsible Self: An Essay in Christian Moral Philosophy* (San Francisco: Harper & Row, 1963), 55–56.

7. Niebuhr, *Responsible Self*, 56.

8. Niebuhr, 61–65.

9. This relates to one of the several insightful critiques of H. Richard Niebuhr offered by Darryl Trimiew in *Voices of the Silenced: The Responsible Self in a Marginalized Community* (Cleveland: Pilgrim Press, 1993).

10. I am indebted to Beth Corrie for this insight.

11. Carla Pratt Keyes, "Proverbs 1:20–33," *Interpretation* 63, no. 3 (July 2009): 282.

12. Several writings and my students' interactions with them have helped to me to see this. Among them are Jennifer Harvey, *Dear White Christians: For Those Still Longing for Racial Reconciliation* (Grand Rapids: Wm. B. Eerdmans Publishing Co., 2014); Shannon Sullivan, *Good White People: The Problem with Middle-Class White Anti-Racism* (Albany: State University of New York, 2014); George Yancy, *Black Bodies, White Gazes: The Continuing Significance of Race in America* (Lanham, MD: Rowman & Littlefield, 2016). Kristopher Norris, "The White Problem in Evangelicalism: Conversion as Alternative to Reconciliation," paper presented to the American Academic of Religion, Evangelical Studies Session (November 2017). Karen Crozier told me this a long time ago.

13. The bull symbolized "divine strength, energy, fertility, and even leadership in the biblical world" (Carol Meyers, *Exodus* [Cambridge: Cambridge University Press, 2005], 259).

14. Kate DiCamillo, *Because of Winn-Dixie* (Sommerville, MA: Candlewick Press, 2000), 122.

15. DiCamillo, *Because of Winn-Dixie*, 122.

16. DiCamillo, 119.

17. DiCamillo, 129.

18. DiCamillo, 132.

19. DiCamillo, 153.

20. *Book of Common Prayer*, 360.

21. *Book of Common Prayer*, 365.

22. I have long been irritated with the divisive and wrongheaded version of grace expressed in the saying "There, but for the grace of God, go I." This is my alternative to that.

23. Maggie Smith, "Good Bones," *Waxwing* 9 (summer 2016) http://waxwingmag.org/items/Issue9/28_Smith-Good-Bones.php#top, accessed July 23, 2018.

24. H. Richard Niebuhr, “Man’s Work and God’s,” in *Theology, History, and Culture*, ed. William Stacy Johnson (New Haven, CT: Yale University Press, 1996), 208.

25. Niebuhr, “Man’s Work and God’s,” 211 (emphasis added).

26. Mary Oliver, “The World I Live In,” *Felicity* (New York: Penguin Books, 2017), 11.

27. Walter Rauschenbusch, *A Theology for the Social Gospel*, reprint ed., 4th printing (Nashville: Abingdon Press, 1990), 186.

Bibliography

Ackerman, David A. *1 and 2 Timothy, Titus: A Commentary in the Wesleyan Tradition*. New Beacon Bible Commentary. Kansas City, MO: Beacon Hill Press, 2016.

Amesbury, Richard, and George M. Newlands. *Faith and Human Rights: Christianity and the Global Struggle for Human Dignity*. Minneapolis: Fortress Press, 2008.

Aristotle, *Nicomachean Ethics*. Translated with an introduction and notes by Martin Ostwald. Englewood Cliffs, NJ: Prentice Hall, 1962.

Aune, David E., ed. *The Blackwell Companion to the New Testament*. Malden, MA: Blackwell Publishing, 2010.

Bartholomew, Craig G., Joel B. Green, and Anthony C. Thiselton, eds. *Reading Luke: Interpretation, Reflection, Formation*. Scripture and Hermeneutics Series. Vol. 6. Grand Rapids: Zondervan, 2005.

Basset, Lytta. *Holy Anger: Jacob, Job, Jesus*. Grand Rapids: Wm. B. Eerdmans Publishing Co., 2007.

Bedford, Nancy Elizabeth. *Galatians*. Belief: A Theological Commentary on the Bible, edited by Amy Plantinga Pauw and William C. Placher. Louisville, KY: Westminster John Knox Press, 2016.

Bush, Robert A. Baruch, and Joseph P. Folger, *The Promise of Mediation: The Transformative Approach to Conflict*. New and rev. ed. San Francisco: Jossey-Bass, 2004.

Buttrick, David. *Speaking Conflict: Stories of a Controversial Jesus*. Louisville, KY: Westminster John Knox Press, 2007.

Cannon, Katie Geneva, Emilie M. Townes, and Angela D. Simms, eds. *Womanist Theological Ethics: A Reader*. Louisville, KY: Westminster John Knox Press, 2011.

Card, Claudia. *Feminist Ethics*. Lawrence: University Press of Kansas, 1991.

Cobb, John B., Jr. *Grace and Theology: A Wesleyan Theology for Today*. Nashville: Abingdon Press, 1995.

Cone, James. "Biblical Revelation and Social Existence." *Interpretation* 28, no. 4 (October 1974): 422–40.

Cone, James. *The Cross and the Lynching Tree*. Maryknoll, NY: Orbis Books, 2011.

Copeland, M. Shawn. *Enfleshing Freedom: Body, Race, and Being*. Minneapolis: Fortress Press, 2010.

Corley, Kathleen E. *Private Women, Public Meals: Social Conflict in the Synoptic Tradition*. Peabody, MA: Hendrickson Publishers, 1993.

Danaher, William J., Jr. "Music That Will Bring Back the Dead? Resurrection, Reconciliation, and Restorative Justice in Post-Apartheid South Africa." *Journal of Religious Ethics* 38, no. 1 (2010): 115–41.

Danaher, William J., Jr. "Resurrection and Reconciliation: Toward a Paschal Theology of Restorative Justice." *Sewanee Theological Review* 50, no. 1 (Christmas 2006): 51–64.

De Gruchy, John W. *Reconciliation: Restoring Justice*. Minneapolis: Fortress Press, 2002.

Dorrien, Gary. *Social Ethics in the Making: Interpreting an American Tradition*. Chichester, UK: Wiley-Blackwell, 2011.

Douglas, Kelly Brown. *Stand Your Ground: Black Bodies and the Justice of God*. Maryknoll, NY: Orbis Books, 2015.

Dunderberg, Ismo, Christopher Tuckett, and Kari Syreeni. *Fair Play: Diversity and Conflicts in Early Christianity*. Boston: Brill, 2002.

Dunning, H. Ray. *Reflecting the Divine Imagine: Christian Ethics in Wesleyan Perspective*. Eugene, OR: Wipf & Stock, 1998.

Esler, Philip Francis. *Community and Gospel in Luke-Acts: The Social and Political Motivations of Lucan Theology*. Society for New Testament Studies Monograph Series, edited by G. N. Stanton. Cambridge: Cambridge University Press, 1987.

Esler, Philip Francis. *Conflict and Identity in Romans: The Social Setting of Paul's Letters*. Minneapolis: Fortress Press, 2003.

Evans, Craig A. *From Jesus to the Church: The First Christian Generation*. Louisville, KY: Westminster John Knox Press, 2014.

Farley, Margaret A. "Feminist Consciousness and the Moral Authority of Scripture." In *Feminist Interpretation of the Bible*, edited by Letty M. Russell, 41–51. Philadelphia: Westminster Press, 1985.

Fowler, James W. *To See the Kingdom: The Theological Vision of H. Richard Niebuhr*. Eugene, OR: Wipf & Stock, 2001.

Francis, Leah Gunning. *Ferguson and Faith: Sparking Leadership and Awakening Community*. St. Louis: Chalice Press, 2015.

Gibbs, Jeffrey A., and Jeffrey J. Kloha. "'Following' Matthew 18: Interpreting Matthew 18:15–20 in Its Context." *Concordia Journal* 29, no. 1 (January 2003): 6–25.

Gilligan, Carol. *In a Different Voice: Psychological Theory and Women's Development*. Cambridge, MA: Harvard University Press, 1993.

Gundry, Robert H. *Matthew: A Commentary on His Handbook for a Mixed Church under Persecution*. 2nd ed. Grand Rapids: Wm. B. Eerdmans Publishing Co., 1994.

Gustafson, James M. "Ways of Using Scripture." In *From Christ to the World: Introductory Readings in Christian Ethics*, edited by Wayne G. Boulton,

Thomas D. Kennedy, and Allen Verhey, 21–26. Grand Rapids: Wm. B Eerdmans Publishing Co., 1994.
Hagner, Donald A. *Matthew 1–13*. Word Biblical Commentary, vol. 33A. Dallas: Word Books, 1993.
Hanson, K. C., and Douglas E. Oakman. *Palestine in the Time of Jesus: Social Structures and Social Conflicts*. 2nd ed. Minneapolis: Fortress Press, 2008.
Harvey, Jennifer. *Dear White Christians: For Those Still Longing for Racial Reconciliation*. Grand Rapids: Wm. B. Eerdmans Publishing Co., 2014.
Harvey, Jennifer. "Which Way to Justice? Reconciliation, Reparations, and the Problem of Whiteness in U.S. Protestantism." *Journal of the Society of Christian Ethics* 31, no. 1 (2011): 57–77.
Hauerwas, Stanley. *A Community of Character: Toward a Constructive Christian Social Ethic*. Notre Dame, IN: University of Notre Dame Press, 1981.
Hauerwas, Stanley, and Samuel Wells. *The Blackwell Companion to Christian Ethics*. Malden, MA: Blackwell Publishing, 2004.
Heitzenrater, Richard P. *Wesley and the People Called Methodists*. Nashville: Abingdon Press, 1995.
Held, Virginia, ed. *Justice and Care: Essential Readings in Feminist Ethics*. Boulder, CO: Westview Press, 1995.
Helmick, Raymond G., SJ, and Rodney L. Peterson, eds. *Forgiveness and Reconciliation: Religion, Public Policy, and Conflict Transformation*. Philadelphia: Templeton Foundation Press, 2001.
Horsley, Richard A. *Jesus and the Powers: Conflict, Covenant, and the Hope of the Poor*. Minneapolis: Fortress Press, 2011.
Illian, Bridget. "Church Discipline and Forgiveness in Matthew 18:15–35." *Currents in Theology and Missions* 37, no. 6 (December 2010): 444–50.
Jennings, Theodore W. *Outlaw Justice: The Messianic Politics of Paul*. Redwood City, CA: Stanford University Press, 2013.
The Kairos Theologians. *The Kairos Document: Challenge to the Church: A Theological Comment on the Political Crisis in South Africa*. Grand Rapids: Wm. B. Eerdmans Publishing Co., 1986.
Katongole, Emmanuel, and Chris Rice. *Reconciling All Things: A Christian Vision for Justice, Peace, and Healing*. Downers Grove, IL: InterVarsity Press, 2008.
Kraybill, Ronald S., Robert A. Evans, and Alice Frazer Evans. *Peace Skills: Manual for Community Mediators*. San Francisco: Jossey-Bass, 2001.
Lederach, John Paul. *The Little Book of Conflict Transformation: Clear Articulation of the Guiding Principles by a Pioneer in the Field*. Intercourse, PA: Good Books, 2003.
Lederach, John Paul. *The Moral Imagination: The Art and Soul of Building Peace*. Oxford: Oxford University Press, 2005.
Lederach, John Paul. *Reconcile: Conflict Transformation for Ordinary Christians*. Harrisonburg, VA: Herald Press, 2014.

Lederach, John Paul, and Angela Jill Lederach. *When Blood and Bones Cry Out: Journeys through the Soundscape of Healing and Reconciliation*. Oxford: Oxford University Press, 2010.

Levad, Amy. *Redeeming a Prison Society: A Liturgical and Sacramental Response to Mass Incarceration*. Minneapolis: Fortress Press, 2014.

MacIntyre, Alasdair. *After Virtue: A Study in Moral Theory*. 2nd ed. Notre Dame, IN: University of Notre Dame Press, 1984.

Marshall, Ellen Ott. *Christians in the Public Square: Faith That Transforms Politics*. Reissue ed. Eugene, OR: Wipf & Stock, 2015.

Marshall, Ellen Ott. "Conflict, God, and Constructive Change: Exploring Prominent Christian Convictions in the Work of Conflict Transformation." *Brethren Life and Thought* 61, no. 2 (Fall 2016): 1–15.

Marshall, Ellen Ott. *Though the Fig Tree Does Not Blossom: Toward a Responsible Theology of Christian Hope*. Reissue ed. Eugene, OR: Wipf & Stock, 2015.

Marshall, Ellen Ott, ed. *Conflict Transformation and Religion: Essays on Faith, Power, and Relationship*. New York: Palgrave Macmillan, 2016.

Mayer, Bernard. *Dynamics of Conflict: A Guide to Engagement and Intervention*. 2nd ed. San Francisco: Jossey-Bass, 2012.

McCarty, James W., III. "The Embrace of Justice: The Greensboro Truth and Reconciliation Commission, Miroslav Volf, and the Ethics of Reconciliation." *Journal of the Society of Christian Ethics* 22, no. 2 (2013): 111–29.

McFarland, Ian A. *The Divine Image: Envisioning the Invisible God*. Minneapolis: Fortress Press, 2005.

Mitchem, Stephanie Y. "'To Make the Wounded Whole': Womanist Explorations of Reconciliation." In *Gender, Ethnicity, and Religion: Views from the Other Side*, edited by Rosemary Radford Ruether. Minneapolis: Fortress Press, 2002.

Myers, Ched, and Elaine Enns. *Ambassadors of Reconciliation: Diverse Christian Practices of Restorative Justice and Peacemaking*. Maryknoll, NY: Orbis Books, 2009.

Myers, Ched, and Elaine Enns. *Ambassadors of Reconciliation: New Testament Reflections on Restorative Justice and Peacemaking*. Maryknoll, NY: Orbis Books, 2009.

Nagel, Thomas. *The View from Nowhere*. Oxford: Oxford University Press, 1986.

Niebuhr, H. Richard. *The Meaning of Revelation*. New York: Macmillan, 1941.

Niebuhr, H. Richard. *The Responsible Self: An Essay in Christian Moral Philosophy*. San Francisco: Harper & Row, 1963.

Omer, Atalia, R. Scott Appleby, and David Little. *The Oxford Handbook of Religion, Conflict, and Peacebuilding*. Oxford: Oxford University Press, 2015.

Ottati, Douglas F. *Jesus Christ and Christian Vision*. Louisville, KY: Westminster John Knox Press, 1996.

Peters, Rebecca Todd, and Elizabeth Hinson-Hasty. *To Do Justice: A Guide for Progressive Christians*. Louisville, KY: Westminster John Knox Press, 2008.

Pfeil, Margaret R. "A Theological Understanding of Restorative Justice." *Journal of Moral Theology* 5, no. 2 (2016): 158–63.

Philpott, Daniel. *Just and Unjust Peace: An Ethic of Political Reconciliation.* Oxford: Oxford University Press, 2012.

Porter, Tom. *The Spirit and Art of Conflict Transformation.* Nashville: Upper Room Books, 2010.

Pranis, Kay. *The Little Book of Circle Processes: A New/Old Approach to Peacemaking.* Intercourse, PA: Good Books, 2005.

Quinn, Jerome D., and William C. Wacker. *The First and Second Letters to Timothy.* Grand Rapids: Wm. B. Eerdmans Publishing Co., 2000.

Ross, Sir David. *Aristotle.* 6th ed. London: Routledge, 1995.

Runyon, Theodore. *The New Creation: John Wesley's Theology Today.* Nashville: Abingdon Press, 1998.

Sawatsky, Jarem. *Justpeace Ethics: A Guide to Restorative Justice and Peacebuilding.* Eugene, OR: Cascade Books, 2008.

Schirch, Lisa. *Ritual and Symbol in Peacebuilding.* London: Kumarian Press, 2005.

Schirch, Lisa, and David Campt. *The Little Book of Dialogue for Difficult Subjects.* Intercourse, PA: Good Books, 2007.

Schreiter, Robert J. *The Ministry of Reconciliation: Spirituality and Strategies.* Maryknoll, NY: Orbis Books, 1998.

Schreiter, Robert J. "A Practical Theology of Healing, Forgiveness, and Reconciliation." In *Peacebuilding: Catholic Theology, Ethics, and Praxis,* edited by Robert J. Schreiter, R. Scott Appleby, and Gerard F. Powers, 366–97. Maryknoll, NY: Orbis Books, 2010.

Schrock-Shenk, Carolyn, and Lawrence Ressler, eds. *Making Peace with Conflict: Practical Skills for Conflict Transformation.* Scottdale, PA: Herald Press, 1999.

Spelman, Elizabeth. *Inessential Woman: Problems of Exclusion in Feminist Thought.* Boston: Beacon Press, 1988.

Stiltner, Brian. *Toward Thriving Communities: Virtue Ethics as Social Ethics.* Winona, MN: Anselm Academic, 2016.

Sullivan, Shannon. *Good White People: The Problem with Middle-Class White Anti-Racism.* Albany: State University of New York, 2014.

Townes, Emilie, ed. *Embracing the Spirit: Womanist Perspectives on Hope, Salvation, and Transformation.* Maryknoll, NY: Orbis Books, 2001.

Villa-Vicencio, Charles. *Walk with Us and Listen: Political Reconciliation in Africa.* Washington, DC: Georgetown University Press, 2009.

Volf, Miroslav. *Exclusion and Embrace: A Theological Exploration of Identity, Otherness, and Reconciliation.* Nashville: Abingdon Press, 1996.

Volf, Miroslav. "The Social Meaning of Reconciliation." *Interpretation* 2, no. 54 (April 2000): 158–72.

Waldron, Jeremy. "The Image of God: Rights, Reason, and Order." In *Christianity and Human Rights: An Introduction,* edited by John Witte Jr. and Frank S. Alexander, 216–35. Cambridge: Cambridge University Press, 2010.

Walker, Margaret Urban. *Moral Contexts*. Lanham, MD: Rowman & Littlefield, 2003.

Yancy, George. *Black Bodies, White Gazes: The Continuing Significance of Race in America*. Lanham, MD: Rowman & Littlefield, 2016.

Zaru, Jean. *Occupied with Nonviolence: A Palestinian Woman Speaks*. Minneapolis: Fortress Press, 2008.

Zehr, Howard. *Changing Lenses*. Scottdale, PA: Herald Press, 1995.

Zehr, Howard. *The Little Book of Restorative Justice*. Intercourse, PA: Good Books, 2002.

Index of Names

Index of Subjects

Cross-referenced names are found in the index of names.

Lightning Source UK Ltd.
Milton Keynes UK
UKHW021610211118
332683UK00005B/454/P

9 780664 263447